Natural Law and the Antislavery Constitutional Tradition

In *Natural Law and the Antislavery Constitutional Tradition*, Justin Buckley Dyer provides a succinct account of the development of American antislavery constitutionalism in the years preceding the Civil War. Within the context of recent revisionist scholarship, Dyer argues that the theoretical foundations of American constitutionalism – which he identifies with principles of natural law – were antagonistic to slavery. Still, the continued existence of slavery in the nineteenth century created a tension between practice and principle. In a series of case studies, Dyer reconstructs the constitutional arguments of prominent antislavery thinkers such as John Quincy Adams, John McLean, Abraham Lincoln, and Frederick Douglass, who collectively sought to overcome the legacy of slavery by emphasizing the natural-law foundations of American constitutionalism. What emerges is a convoluted understanding of American constitutional development that challenges traditional narratives of linear progress while highlighting the centrality of natural law to America's greatest constitutional crisis.

Justin Buckley Dyer is an assistant professor of political science at the University of Missouri, Columbia.

Natural Law and the Antislavery Constitutional Tradition

JUSTIN BUCKLEY DYER

University of Missouri, Columbia

CAMBRIDGE
UNIVERSITY PRESS

CAMBRIDGE
UNIVERSITY PRESS

32 Avenue of the Americas, New York NY 10013-2473, USA

Cambridge University Press is part of the University of Cambridge.

It furthers the University's mission by disseminating knowledge in the pursuit of education, learning and research at the highest international levels of excellence.

www.cambridge.org
Information on this title: www.cambridge.org/9781107454354

© Justin Buckley Dyer 2012

First published 2012
First paperback edition 2014

A catalogue record for this publication is available from the British Library

Library of Congress Cataloguing in Publication data
Dyer, Justin Buckley, 1983–
Natural law and the antislavery constitutional tradition / Justin Buckley Dyer.
p. cm.
Includes bibliographical references and index.
ISBN 978-1-107-01363-6 (hardback)
1. Slavery – Law and legislation – United States. 2. Constitutional history – United States. 3. Antislavery movements – United States. 4. Natural law – Influence. I. Title.
KF4545.S5.D94 2012
342.73087 – dc23 2011030291

ISBN 978-1-107-01363-6 Hardback
ISBN 978-1-107-45435-4 Paperback

To Kyle,
for everything

appeared as "After the Revolution: *Somerset* and the Antislavery Tradition in Anglo-American Constitutional Development," *Journal of Politics* 71, no. 4 (2009): 1422–1434. Various sections in Chapter 4 are drawn from "Slavery and the Magna Carta in the Development of Anglo-American Constitutionalism," *PS: Political Science and Politics* 43, no. 3 (2010): 479–482, and "Lincolnian Natural Right, *Dred Scott*, and the Jurisprudence of John McLean," *Polity* 4, no. 1 (2009): 63–85. Additionally, an early version of Chapter 5 was published as "Revisiting *Dred Scott*: Prudence, Providence, and the Limits of Constitutional Statesmanship," *Perspectives on Political Science* 39, no. 3 (2010): 166–174. Permission from the publishers to use this material is acknowledged.

As always, family and friends have carried me through the research and writing process. The "sun looks down on nothing half so good," C. S. Lewis once ventured, "as a household laughing together over a meal, or two friends talking over a pint of beer." I have been blessed with good meals and interesting conversations too numerous to count, and I appreciate those who have shared them with me. Finally, my largest debt is to my wife, Kyle, who supports me in work and sustains me in life, and to our son, Bennett, who has enriched our lives in ways we could not have imagined.

Contents

Acknowledgments

Many people have had a hand in shaping this book from t
beginning. I thank Jeff Tulis, Sandy Levinson, Gretchen Ritt
and H.W. Perry for offering valuable comments and criticis
while this project was still in its early stages. J. Budziszews
was willing to read and comment on numerous drafts, and h
work on the problem of moral self-deception has shaped n
own thinking on problems of epistemology and natural law. A
J. has taught us throughout his career, there truly are things "w
can't not know." I also owe a special debt of gratitude to Gar
Jacobsohn. The theoretical framework of constitutional dis
harmony that structures the arguments in this book is largely ;
result of his mentorship and guidance. Over the years, Gary ha:
challenged me to think deeply about the aspirations and identity
of our constitutional order, and for that I am grateful.

My colleagues at the University of Missouri have been uniformly encouraging, and I thank John Petrocik, our department
chair, for his continued support. Matthew Moore and Kayla
Crider each provided valuable research assistance, and Kayla's
proofreading saved me from more than a few errors. On the
business side, it has been a pleasure working with Lew Bateman
and Anne Lovering Rounds at Cambridge University Press,
and I appreciate their willingness to incorporate previously
published material in this book. An earlier version of Chapter 2

Prologue

Slavery and the Laws and Rights of Nature

We hold these truths to be self-evident, that all men are created equal, that they are endowed by their Creator with certain inalienable Rights, that among these are Life, Liberty, and the pursuit of Happiness.

Declaration of Independence, 1776

Neither aiming at originality of principle or sentiment, nor yet copied from any particular and previous writing, [the Declaration of Independence] was intended to be an expression of the American mind, and to give to that expression the proper tone and spirit called for by the occasion. All its authority rests then on the harmonizing sentiments of the day, whether expressed in conversation, in letters, printed essays, or in the elementary books of public right, as Aristotle, Cicero, Locke, Sidney, &c.

Thomas Jefferson, 1825

Years ago, the twentieth-century American philosopher Henry Veatch began a bibliographic essay on the Western tradition of natural-law theory by exclaiming, "Surely, the ancient and honorable doctrine of natural law is dead, is it not? And many would add, 'Long dead and well dead!'"[1] But to the contrary, Veatch

---

[1] Henry B. Veatch, "Natural Law: Dead or Alive?" *Literature of Liberty: A Review of Contemporary Liberal Thought* 1, no. 4 (1978), 7.

concluded, funeral orations for the perennial philosophy of natural law had been delivered prematurely, as the post–World War II search for objective standards of political right had led to a renaissance of natural-law thinking in the Western world. Still, natural-law theory today remains at the periphery of academic discussions of ethics and politics, and one of the chief reasons for the continuing disrepute of natural-law doctrines, in addition to trends in epistemology and ontology, is the unhappy association of natural law with certain practices that are repugnant to our modern sensibilities.

The historical defense of slavery as "natural" – and, therefore, just – particularly burdens the contemporary enterprise of natural-law thinking. If something as unjust and immoral as chattel slavery could be defended in terms of nature, then why turn to nature as a guide for political and ethical life? The appeal to Aristotle by some nineteenth-century defenders of race-based and hereditary chatteldom further cements the unfortunate association of natural law with human bondage. Aristotle's doctrine of natural slavery – defended by no less a natural lawyer than Thomas Aquinas – has indeed cast a long shadow over the natural-law tradition, which has been invoked throughout history to defend practices, such as slavery, that are now widely and rightly disparaged.[2]

In this vein, several prominent nineteenth-century American academics enlisted Aristotle in defense of the South's peculiar institution. As George Frederick Holmes wrote in the *Southern Literary Messenger* in 1850, "The main thesis in regard to Slavery is laid down in the most precise terms, and in the form most convenient for discussion, by Aristotle in his Politics. His position is that 'Nature has clearly designed some men for freedom and others for slavery: – and with respect to the latter, slavery is both just and beneficial.'"[3] One of the logical implications of

---

[2] See Aristotle, *Politics* (trans. Simpson) 1253b1–1255b41; Aristotle, *Nichomacheaan Ethics* (trans. Irwin) 1145a15–1154b35; cf. Thomas Aquinas, *Commentary on Aristotle's Politics*, trans. Richard J. Regan (Indianapolis, IN: Hackett Publishing, 2007), 10; 19–41.

[3] George Frederick Holmes, "Observations on a Passage in the Politics of Aristotle on Slavery," *Southern Literary Messenger* 16, no. 4 (1850), 193.

Aristotle's argument, Holmes assumed, was that Africans were naturally slavish and Europeans naturally virtuous, so that the enslavement of Africans by Europeans was not only just but beneficial for the slaves themselves.

From the details of Aristotle's teaching on natural slavery, however, such an assumption is far from warranted. Aristotle's natural slave is a physically able but incontinent individual whose own good can only be realized through the direction of another. The natural master, on the other hand, is nearly the opposite: an extraordinarily virtuous individual who can obtain a "certain mutual benefit and friendship" from the man he would rule.[4] Yet Aristotle invited a comparison between this idealized version of slavery and slavery on the ground, so to speak, when he reflected on the practical difficulty of identifying natural slaves and natural masters; for, as Aristotle asserted, nature has a desire to clearly demarcate men into the categories of free and slave by some easily recognizable indicator of virtue such as body type or birth, but she is "seldom able to realize it."[5] Thus, even if one were to concede along with Aristotle that "by nature some are free and others slaves," still the discussion of natural slavery in terms of virtue would present a strong challenge to slavery as it actually existed in ancient (not to mention modern) societies.

This, of course, is not to vindicate or defend Aristotle's position on slavery, but rather to suggest that there is no easy or obvious connection between Aristotle's doctrine of natural slavery and slavery as it has actually existed in any particular society. There are, as well, important differences between ancient slavery and the form of slavery that took root in seventeenth- and eighteenth-century America. "In antiquity," Tocqueville noted, "the slave belonged to the same race as his master and was often superior to him in education and knowledge. Freedom alone separated them; once freedom was granted, their differences melted away."[6] In America, masters could scarcely contemplate

[4] Aristotle, *Politics*, 1255b14.
[5] Aristotle, *Politics*, 1255b3.
[6] Alexis de Tocqueville, *Democracy in America*, trans. Gerald E. Bevan (London: Penguin Books, 2003), 399–400.

the education of the slave. As Frederick Douglass recounted overhearing his master quip, educated men were unfit for the kind of slavery practiced in the new world.[7] If an American slave nevertheless managed to gain freedom and education, he was still marked off from the ruling population by skin color and excluded from society by a virulent and widespread racism. Moving beyond Aristotle, therefore, we might ask how a natural-law ethical and political theory would apply in this context and make some attempt to distinguish between better and worse formulations of the natural-law arguments that were made during the course of debate on American slavery. Such an inquiry, however, requires at least a preliminary historical consideration of how natural-law thinkers have answered the fundamental (and yet convoluted and controversial) questions, "What is nature?" and "What is law?"

Classical Natural Law

The classical natural-law tradition developed from the wisdom literatures of Athens, Rome, and Jerusalem, which insisted, in different ways, that the order of the universe is such that human reason can discover morally obligatory principles of action that are rooted in human nature. As Paul Sigmund writes, "in all its diverse forms, the theory of natural law represents a common affirmation about the possibility of arriving at objective standards, and a common procedure for doing so – looking for a purposive order in nature and man."[8] Aristotelian ethics and metaphysics were particularly important in later theorizing about the epistemological and ontological foundations of any such natural moral standards. One could not know what was good for a being, Aristotle taught, unless one first had knowledge of a being's nature, which was understood in terms of functionality or purpose. When inquiring into the nature of man, Aristotle

---

[7] See Frederick Douglass, *Narrative of the Life and Times of Frederick Douglass*, ed. David Blight (Bedford Books, 1993), 57.

[8] Paul E. Sigmund, preface to *Natural Law in Political Thought* (Lanham, MD: Winthrop Publishers, 1971), ix.

Contents

Acknowledgments

Many people have had a hand in shaping this book from the beginning. I thank Jeff Tulis, Sandy Levinson, Gretchen Ritter, and H.W. Perry for offering valuable comments and criticism while this project was still in its early stages. J. Budziszewski was willing to read and comment on numerous drafts, and his work on the problem of moral self-deception has shaped my own thinking on problems of epistemology and natural law. As J. has taught us throughout his career, there truly are things "we can't not know." I also owe a special debt of gratitude to Gary Jacobsohn. The theoretical framework of constitutional disharmony that structures the arguments in this book is largely a result of his mentorship and guidance. Over the years, Gary has challenged me to think deeply about the aspirations and identity of our constitutional order, and for that I am grateful.

My colleagues at the University of Missouri have been uniformly encouraging, and I thank John Petrocik, our department chair, for his continued support. Matthew Moore and Kayla Crider each provided valuable research assistance, and Kayla's proofreading saved me from more than a few errors. On the business side, it has been a pleasure working with Lew Bateman and Anne Lovering Rounds at Cambridge University Press, and I appreciate their willingness to incorporate previously published material in this book. An earlier version of Chapter 2 appeared as "After the Revolution: *Somerset* and the Antislavery Tradition in Anglo-American Constitutional Development," *Journal of Politics* 71, no. 4 (2009): 1422–1434. Various sections in Chapter 4 are drawn from "Slavery and the Magna Carta in the Development of Anglo-American Constitutionalism," *PS: Political Science and Politics* 43, no. 3 (2010): 479–482, and "Lincolnian Natural Right, *Dred Scott*, and the Jurisprudence of John McLean," *Polity* 4, no. 1 (2009): 63–85. Additionally, an early version of Chapter 5 was published as "Revisiting *Dred Scott*: Prudence, Providence, and the Limits of Constitutional Statesmanship," *Perspectives on Political Science* 39, no. 3 (2010): 166–174. Permission from the publishers to use this material is acknowledged.

As always, family and friends have carried me through the research and writing process. The "sun looks down on nothing half so good," C. S. Lewis once ventured, "as a household laughing together over a meal, or two friends talking over a pint of beer." I have been blessed with good meals and interesting conversations too numerous to count, and I appreciate those who have shared them with me. Finally, my largest debt is to my wife, Kyle, who supports me in work and sustains me in life, and to our son, Bennett, who has enriched our lives in ways we could not have imagined.

Prologue

Slavery and the Laws and Rights of Nature

We hold these truths to be self-evident, that all men are created
equal, that they are endowed by their Creator with certain
inalienable Rights, that among these are Life, Liberty, and the
pursuit of Happiness.

Declaration of Independence, 1776

Neither aiming at originality of principle or sentiment, nor yet
copied from any particular and previous writing, [the Declaration
of Independence] was intended to be an expression of the
American mind, and to give to that expression the proper tone
and spirit called for by the occasion. All its authority rests then
on the harmonizing sentiments of the day, whether expressed in
conversation, in letters, printed essays, or in the elementary books
of public right, as Aristotle, Cicero, Locke, Sidney, &c.

Thomas Jefferson, 1825

Years ago, the twentieth-century American philosopher Henry
Veatch began a bibliographic essay on the Western tradition of
natural-law theory by exclaiming, "Surely, the ancient and honorable doctrine of natural law is dead, is it not? And many would
add, 'Long dead and well dead!'"[1] But to the contrary, Veatch

---

[1] Henry B. Veatch, "Natural Law: Dead or Alive?" *Literature of Liberty: A
Review of Contemporary Liberal Thought* 1, no. 4 (1978), 7.

concluded, funeral orations for the perennial philosophy of natural law had been delivered prematurely, as the post–World War II search for objective standards of political right had led to a renaissance of natural-law thinking in the Western world. Still, natural-law theory today remains at the periphery of academic discussions of ethics and politics, and one of the chief reasons for the continuing disrepute of natural-law doctrines, in addition to trends in epistemology and ontology, is the unhappy association of natural law with certain practices that are repugnant to our modern sensibilities.

The historical defense of slavery as "natural" – and, therefore, just – particularly burdens the contemporary enterprise of natural-law thinking. If something as unjust and immoral as chattel slavery could be defended in terms of nature, then why turn to nature as a guide for political and ethical life? The appeal to Aristotle by some nineteenth-century defenders of race-based and hereditary chatteldom further cements the unfortunate association of natural law with human bondage. Aristotle's doctrine of natural slavery – defended by no less a natural lawyer than Thomas Aquinas – has indeed cast a long shadow over the natural-law tradition, which has been invoked throughout history to defend practices, such as slavery, that are now widely and rightly disparaged.[2]

In this vein, several prominent nineteenth-century American academics enlisted Aristotle in defense of the South's peculiar institution. As George Frederick Holmes wrote in the *Southern Literary Messenger* in 1850, "The main thesis in regard to Slavery is laid down in the most precise terms, and in the form most convenient for discussion, by Aristotle in his Politics. His position is that 'Nature has clearly designed some men for freedom and others for slavery: – and with respect to the latter, slavery is both just and beneficial.'"[3] One of the logical implications of

[2] See Aristotle, *Politics* (trans. Simpson) 1253b1–1255b41; Aristotle, *Nichomacheaan Ethics* (trans. Irwin) 1145a15–1154b35; cf. Thomas Aquinas, *Commentary on Aristotle's Politics*, trans. Richard J. Regan (Indianapolis, IN: Hackett Publishing, 2007), 10; 19–41.
[3] George Frederick Holmes, "Observations on a Passage in the Politics of Aristotle on Slavery," *Southern Literary Messenger* 16, no. 4 (1850), 193.

Aristotle's argument, Holmes assumed, was that Africans were naturally slavish and Europeans naturally virtuous, so that the enslavement of Africans by Europeans was not only just but beneficial for the slaves themselves.

From the details of Aristotle's teaching on natural slavery, however, such an assumption is far from warranted. Aristotle's natural slave is a physically able but incontinent individual whose own good can only be realized through the direction of another. The natural master, on the other hand, is nearly the opposite: an extraordinarily virtuous individual who can obtain a "certain mutual benefit and friendship" from the man he would rule.[4] Yet Aristotle invited a comparison between this idealized version of slavery and slavery on the ground, so to speak, when he reflected on the practical difficulty of identifying natural slaves and natural masters; for, as Aristotle asserted, nature has a desire to clearly demarcate men into the categories of free and slave by some easily recognizable indicator of virtue such as body type or birth, but she is "seldom able to realize it."[5] Thus, even if one were to concede along with Aristotle that "by nature some are free and others slaves," still the discussion of natural slavery in terms of virtue would present a strong challenge to slavery as it actually existed in ancient (not to mention modern) societies.

This, of course, is not to vindicate or defend Aristotle's position on slavery, but rather to suggest that there is no easy or obvious connection between Aristotle's doctrine of natural slavery and slavery as it has actually existed in any particular society. There are, as well, important differences between ancient slavery and the form of slavery that took root in seventeenth- and eighteenth-century America. "In antiquity," Tocqueville noted, "the slave belonged to the same race as his master and was often superior to him in education and knowledge. Freedom alone separated them; once freedom was granted, their differences melted away."[6] In America, masters could scarcely contemplate

---

[4] Aristotle, *Politics*, 1255b14.
[5] Aristotle, *Politics*, 1255b3.
[6] Alexis de Tocqueville, *Democracy in America*, trans. Gerald E. Bevan (London: Penguin Books, 2003), 399–400.

the education of the slave. As Frederick Douglass recounted overhearing his master quip, educated men were unfit for the kind of slavery practiced in the new world.[7] If an American slave nevertheless managed to gain freedom and education, he was still marked off from the ruling population by skin color and excluded from society by a virulent and widespread racism. Moving beyond Aristotle, therefore, we might ask how a natural-law ethical and political theory would apply in this context and make some attempt to distinguish between better and worse formulations of the natural-law arguments that were made during the course of debate on American slavery. Such an inquiry, however, requires at least a preliminary historical consideration of how natural-law thinkers have answered the fundamental (and yet convoluted and controversial) questions, "What is nature?" and "What is law?"

Classical Natural Law

The classical natural-law tradition developed from the wisdom literatures of Athens, Rome, and Jerusalem, which insisted, in different ways, that the order of the universe is such that human reason can discover morally obligatory principles of action that are rooted in human nature. As Paul Sigmund writes, "in all its diverse forms, the theory of natural law represents a common affirmation about the possibility of arriving at objective standards, and a common procedure for doing so – looking for a purposive order in nature and man."[8] Aristotelian ethics and metaphysics were particularly important in later theorizing about the epistemological and ontological foundations of any such natural moral standards. One could not know what was good for a being, Aristotle taught, unless one first had knowledge of a being's nature, which was understood in terms of functionality or purpose. When inquiring into the nature of man, Aristotle

---

[7] See Frederick Douglass, *Narrative of the Life and Times of Frederick Douglass*, ed. David Blight (Bedford Books, 1993), 57.

[8] Paul E. Sigmund, preface to *Natural Law in Political Thought* (Lanham, MD: Winthrop Publishers, 1971), ix.

answered that man was a rational animal whose proper function was "activity of the soul in accord with reason or requiring reason."[9] In addition to being a rational animal, man was also a political animal, whose individual good required that he live in political community. A man who was able to live apart from the polis, Aristotle famously suggested, would be either a beast or a god.[10] Nature and reason, then, were the starting points for Aristotelian ethics, and politics, which was necessary for human flourishing, was a central and vital aspect of ethical study.

Although Aristotle spoke infrequently about natural law – making reference to a common law "according to nature" only in passing – he did explicitly juxtapose a standard of "natural justice" with a form of "justice by convention."[11] There was, in other words, a standard of justice, understood in terms of nature, that transcended any mere conventional practice. The idea that nature somehow served as a source of moral and political norms developed within the Roman and Christian orbits, as well. In the voice of Laelius, the Roman philosopher and statesman Cicero had taught that "true law is right reason, conformable to nature, universal, unchangeable, eternal" and that God was "its author, its promulgator, its enforcer."[12] Paul, in his letter to the church at Rome, had similarly insisted that there was a law written by God on the hearts of men, and later Christian writers such as Augustine identified that law as the "highest reason, which must always be obeyed."[13] Owing chiefly to the synthesis of Augustinian theology and Aristotelian philosophy in Thomas Aquinas's *Summa Theologiae* (wherein Thomas's brief statement

---

[9] Aristotle, *Nichomachean Ethics*, 1098a13–16.

[10] Aristotle, *Politics*, 1253a25–29.

[11] Aristotle, *Rhetoric* (trans. Roberts), 1372b2–8; Aristotle, *Nichomachean Ethics*, 1134b19–1135a15.

[12] Marcus Tullius Cicero, *The Political Works of Marcus Tullius Cicero: Comprising his Treatise on the Commonwealth; and his Treatise on the Laws*, trans. Francis Barham, 2 vols. (London: Edmund Spettigue, 1841–42). Vol. 1, Book III, Para. 36. http://oll.libertyfund.org/title/546/83303 (accessed April 29, 2011).

[13] Augustine, *On Free Choice of the Will*, trans. Thomas Williams (Indianapolis, IN: Hackett Publishing Company, 1993), 11. See Romans 2.15.

on natural law occupies a mere 8 questions out of more than
500), natural-law theory in the Middle Ages became associated
with a scholastic blend of Aristotelian metaphysics and providential monotheism.

Following Aristotle, Thomas defined man as a "rational
animal" who was directed to his natural end through action
in accordance with reason.[14] Thomas's ethics and politics were
also linked with his natural theology, and he described the
rational order of the cosmos as an eternal law that existed in
the mind of God. Thomas's distinction between four types of
law – eternal, divine, natural, and human – was thus part of an
ontological theory about the rational structure of the universe.
This was separate, however, from the epistemological question
of how humans became acquainted with and participated in
the requirements of this rational order. On that score, Thomas
insisted that humans participated in the eternal law through the
indemonstrable and underived first principles of natural law,
which, like mathematical axioms, formed a part of humanity's
latent knowledge.

Law in whatever form, Thomas taught, was "nothing else
than an ordinance of reason for the common good, made by him
who has care of the community, and promulgated."[15] Natural
law, as law, fit this description: It was ordained by God for the
common good of his creation and promulgated through human
nature. The first principles of natural law were, moreover, right
for all and (at some level) known to all, and they provided the
foundation for practical reason.[16] To be truly law, a legislative
enactment, according this schema, had to be made by legitimate public authority for the common good according to rational
standards of justice. Insofar as a human ordinance diverged from
any of the essential characteristics of law, it was a fraudulent act
of violence rather than a morally binding dictate issued by legitimate authority.

[14] *S.T.*, I-II, Q. 94, Art. 2.
[15] *S.T.*, I-II, Q. 90, Art. 4.
[16] *S.T.*, I-II, Q. 94. Art. 4.

Modern Natural Rights

Several foundational aspects of Thomas's natural-law theory came under attack during the modern era, as enlightenment thinkers attempted to give an account of political right without reference to purposes or ends inherent in nature. The modern trend of distinguishing between the realms of objective material nature and subjective standards of good and right thus initiated a radical departure from the natural teleology of the Aristotelian tradition. If nature did not divulge the purposes of a being, or if natural purposes were irrelevant to morality, then the term "good" could not be employed to describe something that fulfilled its natural function well. Rather, as the seventeenth-century English philosopher Thomas Hobbes wrote, "whatsoever is the object of any man's appetite or desire that is it which he for his part calleth good ... [for there is] nothing simply and absolutely so, nor any common rule of good and evil to be taken from the nature of the objects themselves, but from the person of the man."[17] The Hobbesian turn toward a subjective account of the good led away from the traditional doctrine of natural law and toward a new theory of natural right.

In Hobbes's reformulation, what one had a right to do according to nature was understood quite apart from, and in fact prior to, the laws of nature. Right, in the way Hobbes employed the term, meant "the liberty to do or to forbear," and the foundation of natural right was each man's liberty in the state of nature to use his faculties for the protection of his life and limbs.[18] Indeed, for Hobbes, the *nature* of man did not extend beyond his material existence.[19] Further, every man was himself the judge of what means were conducive to the end of self-preservation, and all things that were conducive to self-preservation were man's liberty or right by nature. The laws of nature, Hobbes thus asserted, were mere maxims that "declare unto us the ways of

---

[17] Thomas Hobbes, *Leviathan*, ed. Edwin Curley (Indianapolis, IN: Hackett Publishing Company, 1994), Chap. 6, Para. 7.

[18] Hobbes, *Leviathan*, 14.3.

[19] See ibid., 14.1.

peace, where the same may be obtained, and of defence where it may not."[20]

Such an argument effectively rendered the old moral code, with the primacy of duty and obligation, meaningless. Natural law became indistinguishable from material self-interest, and the laws of nature were merely prudential guidelines for securing the natural right of self-preservation. At the same time, Hobbes undercut the Aristotelian basis for the legitimate rule of the virtuous over the vicious by emphasizing the natural equality of all men (in terms of relative power) and making irresistible force the sole desideratum of authority.[21] The institution of despotic dominion – along with paternal dominion and the dominion of a sovereign in a commonwealth – was therefore understood in terms of mere force.[22] Accordingly, the laws of a commonwealth were merely the commands of a sovereign power (whatever those commands happened to be).

Within the revolutionary milieu of seventeenth-century England, other theories as well – such as Robert Filmer's patriarchal argument for the divine right of kings – were put forward to justify absolute sovereign power. The general contours of Filmer's argument can be roughly summarized by the chapter headings of his 1680 tract *Patriarcha*: (1) "That the first kings were fathers of families"; (2) "That is it unnatural for the people to govern or choose governors"; and that (3) "Positive laws do not infringe the natural and fatherly powers of kings."[23] In other words, the commonwealth was an extended family, with a natural fatherly authority, sanctioned by God, at the head. Filmer's theory, however, was discordant with the main of the natural-law tradition (whose advocates had long supported a constitutionally mixed regime), and it is perhaps not surprising that English Whigs and American revolutionaries favored the more radical political teachings of Algernon Sidney and John Locke, among others.

[20] Thomas Hobbes, *The Elements of Law*, ed. J.C.A. Gaskin (New York: Oxford University Press, 2008), Part I, Chap 15, Para. 1.
[21] Ibid., I.14.13.
[22] Hobbes, *Leviathan*, 20.14.
[23] Sir Robert Filmer, *Patriarcha; of the Natural Power of Kings* (London: Richard Chiswell, 1680).

Sidney's *Discourses on Government*, published two years before his execution for treason in 1683, read as a point-by-point refutation of Filmer's *Patriarcha*, with chapter headings that declared: (1) "Paternal power is entirely different than political power"; (2) "The people choose their governors by virtue of their natural right to liberty"; and (3) "Kings are entirely subject to the law, which in England means parliament." In contrast to Filmer, Sidney argued that "God and nature" gave freedom to all men and that government, formed by the consent of free men, existed to secure liberty within the bounds of the natural law.[24] In a passage familiar to Thomas Jefferson, Sidney mockingly summarized Filmer's thesis as insisting that some men were "born with crowns upon their heads, and all others with saddles upon their backs."[25] Jefferson, like Sidney, rejected such an assumption, insisting on the "palpable truth that the mass of mankind has not been born with saddles on their backs nor a favored few booted and spurred, ready to ride them legitimately by the grace of God."[26] Yet, although Sidney's arguments against Filmer clearly left an imprint on the American mind, the natural-law theory of Sidney's contemporary, John Locke, perhaps went further than any other to give it shape and form.

"The state of nature has a law of nature to govern it," Locke insisted in his *Second Treatise of Government*, and "... reason, which is that law, teaches all mankind, who will but consult it, that being all equal and independent, no one ought to harm another in his life, health, liberty or possessions."[27] Still, the state of nature was insecure, and, as God had not appointed any one man to rule over the others, each man was necessarily the enforcer and interpreter of the law of nature. In such a state of insecurity, men voluntarily consented to form a government that would

[24] Algernon Sidney, *Discourses Concerning Government*, ed. Thomas West (Indianapolis, IN: Liberty Fund, 1996), Chapter 2, Para. 20.

[25] Ibid., 1.10.

[26] Thomas Jefferson to Robert Weightman (June 24, 1826). http://www.loc.gov/exhibits/declara/rcwltr.html (accessed October 31, 2009).

[27] John Locke, *Two Treatises of Government*, ed. Peter Laslett (New York: Cambridge University Press, 1988), Part II, Chap. 2, Para. 6.

protect their natural rights to life, liberty, and property. A government thus created had no legitimate power to transgress the natural rights of the people, and any man, including a ruler, who showed a design to deprive another of his rights declared war on that man.[28] In Locke's phraseology, "Force without Right, upon a Man's Person, makes a State of War, both where there is, and is not, a common judge."[29] In such a state of war between ruler and ruled, the legitimate power to execute the law of nature devolved back to the offended parties, who could rightfully "appeal to Heaven" (i.e., revolt) and then consent to a different governmental arrangement for the security of their rights.[30]

Locke's profound influence on the American Founders is evidenced by the familiar teaching of the Declaration of Independence that "all men are created equal and ... endowed by their Creator with certain inalienable Rights"; that "to secure these rights, Governments are instituted among Men, deriving their just powers from the consent of the governed"; and that "whenever any Form of Government becomes destructive of these ends, it is the Right of the People to alter or to abolish it, and to institute new Government." The American Declaration was indeed an argument that force without right is illegitimate and that the measure of right was to be found in the "laws of Nature and Nature's God." On this point, the ancient and modern natural-law traditions were in agreement. As Alexander Hamilton had written just months before the Declaration was drafted, "Good and wise men, in all ages have embraced" a theory "that the deity, from the relations we stand to himself and to each other, has constituted an eternal and immutable law, which is indispensably obligatory upon all mankind, prior to any human institution whatever. This is what is called the law of nature.... Upon this law depend the natural rights of mankind."[31]

---

[28] Ibid., II.3.16–17.
[29] Ibid., II.3.19.
[30] Ibid., II.3.20.
[31] Alexander Hamilton, "The Farmer Refuted" (1775) in *The Works of Alexander Hamilton*, ed. Henry Cabot Lodge, 12 vols. (New York: G.P. Putnam's Sons, 1904), 1: 62.

Of course, there were important differences in these ancient and modern formulations of natural law. In the first place, the theory that equal and independent men in a state of nature form a government only because their rights are insecure suggests that men are not naturally political (in the sense that political community is necessary for human well-being). Within the broad sweep of the natural-law tradition, there have been, as well, serious disagreements about the naturalness of slavery and property. According to Aristotle, both slavery and property were rooted in and legitimized by human nature.[32] Aquinas, in contrast, insisted that "the possession of all things in common and universal freedom" were natural for human beings in some primary sense even while acknowledging the legitimate existence of conventional slavery and property rights as a necessary part of communal life in a fallen world.[33] Locke seemed to split the difference between the ancient and medieval views by maintaining the primacy of property (including property in oneself) as a natural right while arguing against the natural dominion of any one man.[34]

Another significant difference between the ancient and modern natural-law traditions is the implicit shift in the notion of freedom as the liberty to rule oneself according to reason to freedom as the absence of external restraints on action. The differences and tensions between these traditions have led to a voluminous secondary literature, and a charge often leveled against the rights-oriented natural-law theories prevalent at the American Founding is that they have led inexorably to the destructive atomistic individualism on display in many Western societies today.[35] Although there is an element of truth in this charge,

---

[32] See, for example, Aristotle, *Politics* 1256a1–1258a34 (arguing that property is natural) and Aristotle, *Politics* 1253b23–1254b39 (arguing that slavery is natural).

[33] *S.T.* I-II, Q. 94, Art. 5. See also *S.T.* II-II, Q. 57, Art. 3.

[34] Locke, *Second Treatise*, II.4–5.

[35] One of the central questions addressed by the secondary literature is whether natural rights are derived from natural law (or vice versa). For a general overview of the debate, see "Symposium: Natural Law v. Natural Rights. What Are They? How Do They Differ?" *Harvard Journal of Law and Public Policy* (1997) 20: 627–731. For prominent criticisms of the hyper-individualism of

the individualistic tendencies of modern natural rights theories
(as received and interpreted by many early Americans) need not
be exaggerated. Reflecting a general American Lockeanism, for
example, John Quincy Adams declared in a Lyceum address in
1842 that "there is a law of nature, or in more proper words, a
law of God, the author of nature, subjected to which the human
being comes into life, and from the power of which he can be
released only by death." According to this "law of nature's God,"
Adams continued, man is "a social being" who "cannot exist
alone." Adams suggested that a child was born utterly dependent
on his parents, whose conjugal union was the result of different
functions (and therefore different obligations) inherent in their
natures. The family, according to Adams, was thus the primary
association without which a man could not live, and the political
community was formed by a compact or agreement among families to better secure their existence and protect the individual
rights of their members.

In the same speech, Adams made it a point to dismiss both
Hobbes and Filmer for granting government the power to transgress the pre-political natural rights of individuals within families, and he suggested that the rival theories of "Sidney and Locke
constitute the foundation of the North American Declaration
of Independence."[36] Even so, in our own day Hobbes cannot
merely be dismissed as an authoritarian, as he was by many of
the American Founders. Hobbes eschewed metaphysics, rooted
legitimate government in consent, and emphasized man's natural equality, which he defined in terms of relative power rather
than dignity. The underlying premises of Hobbes's political
philosophy are, indeed, at the heart of much of modern political thought, and Hobbes offers perhaps the starkest contrast
between the older natural-law tradition and modern materialis-
tic and non-teleological-rights theories.

contemporary rights talk, see, for example, Mary Ann Glendon, *Rights Talk*
(New York: Free Press, 1991) and Alisdair MacIntyre, *After Virtue* (South
Bend, IN: Notre Dame University Press, 1981).
[36] John Quincy Adams, *The Social Compact* (Providence, RI: Knowles and Vose,
1842), 11–12; 29.

It would be a mistake, however, to conclude that classical natural law is somehow inherently antagonistic to individual-rights claims as such, or that Hobbes is representative of the whole of modern natural-rights theory.[37] As John Finnis notes, Hobbes's definition of natural rights as individual liberties with no correlative duties "deprives the notion of rights of virtually all its normative significance."[38] On the other side of this coin, the language of natural rights – despite some of its "dubious seventeenth-century origins" and its unfortunate historical "abuse by fanatics, adventurers, and self-interested persons" – has become part of the natural-law tradition, and the idiom of individual rights can express, or be used to express, traditional ideas about justice and the requirements of the natural law.[39]

The particular focus of this study, however, is on the natural-law arguments made by judges and statesmen, rather than philosophers, and it is at times difficult to tease out what exactly the language of natural law and natural rights is meant to signify in any particular political context. As James Ceaser notes, "Precision, in political life, is not the virtue that it claimed to be in philosophy."[40] Not every American who invoked the natural law in the nineteenth century was as thoughtful or systematic as John Quincy Adams was in his Lyceum Address. To say something was in accord with the laws of nature, during a time when it was generally popular to defend public policy decisions in terms of nature, became an idiomatic way to express approval. Natural law was thus often invoked without a clear indication of what it was or argument about why it was so.

---

[37] For the argument that natural law and natural rights can be reconciled conceptually, see John Finnis, *Natural Law and Natural Rights* (Oxford: Oxford University Press, 1980), 198–230; Anthony Lisska, *Aquinas's Theory of Natural Law: An Analytic Reconstruction* (Oxford: Oxford University Press, 1996), 223–246; and Nicholas Wolterstorff, *Justice: Rights and Wrongs* (Princeton, NJ: Princeton University Press, 2008).

[38] John Finnis, *Natural Law and Natural Rights* (Oxford: Oxford University Press, 1980), 208.

[39] Ibid., 221.

[40] James Ceaser, *Nature and History in American Political Development: A Debate* (Cambridge, MA: Harvard University Press, 2006), 9.

Nevertheless, there was a real and thoughtful tradition of natural-law thinking in nineteenth-century America, and much of this tradition coalesced around the problematic issue of slavery. If all men were created equal in some relevant moral sense, and if legitimate government authority was both founded on the consent of the governed and circumscribed by inalienable natural rights derived from the laws of nature, then the institution of race-based and hereditary chattel slavery stood out as a gross contradiction of the theoretical foundations of American government.[41] But those theoretical foundations can be understood in very different ways, and the notion that natural law is somehow relevant to American politics in general, and constitutional interpretation in particular, continues to be a point of dispute both in the academy and in the broader world of public affairs. By reconstructing some of the animating issues at the heart of the constitutional struggle over American slavery in the nineteenth century, this study seeks to contribute to the ongoing debate about the meaning and place of natural law in the American constitutional regime.

---

[41] It is sometimes suggested that the idea of government based on consent is inherently modern. This is not necessarily the case. For a defense of the compatibility of classical natural law with some consent-based theories of political obligation, see Mark C. Murphy, *Natural Law in Jurisprudence and Politics* (Cambridge: Cambridge University Press, 2006), 91–132. See also Leo Strauss, *Natural Right and History* (Chicago: University of Chicago Press, 1953), 120–164 and particularly 141.

I

Introduction

The Apple of Gold

In his published notes on the debates at the Constitutional Convention, James Madison observed that "the real difference of interest" between states "lay, not between large & small but between N. & Southn.... The institution of slavery & its consequences," Madison noted, "formed the line of discrimination."[1] In certain crucial respects, the Constitution written in Philadelphia during the summer of 1787 thus reflected "a mediation of sectional interests that were based chiefly on slavery."[2] And yet the spirit of compromise, which allowed such a mediation of interests to take place, also led, as Gouverneur Morris protested, to a certain "incoherence." If these moral and political differences "be real," the Pennsylvania delegate had declared, then "let us at once take a friendly leave of each other" rather than "attempting to blend incompatible things."[3]

In the end, however, the convention delegates did seem to blend the incompatible. Slaves were to be represented as property but also as men. Congress could prohibit the importation of slaves from foreign shores, but only after a period of twenty years. The

[1] Max Farrand, ed., *Records of the Federal Convention of 1787*, 3 vols. (New Haven, CT: Yale University Press, 1911), 2: 10 (July 14).

[2] William M. Wiecek, *The Sources of Antislavery Constitutionalism in America, 1760–1848* (Ithaca, NY: Cornell University Press, 1977), 64.

[3] Farrand, ed., *Records*, 1: 604 (July 13).

Constitution guaranteed the return of fugitive slaves, but it did not specify whether this was a matter of interstate comity or an obligation for the national government to enforce. Deeper moral and political principles, too, seemed to exist in an uneasy tension with the various constitutional provisions dealing with slavery. Madison voiced his own concern during debates at the convention that it would be "wrong to admit in the Constitution the idea that there could be property in men,"[4] and the constitutional text spoke of slavery only indirectly with euphemisms and circumlocutions, ostensibly to placate the middle and northern states, whose delegates had "particular scruples" with the word "slavery" appearing in the country's fundamental law.[5]

In later contests over the constitutional status of slavery, the competing principles behind many of the Constitution's compromises afforded plausible arguments for both proslavery and antislavery interpretations. Some insisted that slavery was the "very bond of [the] union,"[6] which could not be removed without destroying the entire constitutional structure, whereas others described the clauses in the Constitution dealing with slavery as mere "scaffolding" necessary for the construction of an otherwise "glorious liberty document."[7] The ambiguity in the relationship between slavery and the Constitution, engendered by the delegates' attempt to blend incompatible principles, left the door open to such variant interpretations, and these competing interpretations often rested on principles that were not explicit in the constitutional text.

For many of the judges, statesmen, and orators who insisted that the Constitution was essentially an antislavery document, such extratextual principles were supplied by theories of natural

---

[4] Jonathan Elliot, ed., *The Debates in the Several State Conventions on the Adoption of the Federal Constitution*, 5 vols. (New Haven, CT: Yale University Press, 1911) 5: 478 (August 25).

[5] Elliot, *Debates*, 4: 176 (James Iredell in the North Carolina ratifying convention). See also, Wiecek, *The Sources of Antislavery Constitutionalism*, 76.

[6] *The Antelope* (1825) 23 U.S. 66, 86 (Georgia Senator John Berrien).

[7] Frederick Douglass, "Should the Negro Enlist in the Union Army?" In Foner, Philip S., ed., *Frederick Douglass on Slavery and the Civil War: Selections from His Speeches and Writings* (Mineola, NY: Dover Publications, 2003), 50.

law. The natural-law principles undergirding the Constitution were antithetical to chattel slavery, it was argued, even though slavery had been protected by the Constitution's various compromises. Indeed, natural law provided the theoretical foundation both for constitutional arguments against slavery and for an antislavery defense of the Constitution's compromises. Even so, the uncomfortable fact remained that considerations of fundamental constitutional commitments, including commitments based on natural law, served in many instances only to highlight the felt tension between ideals and practice.

Slavery and the Contradictions of the American Founding

The tension between normative constitutional principles and the institution of slavery was evident at the beginning of America's fledgling republic, as slaveholding colonists appealed to the universal rights of man to protest government policies designed to reduce them to a state of "slavery." What seems obvious to us now – that it was a gross contradiction to hold some men in chains while declaring the right of all men to live free – was equally obvious to many during the founding era. A conflict between the entrenched and economically profitable system of chattel slavery and the widespread influence of the ideas of natural freedom, equality in natural rights, and government by consent made slavery an acute practical and theoretical problem in postrevolutionary America and presented serious difficulties for constitutional framers after the war. In time, this conflict highlighted certain contradictions between the foundational principles on which Americans had justified their Revolution and the existential reality of American constitutional politics.

The Maryland delegate to the Constitutional Convention, Luther Martin, later identified the fundamental contradiction at the heart of the American Founding. "It was said," Martin recalled,

... that we had but just assumed a place among independent nations, in consequence of our opposition to the attempts of Great-Britain to *enslave us*; that this opposition was grounded upon the *preservation of those rights*, to which God and nature had entitled *us*; not in *particular*, but in *common* with *all the rest of mankind*. That we had *appealed* to the *Supreme being* for his *assistance*, as the *God of freedom*, who could not but *approve* our efforts to preserve the *rights* which he had thus *imparted to his creatures*; that now, when we scarcely had risen from our *knees*, from *supplicating* his *aid* and *protection* – in *forming our government* over a *free people*, a government formed pretendedly on the *principles of liberty* and for *its preservation*, – in *that* government to have a provision, not only putting it *out of its* power to *restrain* and *prevent* the *slave trade*, but *even encouraging that most infamous traffic*, by giving the *States power* and *influence* in the *union, in proportion* as they cruelly *and wantonly sport with the rights of their fellow creatures....*[8]

The constitutional document crafted in Philadelphia was, in fact, replete with concessions to the delegates from South Carolina and Georgia, who insisted that there would be no union if their peculiar institution were to be left to the whims of the national legislature. The most obvious of the concessions to the slave interest included a representation scheme that counted each slave as three-fifths of a person (Article 1§2), a guarantee that the African slave trade would not be federally proscribed for a period of twenty years (Article 1§9), and a provision calling for the interstate rendition of fugitive slaves (Article 4§2). Several of the seemingly innocuous clauses in the Constitution, as well, were either designed to bolster the institution of slavery or had the practical effect of doing so.[9]

[8] Luther Martin, "Genuine Information" (1788) in Herbert Storing, ed., *The Complete Anti-Federalist*, 7 vols. (Chicago: University of Chicago Press, 1981), 2.4.63–71.
[9] See, generally, Paul Finkelman, *Slavery and the Founders: Race and Liberty in the Age of Jefferson* (Armonk, NY: M.E. Sharpe, 1996). As John Kaminski explains, included among the provisions indirectly affecting slavery were those clauses "(1) authorizing Congress to call forth the militia to help suppress domestic insurrections (including slave uprisings); (2) prohibitions on both the federal and state governments from levying export duties, thereby guaranteeing that the products of a slave economy (tobacco, indigo, rice, etc.) would not be taxed; (3) providing for the indirect election of the president through electors based on representation in Congress, which, because of the three-fifths clause, inflated the influence of the white Southern vote; (4) requiring a three-fourths approval of the states to adopt amendments to the Constitution, thus giving the South a veto power over all potential amendments; and (5) limiting the privileges and immunities clause to 'citizens,' thus denying these protections to

The slavery-related clauses in the Constitution of 1787 were not, however, attributable to a general moral obtuseness among members of the founding generation. The fundamental contradiction between the principles of the American Revolution and the system of chattel slavery was widely acknowledged even in the late eighteenth century. "That men should pray and fight for their own Freedom and yet keep others in Slavery," John Jay conceded, "is certainly acting a very inconsistent as well as unjust and perhaps impious part."[10] Likewise, the esteemed law professor St. George Tucker later observed that "[w]hilst we were offering up vows at the shrine of liberty, and sacrificing hecatombs upon her alters ... we were imposing upon our fellow men; who differ in complexion from us, a *slavery*, ten thousand times more cruel than the utmost extremity of those grievances and oppressions, of which we complained."[11]

In pamphlets and newspaper articles, speeches and sermons, both before and after the Revolution, slaveholding and nonslaveholding Americans declaimed the institution as a national curse and a great moral evil. In his *Summary View of the Rights of British Americans*, Thomas Jefferson considered the "abolition of domestic slavery" to be the "great object of desire" in colonial America, and, in his original draft of the Declaration of Independence, Jefferson included as one of the charges against the English Monarch that "[h]e has waged cruel war against

---

slaves and in some cases to free blacks." See John Kaminski, ed., *A Necessary Evil? Slavery and the Debate over the Constitution* (Madison, WI: Madison House, 1995), 45. For a discussion of various scholarly interpretations of the slavery clauses in the Constitution, see also William M. Wiecek, "Slavery in the Making of the Constitution," in *The Sources of Antislavery Constitutionalism in America, 1760–1848* (Ithaca, NY: Cornell University Press, 1977), 62–83 and Michael Zuckert, "Legality and Legitimacy in *Dred Scott*: The Crisis of the Incomplete Constitution," *Chicago-Kent Law Review* 82 (2009): 291–299.

[10] John Jay to Richard Price (September 27, 1785), MS Columbia University. Reprinted in Philip B. Kurland and Ralph Lerner, eds., *The Founder's Constitution*, 5 vols. (Chicago: University of Chicago Press, 1987), 1: 538.

[11] St. George Tucker, "A Dissertation on Slavery" in *Blackstone's Commentaries: With Notes of Reference to the Constitution and Laws of the Federal Government of the United States and of the Commonwealth of Virginia*, 5 vols. (Philadelphia: W.Y. Birch and A. Small, 1803), 2: Appendix, Note H, 31.

human nature itself, violating its most sacred rights of life and liberty in the persons of a distant people who never offended him, captivating & carrying them into slavery in another hemisphere, or to incur miserable death in their transportation thither." [12] The Father of the Constitution, James Madison, denounced chattel slavery as "the most oppressive dominion ever exercised by man over man," and the Father of the Country, George Washington, declared that "there is not a man living who wishes more sincerely than I do, to see a plan adopted for the abolition of it." [13]

Yet few revolutionaries made serious attempts to pluck the moats from their own eyes before they endeavored to remove the beam from the eye of King George. Such inconsistency was useful for critics of the revolution, who chastised the Americans for complaining of their "enslavement" to imperial masters. As Samuel Johnson famously asked during parliamentary debates in Westminster, "how is it we hear the loudest yelps for liberty among the drivers of negroes?" [14] Even as Jefferson accused the King of "waging cruel war against human nature," he personally held legal title to some 200 African slaves, many of whom, like the slaves of Madison and Washington, actively sought refuge in the military camps of the British Royal Army during the war. [15] When given the opportunity to construct a new system of

---

[12] Thomas Jefferson, *A Summary View of the Rights of British America* (Williamsburg, VA: Clementina Rind, 1774), 16–17.

[13] James Madison (June 6, 1787) in Max Farrand, ed., *The Records of the Federal Convention of 1787*, Rev. ed., 4 vols. (New Haven, CT and London: Yale University Press, 1937), 1:135; George Washington to Robert Morris (April 12, 1786) in John C. Fitzpatrick, ed., *The Writings of George Washington from the Original Manuscript Sources 1754–1799* (Washington, 1938), Vol. 28, Electronic Text Center, University of Virginia, www.etext.virginia.edu/ washington/fitzpatrick (accessed March 19, 2009).

[14] Samuel Johnson, *Taxation no Tyranny: An Answer to the Resolutions and Address of the American Congress* (London: T. Cadell, 1775), 89. Johnson was responding, in particular, to the claim that "the subjection of Americans may tend to the diminution of our own liberties." In response, Johnson asked: "If slavery be thus fatally contagious, how is it that we hear the loudest yelps for liberty among the drivers of negroes?"

[15] For the story of American slaves who fled to the British lines during the Revolutionary War, see Simon Schama, *Rough Crossings: Britain, the Slaves, and the American Revolution* (New York: HarperCollins, 2006).

government based on reflection and choice, the Founders then drafted a Constitution that hedged, in various ways, the institution they had singularly denounced as the nefarious imposition of an oppressive Crown.

In his reflections on the Constitutional Convention, Martin – dubbed America's "drunken prophet" by a recent biographer – observed that the slavery clauses in the proposed Constitution had led some delegates to conclude that the legal instrument was

... a *solemn mockery of*, and *insult to*, *that God* whose protection we had then implored, and could not fail to hold us up in *detestation*, and render us *contemptible* to every *true friend* of liberty in the world. It was said, it ought to be considered that *national* crimes can only be, and *frequently are*, *punished* in this world by *national punishments*, and that the *continuance* of the slave trade, and thus giving it a *national sanction* and *encouragement*, ought to be considered as *justly exposing* us to the *displeasure* and *vengeance of Him*, who is equal Lord of all, and who views with equal eye, the poor *African slave* and his *American master*![16]

The inability or unwillingness of the delegates to the Constitutional Convention to right what was widely recognized as a great national evil portended, to some participants, a great national tragedy. "By an inevitable chain of causes and effects," George Mason had warned, "Providence punishes national sins by national calamities."[17]

The Lincolnian Interpretation

Three score and eighteen years later, during his Second Inaugural Address as President of the United States, Abraham Lincoln invoked a similar view of Divine Providence as he offered his own tragic interpretation of the American experiment. Slaves

---

[16] Luther Martin, "Genuine Information" (1788) in Herbert J. Storing, ed., *The Complete Anti-Federalist*, 3 vols. (Chicago: University Press of Chicago, 1981), 2.4.63–71. The biography is Bill Kauffman, *Forgotten Founder, Drunken Prophet: The Life of Luther Martin* (Wilmington, DE: ISI Books, 2008).

[17] George Mason (August 22, 1787) in Max Farrand, ed., *Records of the Federal Convention*, 3 vols. (New Haven, CT: Yale University Press, 1911).

had "constituted a peculiar and powerful interest" in antebellum America, Lincoln observed, and "all knew that this interest was somehow the cause of the war."[18] Quoting Scripture, Lincoln then summarized, in familiar words, his interpretation of the conflict:

"Woe unto the world because of offenses; for it must needs be that offenses come, but woe to that man by whom the offense cometh." If we shall suppose that American slavery is one of those offenses which, in the providence of God, must needs come, but which, having continued through His appointed time, He now wills to remove, and that He gives to both North and South this terrible war as the woe due to those by whom the offense came, shall we discern therein any departure from those divine attributes which the believers in a living God always ascribe to Him? Fondly do we hope, fervently do we pray, that this mighty scourge of war may speedily pass away. Yet, if God wills that it continue until all the wealth piled by the bondsman's two hundred and fifty years of unrequited toil shall be sunk, and until every drop of blood drawn with the lash shall be paid by another drawn with the sword, as was said three thousand years ago, so still it must be said "the judgments of the Lord are true and righteous altogether."[19]

Yet although Lincoln viewed slavery as a particular national evil – providentially punishable, even, by a mighty scourge of war – he did not agree with the position espoused by anti-federalists such as Luther Martin and George Mason that the Constitution was itself the sanctioner and protector of that national evil.

In the Lincolnian interpretation, well known in our own day, the Constitution drew aspirational content from the principles in the opening lines of the Declaration of Independence. In a reflection on Proverbs 25:11, Lincoln wrote of the proclamation that "all men are created equal" and "endowed by their Creator with certain unalienable rights": "The assertion of that principle, at that time, was the word, 'fitly spoken,' which has proved an 'apple of gold' to us. The Union, and the Constitution, are the picture of silver, subsequently framed around it. The

[18] Lincoln, "Second Inaugural Address" (March 4, 1865) in Roy P. Basler, ed., *The Collected Works of Abraham Lincoln*, 8 vols. (New Brunswick, NJ: Rutgers University Press, 1953), 8: 332–333.

[19] Ibid.

picture was made for the apple, not to conceal, or destroy the apple; but to adorn, and preserve it. The picture was made for the apple – not the apple for the picture."[20] Within the context of slavery, then, the aspirations of the American regime were succinctly stated in the Declaration of Independence, and the Constitution was appropriately understood as being framed to realize those aspirations. Accordingly, all of the provisions in the Constitution implicitly touching the slavery issue could be seen as anticipating a time when slavery would become extinct. The fact that the word did not grace the pages of the Constitution was evidence, for Lincoln, that a time without slavery was anticipated, for "covert language was used with a purpose, and that purpose was that ... when it should be read by intelligent and patriotic men, after the institution of slavery had passed from among us – there should be nothing on the face of the great charter of liberty suggesting that such a thing as negro slavery had ever existed among us."[21]

Additionally, the central place Lincoln gave to the political doctrines in the Declaration of Independence was derived, in part, from his belief that they were grounded in truths that transcended a particular time and place and found an enduring basis in human nature. Nature, for Lincoln, in other words, did not merely denote what is but also supplied norms of what ought to be, and reason, rather than passion, provided the means by which man apprehended those practical axioms. As such, the particular norms of a particular polity could be measured against transcendent, rational standards. While Lincoln thought that historically the Declaration articulated principles that were relevant to the exercise of constitutional interpretation, the debate over the natural rights doctrine in the Declaration and its application to African slaves was also part of an "eternal struggle between these two principles – right and wrong – throughout

---

[20] Lincoln, "Fragment on the Constitution and the Union" (January 1861) in Basler, ed., *The Collected Works of Abraham Lincoln*, 4: 168–169.
[21] Lincoln, "Seventh and Last Debate with Stephen A. Douglas at Alton, Illinois" (October 15, 1858) in Basler, ed., *Collected Works of Abraham Lincoln*, 3: 307.

the world."[22] Such an interpretation of the Constitution – as the Frame of Silver constructed around an Apple of Gold – in turn allowed Lincoln to interpret America's fundamental law, despite its imperfections, as a "great charter of liberty."[23]

Lincoln's moderate antislavery interpretation of the Constitution (understood in light of the Declaration of Independence and with a view toward the ultimate extinction of slavery) emerged against the backdrop of radical abolitionism on the one hand and proslavery constitutionalism on the other. As Lincoln observed in his Second Inaugural Address, Americans knew slavery was "somehow the cause of the war" – but, while praying to the same God and reading the same Bible, they did not ascribe blame for the contest over slavery to the same source. Americans who took a principled stand against slavery asserted with one accord that the institution was a violation of the natural moral order, but the paramount disagreement that split the antislavery movement into radical and moderate camps concerned whether or not the Constitution was, as Lincoln insisted, an essentially antislavery document. The question that split radical abolitionists and proslavery constitutionalists, by contrast, was not whether the Constitution was antislavery – they agreed that it was not – but whether slavery was a moral wrong that contravened the laws of nature. For those Americans who insisted that slavery was a social and moral good, the blame for the war could be laid squarely at the feet of the abolitionists and their moderate enablers, such as Lincoln. The nineteenth-century debate over slavery – both within the abolitionist movement and within the polity as a whole – was thus structured, to a large degree, around the meaning and legacy of the natural-law tradition in America and the relationship between the principles of natural law and the Constitution.

Because the philosophical viability of natural-law theories is generally disparaged in contemporary scholarship, however, the fundamental role that disputes over natural law played in the

---

[22] Ibid., 3: 315.
[23] Ibid., 3: 307.

development of antislavery constitutionalism does not receive the attention it deserves. Neither are the implications of the modern philosophical rejection of natural law, within the context of slavery and American constitutionalism, adequately considered. Yet the general premises undergirding modern constitutional scholarship preclude normative judgments about competing historical sources, and, in turn, scholars do not render the same account of the constitutional wrong of slavery that undergirded Lincoln's "Apple of Gold" metaphor.

The Death of Natural-Law Constitutionalism

The coherence of Lincoln's constitutional interpretation required the philosophic vitality of those "Jeffersonian axioms," as he called them. But those axioms – grounded foremost in a belief in natural law – have since died in American constitutional theory, after receiving their deathblow from a man who endured a nearly fatal wound while fighting at Antietam in defense of the Union. The Civil War veteran and Associate Justice of the Supreme Court, Oliver Wendell Holmes, had declared in his seminal article in the 1918 *Harvard Law Review* that those jurists and statesmen who still believed in natural law were "in that naïve state of mind that accepts what has been familiar and accepted by them and their neighbors as something that must be accepted by all men everywhere."[24] The grounds of human judgment, Holmes explained, were based on deep-seated preferences, relative to each man. Thus rights and duties were founded on the arbitrary desires, beliefs, and wishes of society rather than on any "*a priori* discernment of a duty or the assertion of a preëxisting right."[25] Although men may be willing to fight each other and even die for their arbitrary preferences, still, from an enlightened vantage point, Holmes insisted, the other's grounds for fighting "are just as good as ours."[26]

[24] Oliver Wendell Holmes, "Natural Law," *Harvard Law Review* 32 (1918): 41.
[25] Ibid., 42.
[26] Ibid., 41.

Once we have accepted that the grounds of judgment are relative, however, what support may be given to Lincoln's constitutionalism? What becomes of the theory of constitutional aspiration? And on what grounds might we judge the historically competing principles implicit in the constitutional compromises over slavery? The general milieu of modern constitutional theory, in answering these questions, diverges from the Lincolnian view principally on two points. First, the Constitution is understood either to embody equally proslavery and antislavery aspirations or to be dominantly proslavery in orientation. Second, the particular natural-law theory found in the Declaration of Independence is thought to be philosophically discredited. As Gary Jacobsohn noted in *The Supreme Court and the Decline of Constitutional Aspiration*, many of our modern approaches to constitutional interpretation "were developed during a time distinguished by its rejection of eternal principles of natural justice" and therefore "founding aims and principles no longer display a decisive … presence in contemporary constitutional theory."[27]

Herbert Storing observed that part of this rejection of founding aims and principles is based on the modern opinion that "admirable as the Founders may be in other respects, in their response to the institution of Negro slavery, their example is one to be lived down rather than lived up to."[28] Noting that both radical abolitionists and proslavery constitutionalists in the antebellum era viewed the Constitution in essentially proslavery terms, Storing went on to write, "one of the best, and surely most authoritative, expressions of this view came in the opinion of Chief Justice Taney in the famous Supreme Court case of *Dred Scott v. Sandford*."[29] In that famous – and now infamous – opinion, Taney argued that the Framers meant to exclude African slaves from participation in the natural rights spoken of in the

---

[27] Gary J. Jacobsohn, *The Supreme Court and the Decline of Constitutional Aspiration* (Totowa, NJ: Rowman & Littlefield, 1986), 2; 10.

[28] Herbert Storing, "Slavery and the Moral Foundations of the American Republic," in Robert H. Horwitz, ed., *The Moral Foundations of the American Republic* (Charlottesville: University Press of Virginia, 1977), 214.

[29] Ibid., 214–215.

Declaration of Independence, that the Constitution strictly and expressly affirmed a right to own and traffic in slaves, and that no one at the time of the Founding would have thought that the descendents of slaves, whether or not they had progressed to a state of freedom, could ever be considered as part of the people for whom the Constitution was written.

The inegalitarian interpretation of the American regime represented in Taney's opinion has, of course, always had adherents, and modern scholarship has done much to highlight America's racist and ascriptive past.[30] Rogers Smith, in particular, has provided an account of the inegalitarian principles at work during the Founding era with respect to citizenship laws, and, while acknowledging the influence of America's liberal and republican traditions, Smith argues that political elites have quite frequently structured "U.S. citizenship in terms of illiberal and undemocratic racial, ethnic, and gender hierarchies, for reasons rooted in basic, enduring imperatives of political life."[31] Smith therefore interprets American political development through a "multiple traditions" paradigm, which recognizes "varying civic conceptions blending liberal, republican, and ascriptive elements in different combinations."[32] When assessing these competing traditions, moreover, Smith concludes that "it does not appear possible to ground liberal democratic values on any unimpeachable evidence or reasoning from nature, divine will, or human history. This inability to appeal to unchanging, transcendental grounds places liberal democratic civic ideals at a great disadvantage in competition with many ascriptive ones."[33] Once transcendent grounds for liberal civic ideals are abandoned as either philosophically unsound or impossible to ascertain, the "multiple

[30] See, for example, Paul Finkelman, ed., *Proslavery Thought, Ideology, and Politics* (New York: Garland Pub., 1989) and David F. Ericson, *The Debate over Slavery: Antislavery and Proslavery Liberalism in Antebellum America* (New York: New York University Press, 2000).

[31] Rogers Smith, *Civic Ideals: Conflicting Visions of Citizenship in U.S. History* (New Haven, CT: Yale University Press, 1997), 1.

[32] Ibid., 8.

[33] Ibid., 489.

traditions" paradigm seems to imply that the Lincolnian view of constitutional aspirationalism is an unreliable guide to interpreting the Constitution. Without a transcendent basis from which to judge the decency of various competing civic ideals, there seems to be no reason (other than preference) to privilege liberal ideals over illiberal ideals.

Mark Graber candidly embraces this dilemma in his work on the problem of constitutional evil. The task of modern constitutionalism, Graber suggests, is to secure peace between parties with competing conceptions of justice, and slavery engendered controversy in antebellum America precisely because there was no moral or constitutional consensus on the issue. Along with antislavery principles, the "racist and proslavery principles [the Taney Court] relied on" in *Dred Scott*, Graber argues, "had strong roots in both the Constitution and the American political tradition."[34] Aspirational arguments thus could not guarantee antislavery results because "[r]acist and other ascriptive ideologies are as rooted in the American political tradition as liberal, democratic, and republican ideals. Americans cherished white supremacy. Policies preserving racial hegemony were means to valued ends, not temporary expedients."[35] In addition to antislavery aspirationalism, Graber asserts, "Pro-slavery aspirationalism was similarly grounded in the original Constitution."[36] According to this view, then, Lincoln's argument against Taney's opinion in *Dred Scott* may have been effective political rhetoric, but it did not accurately assess the conflicted aspirational character of the Constitution and it did not adequately take into consideration the principal purpose of modern constitutionalism, which is to secure constitutional peace rather than constitutional justice (according to some contestable normative perspective).

An alternative modern theory of constitutional aspirationalism that attempts to bypass this historical dilemma locates

---

[34] Mark Graber, *Dred Scott and the Problem of Constitutional Evil* (New York: Cambridge University Press, 2006), 76.

[35] Ibid., 82.

[36] Ibid., 82.

constitutional aspirations in the contemporary polity rather than in the animating principles of the Constitution itself. Against the Lincolnian interpretation, for example, Hendrik Hartog writes that "1787 is little more than a starting point for a variety of narratives of constitutional struggles over power, justice, autonomy, citizenship, and community."[37] Legitimate constitutional aspirations, according to Hartog, are the "aspirations of autonomous citizens and groups" who hold on to a "faith that the received meanings of constitutional texts will change" in light of those citizens' and groups' evolving "rights-consciousness."[38] According to this alternative view, Lincoln took part in the struggle over constitutional meaning, and he did so within a rhetorical framework of original intent and natural rights, but it is inaccurate, and perhaps irrelevant, to claim that Lincoln's specific aspirational arguments are historically or philosophically true.

The constitutional theory of the late Supreme Court justice William Brennan rests somewhere in between Hartog's mere "starting point for a variety of narratives" and Lincoln's theory that constitutional aspirations were not contingent on the conceptions of each individual generation but were, in some sense, fixed by the events of 1776 and 1787. The amended Constitution, Brennan argued,

... entrenches the Bill of Rights and the Civil War amendments, and draws sustenance from the bedrock principles of another great text, the Magna Carta. So fashioned, the Constitution embodies the aspiration to social justice, brotherhood, and human dignity that brought this nation into being. The Constitution and the Bill of Rights solemnly committed the United States to be a country where the dignity and rights of all persons were equal before all authority.[39]

Brennan also acknowledged, however, that the history of the United States revealed inegalitarian practices, and he insisted

---

[37] Hendrik Hartog, "The Constitution of Aspiration and 'The Rights that Belong to Us All,'" *The Journal of American History*, 74 (1987): 1013–1014.

[38] Ibid., 1015.

[39] William J. Brennan, "Speech to the Text and Teaching Symposium" (October 12, 1985), Georgetown University, Washington, DC, www.fed-soc.org/resources/id.50/default.asp (accessed March 19, 2009).

that the liberal tradition in American politics has too often been "more pretension than realized fact." Nonetheless, Brennan maintained, "we are an aspiring people, a people with a faith in progress." As such, "our amended Constitution is the lodestar for our aspirations" and the Constitution's "majestic generalities and ennobling pronouncements" call forth interpretation in light of the polity's contemporary aspirational ideals. Brennan, in other words, looked to the historical development of the substantive value choices of the Founders in light of the evolving values of contemporary society. Our acceptance of the Founding principles, Brennan asserted, "should not bind us to those precise, at times anachronistic, contours." Quoting Robert Jackson's opinion in *Board of Education v. Barnette* (1943), Brennan argued that the task of contemporary constitutional interpretation is to translate those "majestic generalities of the Bill of Rights, conceived as part of the pattern of liberal government in the eighteenth century, into concrete restraints on officials dealing with the problems of the twentieth century."[40]

Contemporary aspirational theories thus have been occupied with articulating ways in which those majestic generalities might be translated into concrete restraints on government, and Ronald Dworkin has offered the most prominent of these theories. In his work on constitutional interpretation, Dworkin calls for "a fusion of constitutional law and moral theory" and appeals particularly to the constructivist political and moral theory of the late-twentieth-century philosopher John Rawls.[41] Notably, Rawls's theory of justice does not depend on any normative foundation outside of the political culture itself and is therefore fundamentally different than the natural-law theories held by many of the American Founders.[42] Dworkin, like Rawls, insists

[40] Ibid.
[41] Ronald Dworkin, *Taking Rights Seriously* (Cambridge, MA: Harvard University Press, 1978), 149.
[42] As Paul DeHart argues, those who root the foundation of morality solely in political culture or convention share in common a "moral nihilism in the sense that they reject a [moral] standard independent of and normative for human willing." Paul DeHart, *Uncovering the Constitution's Moral Design* (Columbia: University of Missouri Press, 2007), 123. Different assumptions

on bringing "political morality into the heart of constitutional law," with an emphasis on the word political – that is, concerning moral principles derived solely from the political culture.[43] Although Dworkin has embraced the label of "natural lawyer" in a limited sense, he means by this that his theory "makes the content of law sometimes depend on the correct answer to some moral question."[44] The interpretive methodology, however, requires only that judges consider "the political structure of their community in the following, perhaps special way: by trying to find the best *justification* they can find, in principles of political morality, for the structure as a whole."[45] In expounding the Dworkinian approach to constitutional interpretation, Sotirios Barber and James Fleming explain that we must "reflect critically upon our aspirations in striving for the interpretation that makes the Constitution the best it can be."[46]

Aspirationalism and Constitutional Interpretation

In their Dworkinian form, these constitutional aspirations are the proper province of a Herculean judge, who will strive to interpret the principles of morality implicit in contemporary political culture in such a manner as to consistently come to the "correct" constitutional answer. In Lincoln's "Apple of Gold" metaphor, however, the question of whether or not the judiciary is in a unique position to authoritatively interpret the meaning and implications of constitutional aspirations demands a more nuanced answer. Indeed, the relationship between constitutional

about the existence of transcendent moral norms allow for an important distinction between an aspirational theory ultimately rooted in transcendent moral norms (such as the Declaration's "laws of Nature and Nature's God") and an aspirational theory (such as Dworkin's) constructed from a particular political culture independent of anything outside of that culture.

[43] Ronald Dworkin, *Freedom's Law: The Moral Reading of the American Constitution* (Cambridge, MA: Harvard University Press, 1996), 2.

[44] Ronald Dworkin, "Natural Law Revisited," *University of Florida Law Review* 34 (1982): 165–188.

[45] Ibid., 165.

[46] Sotirios Barber and James Fleming, *Constitutional Interpretation: The Basic Questions* (New York: Oxford University Press, 2007), 160.

aspirations and constitutional adjudication became a particularly vexing issue for antislavery judges, who often emphasized the disparity between the deep principles of the Constitution and the particular requirements of the law. Confronted with what Robert Cover called the "moral-formal dilemma," judges emphasized their own impotence in deviating from the will of the people (expressed in the positive law) even when the formal legal requirements contravened principles of justice thought by judges to be embodied in the natural law.

Moderate antislavery public officials such as Lincoln suggested, however, that those very constitutional or statutory requirements could only be properly understood by considering the ends and purposes of the Constitution. In light of the Supreme Court's decision in *Dred Scott*, then, an additional question came to the surface: How shall citizens and public actors react when the Supreme Court interprets the Constitution incorrectly by neglecting to properly consider legitimate constitutional aspirations? Through his celebrated debates with Stephen Douglas regarding the authority of the Supreme Court's decision in *Dred Scott*, Lincoln developed a nuanced view of the proper role of the judiciary in expounding constitutional meaning, and, on the eve of taking office, in the midst of constitutional crisis, Lincoln reflected:

I do not forget the position assumed by some, that constitutional questions are to be decided by the Supreme Court; nor do I deny that such questions must be binding in any case, upon the parties to a suit; as to the object of that suit, while they are also entitled to a very high degree of respect and consideration in all parallel cases by all other departments of the government.... At the same time, a candid citizen must confess that if the policy of the government upon vital questions, affecting the whole people, is to be irrevocably fixed by decisions of the Supreme Court, the instant they are made, in ordinary litigation between parties, in personal actions, the people will have ceased to be their own rulers, having to that extent practically resigned their government into the hands of the eminent tribunal.[47]

---

[47] Abraham Lincoln, "First Inaugural Address" (March 4, 1861) in Basler, ed., *The Collected Works of Abraham Lincoln*, 4: 268.

Having been publicly accused by Douglas of inciting the people to mob violence and attempting to bring the Court into disrepute, Lincoln was forced to develop a coherent theory of judicial review that would respect the authority of the Court while denying the correlative doctrine of judicial supremacy. Lincoln thus argued that although Supreme Court decisions were authoritative and final for the parties involved in litigation, the principles of the Court's decision did not become binding as political rules for the coordinate branches of government unless they also accorded with the core meaning of the Constitution, which was understood in light of the teaching of the Declaration of Independence. As Jacobsohn argues, "Lincoln's response, to ignore the decision as a political rule, was predicated on the view that those sworn to uphold the Constitution have an obligation to advance the cause of constitutional principle, to the end of realizing the ideals of the Declaration of Independence."[48]

But if we reject the natural-law principles in the Declaration, and, more generally, if we reject constitutional teleology, then it appears quite senseless to refer to the ends or purposes – the aspirations – of a written constitution at all. According to Mark Brandon, this precisely was the step taken by the Framers of the Constitution of 1787. "Stated most boldly," Brandon proclaims, "the Constitution represented a point of departure, a quantum step that led constitutionalism out of the old metaphysical paradigm of natural law and into a new paradigm in which constitutionalism is concerned with a particular kind of *enterprise*."[49] This "new constitutionalism" has a "discrete operating logic" that jettisons nature as a source of norms relevant to the constitutional project. Rather than being an attempt to secure rights that have a transhistorical basis, then, the new constitutionalism, on Brandon's account, is defined (without reference to its ends) as a certain type of activity – "an experiment in a particular mode

---

[48] Gary Jacobsohn, "Abraham Lincoln 'On this Question of Judicial Authority,'" *Western Political Science Quarterly* 36 (1983): 68.
[49] Mark Brandon, *Free in the World: American Slavery and Constitutional Failure* (Princeton, NJ: Princeton University Press, 1998), 10.

of establishing, directing, and limiting political power" – that is itself historically contingent.[50]

Accordingly, constitutional failure with respect to slavery did not consist in a failure to protect the equal natural rights of slaves. Rather, the continued existence of slavery represented a failure to abide by the historically contingent standard, internal to the particular enterprise of modern constitutionalism, that the people should, through reflection and choice, be able to "construct their political identities by reference to the Constitution." But this claim, Brandon points out, "does not rest on the notion that the Constitution violated the principle of 'human dignity.' It may well have done so, but within the assumptions of the new constitutionalism, invoking a standard of human dignity is problematic, not least because of its metaphysical roots. Human dignity evokes natural law and natural rights, which are off limits in the new constitutionalism."[51] This new, substantively thin constitutionalism, Brandon further suggests, represents "our current conceptions of what a constitution and constitutional government are."[52]

If Brandon's account of our contemporary conceptions of constitutional government, as well as of the operating logic of the Constitution of 1787, is correct, then the constitutional theory championed by Lincoln was a relic of the new constitutionalism's early dissidents. For on Lincoln's account, the antebellum constitutional order failed because it turned away from the foundational logic of American government, summarized by the political teaching of the Declaration of Independence, that all men are created equal in terms of basic natural rights under the "Laws of Nature and Nature's God." Constitutional success or failure, accordingly, was understood in light of the overarching purpose of the constitutional enterprise, which, at a minimum, was to secure the equal

---

[50] Mark Brandon, "Constitutionalism and Constitutional Failure," in *Constitutional Politics: Essays on Constitution Making, Maintenance, and Change*, eds. Sotirios A. Barber and Robert P. George (Princeton, NJ: Princeton University Press, 2001), 304.

[51] Ibid., 306.

[52] Brandon, *Free in the World*, 11.

natural rights of the governed. Slavery, according to this view, was aberrational to the principles undergirding American constitutionalism, and the continued existence of slavery – not to mention its enlargement and expansion – threatened to undermine the very structure of the constitutional regime.

Lincoln's arguments were shared, moreover, by a larger antislavery constitutional tradition, and what has been overlooked, at times, in the literature on Lincoln is the fact that none of his arguments were original. The Lincolnian emphasis on natural law and natural rights, the antislavery character of the Constitution, the workings of providence in human affairs – even the power to abolish slavery during wartime – all had antecedents in American politics. At the heart of the American antislavery constitutional tradition were the twin notions that (1) slavery is a violation of the natural law and (2) the Constitution (including the provisions protecting slavery) ought to be interpreted in light of the founding commitment to natural law exemplified by (but not necessarily deriving from) the political teaching in the Declaration of Independence. In this light, the abolition of slavery after the Civil War and the adoption of the Reconstruction Amendments were interpreted as the realization of an aspiration latent in the original Constitution. Much of the modern academic literature on constitutional development and theory proceeds, however, from the disparate premises that (1) there is no discernible natural moral order and (2) the original Constitution, if not dominantly proslavery, was, at best, neutral with respect to the competing aspirations of proslavery and antislavery constitutionalists.

Perhaps a related trend in modern scholarship is the insistence on an epistemological separation of facts and values and a nonteleological definition of the objects of study.[53] As George Thomas argues, however, the purpose of modern constitutionalism is precisely to fuse facts and values – or theory and practice – in such

---

[53] For an important discussion of methodology, see George Thomas, "What is Political Development? A Constitutional Perspective," *The Review of Politics* 73 (2011): 275–294 and Karen Orren and Stephen Skowronek, "Have We Abandoned a 'Constitutional Perspective' on American Political Development?" *The Review of Politics* 73 (2011): 295–299.

as way as to create and sustain a political regime through time. The very logic of constitutionalism calls into play certain metaphysical questions about identity that give life to a conception of constitutional development as directed toward certain ends.[54] Jeff Tulis reminds us, as well, that when it comes to studying constitutions, there is an "inextricable connection between descriptive and normative analysis."[55] The following case studies thus partake of a kind of historical and theoretical inquiry that engages both facts and values and acknowledges the inextricable link between the two. Such a link between facts and values was indeed at the heart of the antislavery interpretation of the Constitution of 1787, which grew out of the broader tradition of Anglo-American constitutionalism.

---

[54] For example, how can a constitution maintain its identity through time? Can we identify one change as a "development" and another change as a "deterioration" or "disintegration"? What does it mean for a constitution to fail? For these types of questions, Thomas suggests that developmental approaches "are uniquely positioned to illuminate the logic and experience of a polity in a manner that cannot be captured by more conventional political science methods." Thomas, *What Is Political Development?* 276. For similar discussions, see also Gary Jacobsohn, "Constitutional Identity," *Review of Politics* 68 (2006): 361–397 and J. Budziszewski, *The Line Through the Heart: Natural Law as Fact, Theory, and Sign of Contradiction* (Wilmington, DE: ISI Books, 2009), 145–159.

[55] Jeffrey K. Tulis, "On the State of Constitutional Theory," *Law & Social Inquiry* 16 (1991): 714. For a general discussion of the necessary connection between normative and descriptive analysis, see also J. Budziszewski, "Homily on Method," *Journal of Politics* 46 (1984): 739–759 and George Thomas, "The Qualitative Foundations of Political Science Methodology," *Perspectives on Politics* 3 (2004): 855–866.

2

Somerset and the Antislavery Constitutional Tradition

By declaring in *Somerset v. Stewart* (1772) that the nature of slavery is "so odious ... nothing can be suffered to support it but positive law," Lord Chief Justice Mansfield placed himself firmly in that jurisprudential tradition that distinguishes between the law of nature and the law posited in any particular jurisdiction.[1] Despite Mansfield's declaration, "*fiat justitia ruat caelum,*"[2] however, the judgment in *Somerset* merely maintained that slaves brought to England could not be forcibly removed from the Island without *habeas corpus* review. As the Chief Justice recognized, "The setting 14,000 or 15,000 men at once free loose by a solemn opinion, is much disagreeable in the effects it threatens," and the Court's judgment in *Somerset* was tempered by a due regard for political expedience.[3]

Whatever the limited holding of the case, the *Somerset* judgment did seem to imply that the master-slave relationship rested on a dubious legal foundation because of slavery's contrariness both to natural law and to the substantive principles of the English Constitution. After the American Revolution, moreover, the "decision took on a life of its own and entered

---

[1] 1 Lofft 19. William Murray, Lord Mansfield, served as Chief Justice of the Court of King's Bench, the highest common-law tribunal in England.
[2] Translated "Let justice be done though the heavens may fall."
[3] 1 Lofft 17.

the mainstream of American constitutional discourse," playing a particularly important role in American antislavery constitutionalism.[4] As Don Fehrenbacher notes, *Somerset* "became a major weapon in the arsenal of abolitionism, lending support to the argument that slavery was contrary to natural law and without legal status beyond the boundaries of the jurisdiction establishing it by positive law."[5] At the dawn of the nineteenth century, the legislative criminalization of the transatlantic slave trades by the United Kingdom (1807) and the United States (1808) opened the door to novel legal attacks on slavery based on this jurisprudential distinction between the law of nature and the local positive law.[6]

Although Mansfield's rhetorical attack on the nature of slavery in *Somerset* was subsequently treated as *dictum* that did not decide any specific point of law, the particularities of the newly suppressed slave trade and the ambiguities of international law brought forth cases in the early nineteenth century in which judges were invited to consider whether anything but positive law could be suffered to support the legal status of slavery. One type of novel legal case that was brought before judges in England

---

[4] William M. Wiecek, *The Sources of Antislavery Constitutionalism in America, 1760–1848* (Ithaca, NY: Cornell University Press, 1977), 21.

[5] Don Fehrenbacher, *Slavery, Law, & Politics: The Dred Scott Case in Historical Perspective* (New York: Oxford University Press, 1981), 28.

[6] During the first quarter of the nineteenth century, judges in the South as well as the North interpreted the principle of *Somerset* as declaring that slaves were effectively manumitted by their residence in free jurisdictions. For a description of *Somerset*'s reception in the southern states, see Paul Finkelman, *An Imperfect Union: Slavery, Federalism, and Comity* (Chapel Hill: The University of North Carolina Press, 1981), 187–234. Finkelman notes that the theoretical attack on the nature of slavery, which was the logical outgrowth of the principle in *Somerset*, also elicited a moral and political defense of slavery such that by the mid-1850s, courts "openly debated whether free blacks were 'outlaws' or if they had any rights at all" (234). There are other events that cut against this trend as well, such as the passage of the Fugitive Slave Act of 1793, which sought to enforce interstate extradition of criminals and rendition of fugitive slaves as required by Article IV§2 of the U.S. Constitution. For an exploration of the legislative history of this congressional act, see Paul Finkelman, "The Kidnapping of John Davis and the Adoption of the Fugitive Slave Law of 1793," *The Journal of Southern History* 56 (1990): 397–422.

and the United States involved slaves asserting their own claim to freedom by virtue of their temporary residence in jurisdictions that did not explicitly protect or sanction slavery through positive legislation. Absorbing the premise in *Somerset* that the status of slavery depends on local law, these individuals petitioned for their own freedom. "Once free for an hour, free forever" became the rallying cry of the Anglo-American abolitionist movement. As freemen, they claimed, any reintroduction into a state of slavery constituted an illegal assault subject to *habeas corpus* review and judicial redress.

In contrast to the narratives sketched by Whiggish constitutional histories, the path of constitutional development in these early slave trade cases was often disjointed and the cases emerged within convoluted political and historical contexts.[7] As Ken Kersch notes in the introduction to his revisionist account of the development of post-New Deal civil liberties jurisprudence,

To the extent that political practice implicates important creedal principles ... it also entails both contestation over the meanings of those principles and the perpetual imperative of making tragic choices between those principles – such as liberty and equality or privacy and publicity – when, as is commonly the case, one conflicts with another. The meanings are defined and choices made in concrete political circumstances and institutional contexts, with the decision in each case shot through with pull of specific, historically situated goals, aversions, hopes, and fears.[8]

The development of Anglo-American antislavery constitutionalism in early nineteenth-century slave trade cases is particularly amenable to an analysis that emphasizes the influence of creedal principles on the tragic constitutional choices made within concrete political and historical contexts. Antislavery jurists often invoked

---

[7] See, for example, Ken Kersch, *Constructing Civil Liberties: Discontinuities in the Development of American Constitutional Law* (New York: Cambridge University Press, 2004). Quoting the historian Herbert Butterfield, Kersch describes Whig history as the "endeavor to cut 'a clean path through ... complexity' through 'an over-dramatization of the historical story' that pits the forces of progress against the forces of reaction...." (2). Cf. Herbert Butterfield, *The Whig Interpretation of History* (New York: Norton, 1965).

[8] Kersch, *Constructing Civil Liberties*, 11.

political and moral ideals to challenge contradictory institutional and social practices, but, as historically situated actors, they were seldom faced with simple, unidimensional choices between freedom and slavery or egalitarianism and ascriptive hierarchism.

In several cases that involved slaves asserting their own claims to freedom, the lack of explicit, controlling legislative provisions further brought to the fray questions of higher background rules and fundamental constitutional commitments implicit in each tradition, including considerations of natural law. There was often a tension between the universal and the particular elements at play in these cases, and this tension was brought to light by a judicial consideration of the relationship between the particular requirements of the positive law (as well as other prudential or strategic considerations) and the universal principles of liberty thought by judges to be embodied in the natural law. As scholars such as Samuel Huntington and Gary Jacobsohn have argued in difference contexts, the tension between the universal and the particular elements in constitutional orders often creates a kind of constitutional disharmony. Indeed, from a comparative perspective, Jacobsohn suggests that the problem of disharmony is a "universal constitutional condition," and Huntington, within the American context, notes that the "gap between promise and performance creates an inherent disharmony, at times latent, at times manifest, in American society."[9]

The practice of slavery in the Anglo-American world during the early nineteenth century provides a stark example of discord between normative constitutional principles and existential realities, a disharmony John Quincy Adams later characterized as a great "conflict between the principle of liberty and the fact of slavery."[10] The notion that American ideals have been at odds with American practice is, however, a contested premise.

[9] Gary J. Jacobsohn, *Constitutional Identity* (Cambridge, MA: Harvard University Press, 2010), 86; Samuel P. Huntington, *American Politics: The Promise of Disharmony* (Cambridge, MA: Harvard University Press, 1981), 12.

[10] John Quincy Adams, *Memoirs of John Quincy Adams* (December 13, 1838), ed., Charles Francis Adams (Philadelphia: J.B. Lippincott & Company), 10:39.

Scholars associated with Critical Race Theory, in particular, have challenged the thesis that liberal ideals are necessarily opposed to slavery and other forms of racially ascriptive hierarchies.[11] In addition, the empirical claim that the ideals (as opposed to the practices) of Americans have predominately been liberal has been challenged by scholars such as Rogers Smith, who argue that "American politics is best seen as expressing the interaction of multiple political traditions, including *liberalism, republicanism,* and *ascriptive forms of Americanism,* which have collectively comprised American political culture, without any constituting it as a whole."[12]

Mark Graber's recent revisionist account of the Supreme Court's proslavery ruling in *Dred Scott v. Sandford* (1857) highlights some of the normative questions that emerge from viewing American constitutional development through a multiple-traditions paradigm. American antislavery constitutionalism in the nineteenth century rested on the premise that even the slavery-related clauses in the Constitution aspired toward a certain liberal constitutional vision that was not yet a reality. One specific interpretive difficulty attending such a theory of constitutional aspiration is Graber's claim that, with respect to slavery, illiberal as well as liberal principles were equally rooted in the American political tradition.

Many such revisionist accounts – whether stemming from Critical Race Theory or from the multiple-traditions approach – focus on the Jacksonian, Civil War, or Reconstruction eras. The

---

[11] See, for example, John Hope Franklin, *Race and History: Selected Essays, 1938–1988* (Baton Rouge: Louisiana State University Press); Jennifer Hochschild, *The New American Dilemma: Liberal Democracy and School Desegregation* (New Haven, CT: Yale University Press, 1984); Charles W. Mills, *The Racial Contract* (Ithaca, NY: Cornell University Press, 1997).

[12] Rogers Smith, "Beyond Myrdal, Tocqueville, and Hartz: The Multiple Traditions in America," *The American Political Science Review* 87 (1993): 549–566. Cf. Alexis de Tocqueville, *Democracy in America*, trans. Gerald E. Bevan (New York: Penguin Books, 2003); Gunnar Myrdal, *An American Dilemma: The Negro Problem and American Democracy* (New York: Harper and Row, 1944); Louis Hartz, *The Liberal Tradition in America* (New York: Harcourt, 1955).

defense of slavery as a positive good as well as an entrenched constitutional value, rather than a necessary evil temporarily protected by constitutional compromise, was, however, much less prevalent in the first quarter of the nineteenth century. Even a young Roger Taney, author of the Court's notorious proslavery opinion in *Dred Scott*, assented to the tenets of the antislavery constitutional tradition while working as a lawyer in 1819. "A hard necessity," Taney argued,

... compels us to endure the evil of slavery for a time. It was imposed upon us by another nation, while we were yet in a state of colonial vassalage. It cannot be easily or suddenly removed. Yet while it continues it is a blot on our national character, and every real lover of freedom confidently hopes that it will be effectually, though it must be gradually, wiped away; and earnestly looks for the means, by which this necessary object may best be attained. And until it shall be accomplished: until the time shall come when we can point without a blush, to the language of the Declaration of Independence, every friend of humanity will seek to lighten the galling chain of slavery, and better, to the utmost of his power, the wretched condition of the slave.[13]

Only later did Taney adopt the position, which informed his *Dred Scott* opinion, that "it is too clear for dispute, that the enslaved African race were not intended to be included" under the egalitarian principles of the Declaration of Independence.[14]

The formative but limited impact of *Somerset* on Anglo-American constitutional development during the first quarter of the nineteenth century supplements and challenges traditional "Whiggish" constitutional narratives of inevitable liberal progress and various revisionist accounts that suggest proslavery principles are *as rooted* in the Anglo-American constitutional

---

[13] Roger B. Taney, "Speech in Defense of the Rev. Jacob Gruber." In Clement Eaton, *Freedom of Thought in the Old South* (Durham, NC: Duke University Press, 1940), 131. Gruber was a Free Black Methodist preacher indicted for attempting to "unlawfully and maliciously incite the slaves" at a Methodist camp meeting in Maryland.

[14] *Dred Scott v. Sandford*, 60 U.S. 393 (1857), 407 (Taney, J.). For an insightful article on Taney's changing views on slavery, see Timothy S. Huebner, "Roger B. Taney and the Slavery Issue: Looking Beyond – and Before – *Dred Scott*," *The Journal of American History* 97 (2010): 17–38.

tradition as antislavery principles. The early-nineteenth-century trend of judicially extending the general principles of liberty implicit in *Somerset* was halted by conservative decisions in the American case of *The Antelope* (1825) and the English case of *The Slave Grace* (1827), which are remarkably similar in principle despite their emergence in different constitutional contexts.[15] Rather than reflecting the vindication of proslavery aspirations, equally rooted in the constitutional tradition, these conservative opinions represent misguided judicial efforts to hold together increasingly disharmonic constitutional orders. As an interpretative paradigm, the concept of constitutional disharmony is helpful in explaining the ways in which the English and American constitutions contained internally discordant elements while nonetheless emphasizing the "primacy of particular aspirations within an ongoing dynamic of disharmonic contestation."[16] The increasing disharmony in the constitutional orders did, of course, reflect competing constitutional visions, but it would be a mistake to treat all constitutional visions as equal or to fail to discriminate between those principles which are fundamental and those which are aberrational to the foundations of Anglo-American constitutionalism. In reality, the fundamental principles undergirding the English and American claims to constitutional liberty offered a strong normative challenge to the existing institution of chattel slavery.

[15] In depicting this early-nineteenth-century contest over constitutional principles and the practice of human bondage, I employ the term "liberal" – as distinguished from *liberalism* – in a very broad sense to connote a partisanship for liberty as opposed to slavery. I use the term "conservative," on the other hand, as a relative term that connotes the conservation of the *status quo* with respect to slavery. In any historical work, the terms "liberal" and "conservative" are potentially anachronistic, not least because of the association of those terms with contemporary politics or political theory. As Rogers Smith notes, "the term *liberalism* (as opposed to *liberty* or *liberal*) was in fact infrequently used in English-speaking countries until the last half of the nineteenth century." See Rogers Smith, "Liberalism and Racism: The Problem of Analyzing Traditions," in David F. Ericson and Louisa Bertch, eds., *The Liberal Tradition in American Politics: Reassessing the Legacy of American Liberalism* (New York: Routledge, 1999), 15.

[16] Gary Jacobsohn, *Constitutional Identity*, 107.

Anglo-American Constitutionalism
and the Challenge of Slavery

If English and American constitutional thought rests on any shared constitutional principle, it is that subject and sovereign alike are to be ruled by the law. In the thirteenth century, the English jurist and legal commentator Henry de Bracton wrote, "For the King ought not to be under man but under God and under the law, because the law makes the king. Let the King therefore bestow upon the law what the law bestows upon him, namely dominion and power, for there is no King where will rules and not law."[17] Bracton no doubt had in mind some of the recent provisions of Magna Carta (1215), which provided a formal codification of this principle. The rebel Barons who imposed the Magna Carta on King John were animated by a desire to limit arbitrary executive power, and in Chapter 39 of that document they secured a promise from the Monarchy that "No free man shall be arrested or imprisoned, or disseised or outlawed or exiled or in any way victimised, neither will we attack him or send anyone to attack him, except by the lawful judgment of his peers or by the law of the land."[18] In the fourteenth century, Chapter 39 was redrafted by Parliament to apply not only to free men but to any man "of whatever estate or condition he may be," and this process of reinterpretation continued throughout the next several centuries as Parliament expanded "the Charter's special 'liberties' for the privileged classes to general guarantees of 'liberty' for all the king's subjects."[19]

The principle that individuals ought not be "in any way victimised" but "by the law of the land" was given legal force in the common law through the writ of *habeas corpus*, which allowed an individual to legally challenge the grounds of his detention

---

[17] Henry de Bracton, *On the Laws and Customs of England* (written between 1235 and 1259), quoted in Albert White, *The Making of the English Constitution: 449–1485* (New York: Knickerbocker Press, 1908), 268.

[18] *Magna Carta* (1215), Article 39, reprinted in appendix to Ralph Turner, *Magna Carta Throughout the Ages* (London: Pearson, 2003), 231.

[19] Ralph Turner, *Magna Carta*, 3.

or molestation. According to Blackstone, that Great Charter in its variety of manifestations throughout the years "was for the most part declaratory of the fundamental laws of England."[20] Furthermore, the Charter's principle of individual liberty was so well enshrined in the canons of jurisprudence operative in the American colonies (and later states) that the U.S. Constitution simply assumed the principle was operative in the newly created federal regime as well.[21] Article I provided that "The privilege of the Writ of *Habeas Corpus* shall not be suspended, unless when in Cases of Rebellion or Invasion the public Safety may require it,"[22] and, in a concession to the Anti-Federalists, the Fifth Amendment to the Constitution succinctly reiterated the principle behind *habeas corpus* review: "No person . . . shall be deprived of life, liberty, or property without due process of law."

As Bernard Bailyn notes, "The colonists' attitude to the whole world of politics was fundamentally shaped by the root assumption that they, as Britishers, shared in a unique inheritance of liberty." That liberty was secured to them by the English

---

[20] William Blackstone, *Commentaries on the Laws of England*, 4 vol. (Oxford: Clarendon Press, 1765–1769), 1: 123–124.

[21] In his *Commentaries*, Blackstone insisted that the common law of England was inoperative in the American colonies, "they being no part of the mother country, but distinct (though dependent) dominions." William Blackstone, *Commentaries on the Laws of England*, 1: 105. Still, as Robert Lowry Clinton notes, "the substantive law applied in colonial courts was largely that of English common law, appropriately modified to suit novel American conditions." Robert Lowry Clinton, *God and Man in the Law: The Foundations of Anglo-American Constitutionalism* (Lawrence: University Press of Kansas, 1997), 91. Indeed, early commentators on American law made just this claim. The "common law, as far as it is applicable to our situation and government," James Kent declared in one such representative statement, "has been recognized and adopted, as one entire system, by the people of [Virginia]." James Kent, *Commentaries on American Law*, 4 vols. (New York, 1826–1830), 1: 440. For a more detailed treatment of the common-law heritage of American constitutionalism, see James R. Stoner, Jr., *Common Law and Liberal Theory: Coke, Hobbes, and the Origins of American Constitutionalism* (Lawrence: University Press of Kansas, 1992) and *Common Law Liberty: Rethinking American Constitutionalism* (Lawrence: University Press of Kansas, 2003).

[22] United States Constitution, Art. 3§9.

Constitution, which was "the constituted – that is, existing – arrangement of governmental institutions, laws, and customs together with the principles and goals that animated them."[23] It is true that legal commentators such as Bracton, Coke, and Blackstone had identified the common law with principles of natural law, and a "belief that a proper system of laws and institutions should be suffused with, should express, essences and fundamentals – moral rights, reason, justice – had never been absent from English notions of the constitution."[24] Nevertheless, English constitutional thought also had never considered the laws and institutions of England as something theoretically distinct or separate from the English Constitution. As the colonists began enumerating grievances against those very English laws and institutions (often invoking the authority of natural law), it soon became evident that it would be politically foolish and perhaps theoretically misguided to ground their claim to rights in the English Constitution itself.

Gordon Wood argues that "[b]y 1776, the Americans had produced out of the polemic of the previous decade a notion of a constitution very different from what eighteenth century Englishmen were used to – a notion of a constitution that has come to characterize the very distinctiveness of American political thought."[25] In their rhetorical battle with the Crown, Americans attempted to separate "principles from government, constitutional from legal." This new understanding of a constitution outlived the circumstances that gave rise to it, and, in 1787, the delegates to the constitutional convention endeavored to lift some principles out of the political environment by enshrining them as fundamental or higher "constitutional" laws. The constitution was no longer synonymous with the

---

[23] Bernard Bailyn, *The Ideological Origins of the American Revolution*, 2nd ed. (Cambridge, MA: Harvard University Press, 1992), 66.

[24] Ibid., 69.

[25] Gordon Wood, *The Creation of the American Republic: 1776–1787*, 2nd ed. (Chapel Hill: The University of North Carolina Press, 1998), 260. Wood goes on to note, "So enthralled with their idea of a constitution as a written superior law set above the entire government against which all other law is to be measured that it is difficult to appreciate a contrary conception."

government, and ordinary legislation now could be measured against some set of enshrined higher background rules. In place of the traditional understanding of a constitution, the Americans championed "a deliberately contrived design of government and a specification of rights beyond the power of ordinary legislation to alter."[26] This new understanding is what modern commentators have broadly come to call "constitutionalism" as opposed to the older understanding, which merely connoted an experiential constitution – or institutional arrangement – of government.

Englishmen, of course, took pride in their own particular constitution. It was through the English Constitution, after all, that the principles of Magna Carta were continually reaffirmed. Blackstone had observed that "[t]he absolute rights of every Englishman ... are coeval with our form of government," and the liberties of Englishmen were associated principally with "that great charter of liberties."[27] Indeed, that charter of liberties inculcated principles that were identical with the principles undergirding the new American constitutionalism: limited government, supremacy of the rule of law, and condemnation of arbitrary power. But the "security of rights under the old constitutional system had been custom," and when Parliament began to move against ancient custom, the American colonists perceived that their rights were not secured by any fundamental restraint on the will of Parliament.[28]

That narrative, at least, informed the polemic issued against the English Constitution by the Americans. James Wilson, one of the early expounders of American law, summarized this position

---

[26] Bailyn, *Ideological Origins*, 68.

[27] Blackstone, *Commentaries on the Laws of England*, 1: 123.

[28] John Phillip Reid, *Constitutional History of the American Revolution* (Madison: The University of Wisconsin Press, 1986), 9. Thomas Paine, for example, argued that "it is wholly owing to the constitution of the people, and not the constitution of the government that the crown is not as oppressive in England as in Turkey," and Paine drew a stark distinction between a constitution antecedent to government and the English Constitution, which, according to Paine, was synonymous with unlimited government. See Thomas Paine, "Common Sense" (1776) in William M. Vander Weyde, ed., *The Life and Works of Thomas Paine*, vol. 2 (New Rochelle, NY: Thomas Paine National

when he wrote, "The order of things in Britain is exactly the reverse of things in the United States. Here, the people are masters of the government. There, the government is master of the people."[29] In his opinion in *Chisholm v. Georgia* (1794), Wilson explained that the new American science of jurisprudence rested on a fundamentally different foundation than had the jurisprudence of the mother country: "To the Constitution of the United States the term SOVEREIGN, is totally unknown."[30] In England, it was said that "the King or sovereign is the fountain of Justice," but "another principle, very different in its nature" was operative in America. That principle, according to Wilson, was that "The sovereign, when traced to his source, must be found in the man."[31] The people, in their corporate capacity, were to be sovereign over the government, and, as Hamilton argued in *Federalist* no. 78, the will of the people was "declared in the constitution" such that this declaration enjoyed preeminence over "the will of the legislature declared in its statutes."[32]

Despite the American parry against the doctrine of Parliamentary sovereignty, however, the substantive principles of the English Constitution were still understood by Englishmen to consist of those same principles underlying American constitutional thought. The mode of government operation was different, to be sure: In England, "Every act of Parliament was in a sense a part of the constitution, and all law, customary and statutory, was thus constitutional."[33] Yet the rights of Englishmen, established and secured by Parliament, were nevertheless understood to be "founded on nature and reason" even if they were at times existentially denied and left insecure, "their establishment, excellent as

Historical Association, 1925). The differences between the American and English Constitutions on this score have perhaps been overemphasized. See, in particular, Charles McIlwain, *Constitutionalism Ancient and Modern* (Ithaca, NY: Cornell University Press, 1947), 1–22.

[29] James Wilson, *The Works of the Honourable James Wilson*, 3 vols. (Philadelphia, 1804), 1: 425.

[30] *Chisholm v. Georgia* (1794), 2 U.S. 419, 454 (Wilson, J.).

[31] Ibid., 458.

[32] *Federalist* no. 78 (ed. Rossiter), para. 13.

[33] Wood, *Creation of the American Republic*, 261.

it is, still being human."[34] The principal disagreement between the American and English jurists, then, was a disagreement on how effectively to secure those rights, founded on nature and reason, through the creation and maintenance of a constitutional order.

For both Americans and Englishmen, the existence of legal slavery provided a challenge to the fundamentals of their own constitutional thought. The principles of African slavery, as it was found in the English colonies, including the American colonies, were diametrically opposed to Anglo-American constitutional principles. This particular system of chattel slavery established the private despotism of one man over another; the rule of private human will instead of the rule of law; and the expansion and enlargement of arbitrary power. If a system of chattel slavery was to subsist under a regime of liberty, then the questions properly arose: Are the rights to liberty merely conventional rights, inhering in Englishmen *qua* Englishmen (or Americans *qua* Americans), or do some fundamental rights inhere in man as such? Further, if there are rights that inhere in man *qua* man, do these rights apply to Africans, and, if so, are these rights justiciable in courts of law? These questions uncover a tension between universal and particular elements at work in the English and American claim to liberty. To maintain a system of chattel slavery and simultaneously assert a constitutional right to be free from arbitrary exercises of force, one had to either deny the humanity of the slave or deny the relevance of human status to the claim of liberty under the Constitution. In this respect, one could deny the Africans' participation in the universal rights of man, altogether deny the existence of any such universal rights, or concede that universal rights do apply to the Africans while nevertheless asserting that such rights are not secured by the particular constitution in question.

It is this tension between the universal and the particular that Blackstone attempted to navigate in that section of his *Commentaries* titled "Of Master and Servant." "The principle aim of society," Blackstone wrote, "is to protect individuals in

[34] Blackstone, *Commentaries on the Laws of England*, 1:123.

the enjoyment of those absolute rights, which were vested in them by the immutable laws of nature."[35] Those absolute rights inhering in man by nature served to underpin that spirit of liberty, which, Blackstone declared, "is so deeply implanted in our constitution, and rooted even in our very own soil, that a slave or a negro, the moment he lands in England, falls under the protection of the laws, and with regard to all natural rights becomes *eo instanti* a freeman."[36] In a subsequent edition, Blackstone qualified his teaching on natural liberty with a concession that a master may have certain rights to a slave's labor under the English Constitution, although he still maintained that the Constitution afforded certain legal protections to all English residents, including slaves.[37] Perhaps Blackstone had in mind some limited or qualified right of a master to the services of a slave when he wrote that "pure and proper slavery does not, nay cannot, subsist in England: such I mean, whereby an absolute and unlimited power is given to the master over the life and fortune of the slave."[38]

The imperial relationship between England and the American colonies further complicated Blackstone's analysis. The esteemed lawyer insisted that the common law of England was inoperative in the American colonies, "they being no part of the mother

[35] Ibid., 1: 120.

[36] Ibid., 1: 123.

[37] See William Blackstone, *Commentaries on the Laws of England*, 4 vols., 3rd ed. (Oxford: Clarendon Press, 1769), 1: 127. In the third edition, the relevant passage quoted above in note 36 is changed to read: "And this spirit of liberty is so deeply implanted in our constitution, and rooted even in our very soil, that a slave or a negro, the moment he lands in England, falls under the protection of the laws, and so fare becomes a freeman; though the master's right to his service may probably still continue." Wiecek notes that the first edition of Blackstone's *Commentaries* did not include the disclaimer that "the master's right" to the service of the slave might still have a legitimate basis in England, and the claim to liberty for the slave in the first edition was categorical. But, Wiecek writes, Blackstone was so "troubled by the potential antislavery uses to which the libertarian part of his writings" were being put by abolitionist leaders such as Granville Sharp that he tempered this passage in the third edition of the *Commentaries* to concede a limited right of a master to the services owed by a slave. See Wiecek, *The Sources of Antislavery Constitutionalism*, 27.

[38] Ibid., 1: 423.

country, but distinct (though dependent) dominions,"[39] and, in a later edition of his *Commentaries*, Blackstone maintained that rights of colonial masters were left untouched by the antislavery principles underpinning the English Constitution.[40] Still, American jurists such as James Wilson taught (quite apart from Blackstone) that the entire basis of American law rested on an understanding that "man, fearfully and wonderfully made, is the workmanship of his all perfect Creator," and that arbitrary power degrades "man from the prime rank, which he ought to hold in human affairs."[41] Wilson considered man, in his individual capacity, to be central to the construction of American law. "A state," Wilson reflected, "… is the noblest work of Man; But Man himself, free and honest, is, I speak as to this world, the noblest work of God."[42] Wilson also understood the inconsistency of the primacy of man in the constitutional order with the existence of African slavery, having approvingly quoted the abolitionist French statesman Jacques Necker in the Pennsylvania Ratifying Convention, saying to his fellow legislators that "we pride ourselves on the superiority of man, and it is with reason that we discover this superiority in the wonderful and mysterious unfolding of the intellectual faculties; and yet the trifling difference in the hair of the head, or in the color of the epidermis, is sufficient to change our respect into contempt."[43] Like Blackstone, however, Wilson perceived his own Constitution as a repudiation of the principles on which the institution of slavery rested: The clause in Constitution dealing with the importation of persons into the states, Wilson asserted, lay "the foundation for banishing slavery out of this country."[44]

---

[39] Blackstone, *Commentaries on the Laws of England*, 1:105.

[40] Blackstone, *Commentaries on the Laws of England* (3rd ed. 1769), 424–425. For additional commentary on this point, see William M. Wiecek, "*Somerset*: Lord Mansfield and the Legitimacy of Slavery in the Anglo-American World," *The University of Chicago Law Review* 42 (1974): 86–146, particularly the discussion on p. 99.

[41] *Chisholm v. Georgia* (1794), 455; 461 (Wilson, J.).

[42] Ibid., 462–463.

[43] *Elliot's Debates* 2: 485.

[44] Ibid., 2: 452.

The antislavery sentiments of eminent and formative jurists such as Blackstone and Wilson notwithstanding, the fact remained that the rights of a master over his slave had long been customarily recognized in the British Empire, and compromises with the slave interest were imbedded – as scaffolding perhaps, but imbedded nonetheless – in the fundamental law of the American regime.[45] After the legislative criminalization of the transatlantic slave trades in the United Kingdom and the United States in the early nineteenth century, the tension between the universal rights of man and the conventional rights of particular men became quite pronounced through legal battles over the status of captured or imported slaves. In several cases, lawyers for plaintiffs suing for their own freedom urged the courts to consider Mansfield's judgment in *Somerset* as establishing the principle on which the slaves asserted their claim to liberty. In *The Antelope* (1825) and *The Slave Grace* (1827), judges recognized that there was a tension between the conventional rights of the master and the natural rights of the slave, but nevertheless asserted that they were compelled by "the path of duty" – to use a phrase from Marshall's opinion in *The Antelope* – to vindicate the conventional rights of the slave owners.

The *Somerset Judgment*

James Somerset was an African-born Virginia plantation slave who was brought to England by his master in the late 1760s. After a foiled runaway attempt, Somerset was bound and held

---

[45] Abolitionists such as Frederick Douglass later argued that "the Federal Government was never, in its essence, anything but an anti-slavery government.... It was purposely so framed as to give no claim, no sanction to the claim of property in man. If in its origin slavery had any relation to the government, it was only as the scaffolding to the magnificent structure, to be removed as soon as the building was completed." See Frederick Douglass, "Address for the Promotion of Colored Enlistments." In Philip S. Foner, ed., *The Life and Writings of Frederick Douglass*, 4 vols. (New York: International Publishers), 3: 361–366. The claim that the Constitution of 1787 was essentially antislavery is, of course, controversial. Cf. Paul Finkelman, *An Imperfect Union*, 236–284 and Mark Graber, *Dred Scott and the Problem of Constitutional Evil* (New York: Cambridge University Press, 2006), 91–168.

on board an English vessel that was scheduled to set sail for Jamaica, where he was to be sold as punishment for his conduct. After hearing of Somerset's situation, Granville Sharp along with several other antislavery leaders successfully petitioned Lord Mansfield to issue a writ of *habeas corpus* to review the legality of Somerset's detention.[46] Sharp's friend, Francis Hargrave, served as counsel for Somerset, and Hargrave's argument – developed in collaboration with Sharp – rested on several key premises that had gained acceptance in England's nascent anti-slavery societies.

In his argument before the Court, Hargrave first asserted that a master's claim over his slave was "opposite to natural justice" and that this understanding was corroborated by the writings of various philosophers such as Grotius, Montesquieu, Pufendorf, Rutherford, and Locke. Next, he suggested that "the genius and spirit of the constitution" forbade the existence of slavery in England, because the perpetuation of slavery depended on slave codes that established "arbitrary maxims and practices" that were repugnant to the rule of law under the English Constitution.[47] Because slavery was contrary to the law of nature, moreover, Hargrave argued that the legal claim of a master over a slave depended on the local law in force (instead of some abstract property right in a slave), and the law of England "does not invest another man with despotism."[48] Furthermore, because "the right of the master [in this case] depends on the condition of slavery ... in *America*,"[49] the master's absolute claim over his slave was voided by virtue of their residence in England. Thus, under English law the slave was afforded judicial

---

[46] Granville Sharp had been putting together arguments that would attack slavery as "plainly contrary to the laws and constitution of this kingdom," and Somerset's case provided an opportunity to put these arguments before a judicial tribunal. See Granville Sharp, *A Representation of the Injustice and Dangerous Tendency of Tolerating Slavery; or of Admitting the Least Claim of Private Property in the Persons of Men, in England* (London: Benjamin White and Robert Horsfield, 1769), 40–41.

[47] 12 Geo. 3 K.B., 2.

[48] Ibid., 3.

[49] Ibid., 4.

protection from arbitrary detention and deportation against his will: "From the submission of the negro to the laws of England, he is liable to all their penalties, and consequently has a right to their protection."[50] In this way, Somerset's attorneys initiated a two-pronged assault on slavery in England by arguing that it was repugnant to the "natural rights of mankind" as well as contrary to the particular genius of the English Constitution.[51]

Mansfield was favorably inclined to the arguments put forward by Somerset's attorneys, although he recognized the danger of positing a principle that would effectively free the 14,000–15,000 slaves being held in England. The counsel for Somerset's master had warned that "[t]here are very strong and particular grounds of apprehension, if the relation in which [the slaves] stand to their masters is utterly to be dissolved on the instant of their coming into *England*."[52] While noting "the disagreeable effects" that such a situation threatened, including "the many thousands of pounds" that would be lost by slave owners, Mansfield maintained that practical considerations could not alter his judicial duty: "Compassion will not, on the one hand, nor inconvenience on the other, be to decide; but the law."[53] And in interpreting the law, Mansfield reiterated many of the arguments put forward by Hargrave:

The state of slavery is of such a nature, that it is incapable of being introduced on any reasons, moral or political; but only positive law, which preserves its force long after the reasons, occasion, and time itself from whence it was created, is erased from memory; It's so odious, that nothing can be suffered to support it but positive law. Whatever inconveniences, therefore, may follow from a decision, I cannot say this case

---

[50] Ibid., 5.

[51] Ibid., 2. Hargrave's co-counsel, Mr. Alleyne, particularly emphasized the first point, asserting that a man cannot part with his natural rights "without ceasing to be a man; for they immediately flow from, and are essential to, his condition as such." He then went on to summarize the argument being put forward on behalf of Somerset: "Slavery is not a natural, 'tis a municipal regulation; an institution therefore confined to certain places, and necessarily dropped by a passage into a country where such municipal regulations do not subsist." See ibid., 6.

[52] Ibid., 10.

[53] Ibid., 8, 17.

is allowed or approved by the law of England; and therefore the black must be discharged.[54]

Mansfield's judgment said nothing of slavery in the English colonies; neither did it hint at any legal implications for the colonial slave trade. The Chief Justice also specifically asserted that a limited right of a master to the services of his slave did exist in England.[55] It was the particular act of binding Somerset in order to sell him abroad that Mansfield declared to be "so high an act of dominion" that "it must be recognized by the law of the country where it is used."[56] In its direct application, then, the famous *Somerset* decision merely established that slaves held in England could challenge their detention or treatment on grounds of *habeas corpus* – not an unsubstantial ruling but also not the ruling that abolitionists like Sharp and Hargrave were looking for. Nonetheless, Mansfield's teaching that slavery was contrary to natural law – and correlatively that nothing could establish slavery except positive law – had a reverberating influence on Anglo-American antislavery constitutionalism.

Antislavery Constitutionalism after the Closing of the Slave Trades

A half-century after the judgment in *Somerset v. Stewart*, the Anglo-American constitutional debate over slavery continued to occur within the framework established by Mansfield. A series of legislative enactments concerning the slave trades in England and the United States had brought forth novel legal cases that required judges to decide whether anything but positive law could support the status of slavery. Relying on Mansfield's reasoning in *Somerset*, antislavery lawyers argued that slaves became free by virtue of their temporary residence in jurisdictions that did not explicitly protect slavery. As freemen,

---

[54] Ibid., 19.

[55] Mansfield began his opinion by asserting that "Contract for sale of a slave is good here; the sale is a matter which the law properly and readily attaches, and will maintain the price according to the agreement." See ibid., 17.

[56] Ibid., 19.

it was then argued, these persons could not be forcibly transported into another jurisdiction for the purposes of dealing
with them as slaves. In the absence of specific legislative provisions guiding the particularities of these cases, English and
American jurists considered questions of fundamental law as
well as what was ambiguously termed the "law of nations."[57]
Often these considerations required looking beyond any particular text to the animating principles of the Constitution – or,
perhaps more broadly, to the animating principles of modern
constitutionalism.

In the fifty or so years that had passed since Mansfield issued
his decision in *Somerset*, there was a clear line of legislative and
judicial activity in England and the United States tending toward
an expansion of liberty for human beings as such.[58] In March
1807, both the British Parliament and the U.S. Congress passed
legislation that criminalized the transatlantic slave trades.[59] The
earliest judicial decision coming out of this legislation was the

---

[57] For a discussion of the various ways in which the "law of nations" was
understood in the nineteenth century, see Henry Wheaton, *Elements of
International Law* (Philadelphia: Carey, Lea & Blanchard, 1836). The law of
nations, according to Wheaton, consisted of "the rules and principles which
govern, or are supposed to govern, the conduct of states in their mutual intercourse in peace and in war." This law, Wheaton further summarized, was
"supposed to be founded on the higher law sanction of the Natural Law,"
and it included both international positive law (e.g., treaties) and principles
of natural justice (iii).

[58] For an overview of some of the antislavery legislation during the revolutionary
period, see Fehrenbacher, *Slavery, Law & Politics*. "The antislavery tendencies
of the revolutionary period," Fehrenbacher notes, "were not inconsiderable.
State after state took steps to end the African slave trade. Abolition of slavery
itself was achieved in New England and Pennsylvania, and it seemed only a
matter of time in New York and New Jersey. Virginia gave strong encouragement to private manumissions by removing earlier restrictions upon them,
and both Maryland and Delaware subsequently followed her example. By the
1790's, abolition societies had appeared in every state from Virginia north-
ward, with prominent men like Benjamin Franklin and John Jay in leading
roles. And Congress in 1787 prohibited slavery in the Northwest Territory
with scarcely a dissenting vote" (8–9).

[59] The Congressional act was to go into effect on June 1, 1808. See U.S.
Constitution, Art. I§9, prohibiting the abolition of the slave trade by the
national legislature until 1808.

English case of *The Amedie* in 1810.[60] Following the logic of *Somerset*, Sir William Grant wrote for the high court of admiralty that the slave trade – because of its contrariness to natural law – "cannot, abstractedly speaking, be said to have a legitimate existence."[61] Trafficking in slaves was thus held to be *prima facie* illegal unless the claimant could prove that his title or right to property in a certain slave was expressly declared by the "particular law of his own country."[62] According to Grant, then, the judicial posture on claims for the "restoration of human beings" was to be in favor of liberty unless it could be unequivocally shown that the individuals were being held as slaves under some expressly decreed provision of local municipal law. This principle was reiterated by Sir William Scott, Lord Stowell, in *The Fortuna* (1811) and *The Donna Marianna* (1812) before entering American constitutional jurisprudence through Joseph Story's opinion in *La Jeune Eugenie* (1822).[63]

Justice Story's antislavery views were well known long before his hearing of this case.[64] Before a Boston Grand Jury in 1819, Story had proclaimed:

Our constitutions of government have declared, that all men are born free and equal, and have certain unalienable rights, among which are the right of enjoying their lives, liberties, and property, and of seeking and obtaining their own safety and happiness. May not the miserable African ask, 'Am I not a man and a brother?' We boast of our noble

---

[60] *The Amedie* (1810), 1 Acton 240. The *Amedie* was sailing under the flag of the United States with a cargo of 105 slaves. A British cruiser confiscated the ship and cargo and brought the cargo, including the slaves, into a vice-admiralty court for adjudication.

[61] Ibid.

[62] Ibid.

[63] *The Fortuna* (1811), 1 Dodson 81; *The Donna Mariana* (1812), 1 Dodson 91; *La Jeune Eugenie*, 26 Federal Cases, 832–851. *La Jeune Eugenie* was an American-made vessel sailing under a French flag, which was captured by an American schooner off the coast of Africa on suspicion of engaging in the slave trade.

[64] See Chapter 4 for a discussion of Story's seemingly proslavery opinion in *Prigg v. Pennsylvania* (1842). Certainly, the disparity between Story's early antislavery assertions and the decision he rendered in *Prigg* presents a challenge to my thesis concerning the relevance and operational impact of the antislavery tradition in constitutional adjudication.

struggle against the encroachments of tyranny, but do we forget that it assumed the mildest form in which authority ever assailed the rights of its subjects; and yet there are men among us who think it no wrong to condemn the shivering negro to perpetual slavery?[65]

It perhaps is not surprising, then, that Story condemned the nature of the slave trade with forceful rhetoric in his *La Jeune Eugenie* opinion. The slave trade, Story asserted,

... begins in corruption, and plunder, and kidnapping. It creates and stimulates unholy wars for the purpose of making captives. It desolates whole villages and provinces for the purpose of seizing the young, the feeble, the defenceless, and the innocent. It breaks down all the ties of parent, and children, and family, and country. It shuts up all sympathy for human suffering and sorrows. It manacles the inoffensive females and the starving infants. It forces the brave to untimely death in defence of their humble homes and firesides, or drives them to despair and self-immolation. It stirs up the worst passions of the human soul, darkening the spirit of revenge, sharpening the greediness of avarice, brutalizing the selfish, envenoming the cruel, famishing the weak, and crushing to death the broken-hearted. This is but the beginning of the evils.... All the wars, that have desolated Africa for the last three centuries, have had their origin in the slave trade. The blood of thousands of her miserable children has stained her shores, or quenched the dying embers of her desolated towns, to glut the appetite of slave dealers.[66]

This litany of evils was relevant precisely because Story assumed the premise of Mansfield's judgment that a practice contrary to natural law could not obtain a lawful existence unless it was established by positive legislation. In this case, Story was urged by the defendant's counsel to look to "the law of nations" for guidance in his decision. In an application of *Somerset's* principle to international law, Story argued that the law of nations rested on "the eternal law of nature" and found its bearings from "the general principles of right and justice." Whatever might be "deduced from the nature of moral obligation" was part of international law unless those moral obligations were "relaxed or waived by the consent of nations." In other words,

---

[65] William W. Story, ed. *The Life and Letters of Joseph Story*, 2 vols. (Boston, 1851), 340–341.

[66] *La Juene Eugenie* (1822) 26 Federal Cases 832, 845 (Story, J.).

the judicial consideration with respect to international law and slavery remained the same as it was with respect to domestic slavery: Nothing could be suffered to support it except positive legislation. Story's diatribe against the evils of slavery was all by way of showing that slavery was inconsistent with the "nature of moral obligation" under the "eternal laws of nature" such that it could not be said to be countenanced by international law in the absence of a specific treaty provision.[67]

As a constitutional matter, Story's argument in *La Jeune Eugenie* was consistent with the teachings of other antislavery American jurists, such as James Wilson. The classical understanding of the foundation of American constitutional government was that the people at large grant to the government certain limited and enumerated powers. To use Jefferson's language from the Declaration of Independence, governments derive their just powers from the consent of the governed, and any legitimate exercise of government power ultimately rests on a normative understanding of man's equality under "Nature and Nature's God." For Wilson, this constitutional teaching marked the beginning of an entirely new science of jurisprudence, which rested on an understanding that "States and Government were made for man," and correlatively that a State "derives all its acquired importance" from man's "native dignity."[68] The principles of this new science of jurisprudence challenged the very existence of a system of chattel slavery. As long as slavery was given a legal basis by the slave codes of local municipalities under the Constitution, it was to be judicially tolerated, but, according to Wilson, the presuppositions underpinning the Constitution presented "the pleasing prospect that the rights of mankind will be acknowledged and established throughout the Union."[69]

While England's Constitution rested on the disparate foundation of parliamentary sovereignty, there, too, in conjunction with legislative provisions circumscribing the slave trade, was

[67] Ibid., 846.
[68] *Chisholm v. Georgia* (1794), 455 (Wilson, J.).
[69] *Elliot's Debates*, 2: 484.

a development of constitutional claims based on native human dignity. Sir William Grant, in *The Amedie*, reflected:

> The slave trade has ... been totally abolished in this country, and our legislature has declared, that the African slave trade is contrary to the principles of justice and humanity. Whatever opinion, as private individuals, we before might have entertained upon the nature of this trade, no court of justice could with propriety have assumed such a position, as the basis of any of its decisions, whilst it was permitted by our own laws. But we do now lay down as a principle, that this is a trade, which cannot, abstractedly speaking, have a legitimate existence. I say, abstractedly speaking, because we cannot legislate for other countries.[70]

Grant reiterated the logic of *Somerset* that a right to ownership of or traffic in another human being is illegitimate when considered in the abstract, even though it nevertheless may be sanctioned by positive legislation. Therefore, consistent with this doctrine, a libellant applying for the restoration of "human beings ... carried unjustly to another country for the purpose of disposing of them as slaves" bore the burden of showing "that by the particular law of his own country he is entitled to carry on this traffic."[71] The burden of proof now rested on the slave master, and the judicial presumption was a presumption in favor of liberty.

The Conservative Impulse of the 1820s

The logic of the principle posited by Mansfield in the *Somerset* decision had taken such shape by 1824 that Justice Best, writing in *Forbes v. Cochrane and Cockburn*, could assert uncontroversially that *Somerset* had established "on the high ground of natural right" that "slavery is inconsistent with the English constitution."[72] In the American context, as well, it was generally recognized that slavery was – as Justice Story wrote in *La Jeune Eugenie* – a practice that blunted "the interests of universal justice."[73] It was also telling that the lawyer representing the

[70] *The Amedie*, I Acton 240.
[71] Ibid.
[72] *Forbes v. Cochrane and Cockburn* (1824), 2 Barnewall & Cresswell 448.
[73] *La Jeune Eugenie*, 850.

slave traders did not attempt to contradict Story's assertion: "[A] justification of slavery, or the slave trade," he said, "is not intended. I concur entirely in the views of the libellant's counsel on these subjects; and readily acknowledge, that at no time, nor at any occasion, have the noble and honorable sentiments, which spring up in cultivated minds, been more eloquently and ably impressed, than in this case." But, he went on to admonish, "[i]n deciding new and unprecedented cases, some consideration is due to expediency and convenience.... By the judgment which the libellants desire to have given, in the present state of the world, the progress of assent to effect abolition may be seriously retarded."[74] The argument put to Justice Story against judicially extending the logic of the principles growing out of the *Somerset* decision was thus an argument of expediency – a desire not to halt the progress of humanity by pouring the new wine of abolition too quickly into the old wineskin of constitutional compromise. Perhaps abstract constitutional principles had advanced in cultivated minds, but the actual constitution of at least one part of society was nevertheless very much committed to preserving the institution of slavery. Indeed, the proper maintenance of constitutional order amid such bifurcated interests was a real consideration, and if moving the principles of liberty forward too quickly at the judicial level was a serious danger to the constitutional order, given the present state of the world in the early 1820s, then a judicial remedy to the danger of progress was initiated by Chief Justice Marshall's opinion in *The Antelope.*

The case of *The Antelope* involved a pirate ship carrying 280 Africans previously captured from American, Portuguese, and Spanish vessels, which was found off the coast of the United States and brought into Savannah for adjudication. Portuguese and Spanish claimants initiated the suit under a treaty provision in which the United States agreed to return property rescued from pirates. The U.S. Attorney General, contra the Spanish and Portuguese, represented the Africans "as having been transported

[74] Ibid., 839.

from foreign parts by American citizens, in contravention to the laws of the United States, and as entitled to their freedom by those laws, and by the law of nations."[75] When oral arguments began before the Supreme Court, Francis Scott Key, the government lawyer appointed to represent the Africans, laid out an argument that had become familiar in similar cases. Key argued that there was a substantive difference between the *onus* required for proving legal ownership of things on the one hand and proving legal ownership of men on the other. "In some particular and excepted cases, depending upon the local law and usage, [men] may be the subjects of property and ownership; but by the law of nature all men are free."[76] To legally claim title to the Africans, then, the plaintiffs had to demonstrate more than "mere possession"; that is, they had to "show a law, making such persons property, and that they acquired them under such law."[77] After referencing the opinions in *The Amedie, The Fortuna, The Donna Marianna,* and *La Jeune Eugenie,* Key asserted that where the determinative law suffered from any ambiguity, "the fair abstract question arises, and their claim may well be repudiated as founded in injustice and illegality."[78] Finally, Key argued that even if some of the Africans were the legal property of the claimants under the laws of the United States, still, as the Spanish and Portuguese were unable "to identify their own, they are not entitled to restitution of any as slaves, since among them may be included some who are entitled to their freedom."[79]

John Berrien, the sitting U.S. Senator from Georgia who served as the lawyer representing the Spanish and Portuguese slave traders, attacked Key's claims by offering a constitutional argument that protected the right to property in a slave as fundamental, denied the existence of universal rights, and denied the competence of a court to consider arguments based on private notions of morality. "For more than twenty years this traffic was

[75] *The Antelope* (1825), 68.
[76] Ibid., 73.
[77] Ibid., 74.
[78] Ibid., 77.
[79] Ibid., 80–81.

protected by your constitution, exempted from the whole force of your legislative power; its fruits yet lay at the foundation of that compact.... Paradoxical as it may appear," Berrien asserted, the slaves "constitute the very bond of your union."[80] Whatever one's "peculiar notions of morality," a court was to be guided by the law, and, in a reversal of the principle in *Somerset*, Berrien maintained that the slave trade was "not contrary to the positive law of nations; because there is no general compact inhibiting it."[81] Rather than taking a stance *in favorem libertatis*, the legal presumption, according to Berrien, tended in favor of slavery unless the right to slavery was specifically circumscribed by positive legislation.

Of course, the right in question was not construed as a right to slavery as such but rather as a right to property. As Marshall articulated in the opening lines of his opinion, this was a case in which "the sacred rights of liberty and property come in conflict with each other."[82] But in so depicting the point of conflict, Marshall assumed an answer to the very question in controversy; for the argument made on behalf of the Africans was that a human being, by his very nature, was not a legitimate species of property (whereas he was the bearer of rights, including, presumably, the right himself to own property). U.S. Attorney General William Wirt, arguing alongside Key on behalf of the Africans, asserted "that no legitimate right can grow out of a violation" of the principles of "justice and humanity," and, foreshadowing an argument later made by Abraham Lincoln, Wirt summarily declared that it was impossible to "derive a right, founded upon wrong."[83] Under this construction, any alleged conflict between these two rights seemed chimerical at best.

---

[80] Ibid., 86.

[81] Ibid., 90.

[82] Ibid., 114.

[83] Ibid., 112–113. Cf. Roy P. Basler, ed., *The Collected Works of Abraham Lincoln*, 8 vols. (New Brunswick, NJ: Rutgers University Press, 1953), 3:226 and 3:257. In his debates with Stephen Douglas, Lincoln argued "if you admit that [slavery] is wrong, he cannot logically say that anybody has a right to do wrong."

Marshall as well conceded that "every man has a natural right to the fruits of his own labour ... and that no other person can rightfully deprive him of those fruits, and appropriate them against his will, seems to be the necessary result of this admission."[84] Yet by admitting that slavery had no rightful basis in the abstract, the conflict between the two "sacred" rights articulated by Marshall appeared to be a conflict between the universal rights of the slaves on the one hand and the conventional rights of the slave owners on the other. The word *sacred* – with all of its religious connotations – was perhaps not an appropriate adjective for the rights in question; yet there was a manner in which the universal and the particular elements at play conjured sentiments of a religious fervor, and, according to Marshall, any judicial resolution of a case involving these competing claims had to be founded on established custom. "Whatever might be the answer of a moralist to this question," Marshall proclaimed, "a jurist must search for its legal solution, in those principles of action which are sanctioned by the usages, the national acts, and general assent, of that portion of the world in which he considers himself as a part, and to whose law the appeal is made."[85]

By making custom the sole standard of international law, Marshall jettisoned the part of Story's *La Jeune Eugenie* opinion that had argued that custom was determinative only "in things indifferent or questionable" that were not in contravention of "the general principles of right and justice" – unless those principles of right and justice were specifically relaxed by international statute (i.e., by treaty).[86] No one involved in *The Antelope* claimed that the Spanish ought not to be able to reclaim their property under the explicit treaty provision, however. What was central to this case was the question, what types of things legitimately count as property? Under international custom, Marshall declared, slaves were a legitimate species of

[84] Ibid., 120.
[85] Ibid., 121.
[86] *Le Juene Eugenie*, 846.

property because ownership in slaves was not yet universally proscribed. Accordingly, Marshall approved the Circuit Court's decision along with the Circuit Court's remedy, which treated the individual Africans as fungible goods – dividing them up by the proportion claimed by Spain (93/280) while making adjustments for the 114 who had died while in legal custody in Georgia.[87]

James Kent, in his *Commentaries on American Law*, later described the progression from the English slave trade cases in the early nineteenth century to the American cases heard by Story and Marshall in the 1820s. "In the case of *La Jeune Eugenie*," Kent concluded:

[I]t was decided in the Circuit Court of the United States, in Massachusetts, after a masterly discussion, that the slave trade was prohibited by universal law. But, subsequently, in the case of the *Antelope*, the Supreme Court of the United States declared that the slave trade had been sanctioned, in modern times, by the laws of all nations who possessed distant colonies; and a trade could not be considered contrary to the law of nations, which had been authorized and protected by the usages and laws of all commercial nations.[88]

The English correlate of the *Antelope* decision had been handed down by Lord Stowell several years previously in a case involving a French vessel captured by a British cruiser off the coast of Africa. Limiting and modifying his own precedent in *The Fortuna* and *The Donna Marianna*, Stowell declared in the case of *Le Louis* (1817) that the law of nations rested on a "legal standard of morality," which was "fixed and evidenced by

[87] "Read literally," John Noonan notes, "Marshall's decree approved the lottery." There was, however, sufficient ambiguity in the opinion to require interpretation by the lower courts. A year after its original decision, the Supreme Court issued a directive clarifying that the slaves would "be designated by proof made to the satisfaction of that court." Under this formula, the lower court eschewed a lottery system and "without discussion of the admissibility of the evidence, without analysis of its ambiguities, without explication of the standard of proof which they were employing ... held that 39 Africans had been designated by proof to their satisfaction as Spanish property." Noonan, *The Antelope*, 117; 121; 127–128.

[88] James Kent, *Commentaries on American Law*, 4 vols. (New York: O. Halsted, 1826–1830), 1: 187.

general and ancient and admitted practice." Still, wishing not to be "misunderstood or misrepresented," Stowell insisted that he was no "professed apologist for this practice [of slavery]." Yet, to "press forward to a great principle by breaking through every other great principle that stands in the way of its establishment ... in short, to procure an eminent good by means that are unlawful; is as little consonant to private morality as to public justice."[89] As Henry Wheaton later reported, Stowell's decision in *Le Louis* rested on the principle that "no one nation had a right to force the way to the liberation of Africa, by trampling on the independence of other states."[90] Search of foreign vessels in times of peace threatened to strain relations among European nations, and Stowell was cautious about applying natural principles of justice to foreign citizens in English courts of admiralty.

Beyond the difficult questions of international relations implicated by the regulation of the slave trade, the criminalization of the practice also brought forth novel questions of jurisprudence, directly touching on the principle laid down in *Somerset*. In a letter to Joseph Story, Stowell reflected on one such case:

The fact is, I have been, at this late hour of my time, very much engaged in an undertaking perfectly novel to me, and which has occasioned me great trouble and anxiety, and that was the examination of a new question, namely – whether the emancipation of a slave, brought to England, insured a complete emancipation to him upon return to his own country, or whether it only operated as a suspension of slavery in this country, and his original character devolved upon him again, upon his return to his native Island.[91]

A similar scenario had confronted Stowell in a case decided the previous year when Grace, a domestic slave under the laws of Antigua who had nonetheless resided with her master in England for eleven years, was detained by customs authorities upon her return to Antigua for having been illegally imported in contravention of the Slave Trade Act of 1807. The claim made on behalf

[89] *Le Louis* (1817), 2 Dodson 210, 249–250.
[90] Wheaton, *Elements of International Law*, 116.
[91] Stowell, Letter to Story (May 17, 1828) in William W. Story, ed., *Life and Letters of Joseph Story*, 571.

of Grace's freedom was that the laws of England did not protect slavery; that Grace therefore had been divested of her status as a slave when she moved from England; and that as a freewoman she could not be imported into any jurisdiction for the purposes of dealing with her as a slave. The question of this case, again, was essentially whether anything could be suffered to support slavery but positive law, and Grace's lawyers urged the court to treat the principle posited in *Somerset*, in conjunction with the legislative abolition of the slave trade, as protecting Grace's freedom under the laws of England.

As Stowell recognized in his judicial opinion, "this notion of a right to freedom by virtue of a residence in England is universally held out as a matter which is not to be denied."[92] But, Stowell contended, the nature and extent of that freedom was at issue, and it had been established by custom and usage that "residence in England conveys only the character so designated during the time of that residence, and continues no longer than the period of such residence."[93] In other words, the laws of England offered a dispensation of freedom that was temporarily sustained, only because the means of maintaining chatteldom were not "practicable" on the Island, and this understanding was corroborated by the fact that colonial masters actually did bring their slaves with them to England when they traveled, and they frequently returned home with the master-slave relationship intact.[94]

To maintain this position, Stowell dismissed Mansfield's claim regarding the odious nature of slavery as a mere "*obiter dictum* that fell from that great man." Additionally, rather than undertaking a consideration of those abstract, universal principles asserted by Mansfield, Stowell maintained that "ancient custom

---

[92] *The Slave Grace* (1827), 2 Haggard 94, 103–104.

[93] Ibid., 103–104.

[94] Stowell observed, "Persons though possessed of independence and affluence acquired in the mother-country, have upon a return to a colony been held and treated as slaves; and the unfortunate descendents of these persons, if born within the colony, have come slaves into the world, and in some instances have suffered all the consequences of real slavery; and the proprietors of these slaves are not called upon to give up to the public all the slaves that they have thus acquired." See ibid., 111.

is generally recognized as the just foundation of all law," and that those principles buttressing the English claim to liberty were conventional principles that applied only to particular people.[95] "This cry of 'Once free for an hour, free forever!'" Stowell wrote, "... is mentioned as a peculiar cry of Englishmen as against those two species of property [i.e., villenage and slavery]. It could interest none but the people of this country: and of these only the masters."[96] In conclusion, Stowell declared, "It may be a misfortune that she was a slave" – a sentiment that would have been seconded by Marshall – "but being so, she in the present constitution of society had no right to be treated otherwise."[97]

Constitutionalism Amid "What is Passing in the World"

From a comparative perspective, both Marshall's and Stowell's opinions appear to represent a stark limitation on the efficacy of universal principles in constitutional adjudication. Neither opinion, for example, denied the validity of the principle cited by Marshall that "every man has a natural right to the fruits of his own labour." Nor did they deny that such a principle applied universally, and Stowell went so far as to declare himself a "friend of abolition generally." Whereas the substance of Stowell's opinion would seem markedly inconsistent with such rhetoric, a conservative decision in such a novel case is perhaps consistent with some of the principles undergirding the English Constitution, particularly the principle of Parliamentary sovereignty and the high regard for English custom. Indeed, Stowell's opinion in *The Slave Grace* was soon rendered irrelevant by the 1833 Parliamentary act abolishing slavery throughout the British Empire. However, the judicial remedy seemingly approved by Marshall – a simple lottery system – was particularly inconsistent with the logic of American constitutionalism and the American constitutional emphasis on, as Wilson put it, "the prime rank

---

[95] Ibid., 107.
[96] Ibid., 115.
[97] Ibid., 100.

of man in human affairs." That two similar cases limiting the applicability of universal principles – after a series of cases tending in the opposite direction – would emerge in different constitutional contexts also reinforces the notion that there are important extra-constitutional factors involved in the construction and application of legal rules and principles. Nevertheless, the articulation of constitutional principles at the judicial level plays a formative role in constitutional maintenance and constitutional change, and considerations of this sort led Stowell and Marshall to render decisions tending toward the maintenance of a tension implicit in a fragile constitutional order.

In his argument before Marshall in *The Antelope*, Attorney General Wirt urged the Court not to "shut their eyes to what is passing in the world," and he asserted that the "Africans stand before the Court as if brought up before it upon a habeas corpus."[98] In so doing, Wirt brought the logic of Anglo-American constitutionalism full circle by drawing on the principles behind *habeas corpus* review. If the Africans were able to "stand before the Court as if brought up ... upon a habeas corpus," the only reason was because judicial protection from arbitrary force was a protection that ought not to have depended on one's status as an Englishman or an American but simply on one's status as a man. What evidence, then, should have been required to prove that a man was held by the law of the land and not by mere arbitrary force? As Key took up this argument, he suggested that it surely was not "mere possession" that made one's claim over another rightful. For other goods and chattels, he conceded, mere possession may have been all that was required to demonstrate ownership, "[b]ut these are men ... and by the law of nature all men are free."[99] In so linking the plight of the Africans with the logic of Anglo-American constitutionalism, Wirt and Key sought constitutional recognition of the principles at work in "the great moral and legal revolution which is now going on in the world."[100]

[98] *The Antelope*, 110, 108.
[99] Ibid., 73.
[100] Ibid., 75.

Such a revolution, however, was not the only thing going on in the world. The Americans were undergoing a heated domestic debate over the institution of slavery, and there was much anxiety about its final resolution. The opposing factions had been quieted, for a moment, by Henry Clay's Missouri Compromise, but Thomas Jefferson acknowledged the residual tension in the bi-sectional arrangement when he wrote: "This momentous question, like a fire bell in the night, awakened and filled me with terror. I considered it at once as the death knell of the Union ... A geographical line, coinciding with a marked principle, moral and political, once conceived and held up to the angry passions of men, will never be obliterated; and every new irritation will mark it deeper and deeper."[101] The Missouri Compromise held together a tenuous union of desultory commitments within a larger constitutional order, and from one perspective, "any cause which focused feelings on the rights of slaves could be seen as inflammatory."[102]

The cause in the world that particularly focused feelings on the rights of slaves was legislation passed in America and England that heightened penalties for slave trading and declared the slave trade itself to be piracy – a crime that carried with it a sentence of death. The 1820s was also the era of the Monroe Doctrine, and any case dealing with the slave trade involved "difficult issues of visitation and search of foreign vessels in time of peace."[103] On the English side, antislavery legislators had turned their attention to the abolition of slavery in the English colonies, and there were powerful factions and vested interests opposing any such move. It is within these contexts that the decisions in *The Antelope* and *The Slave Grace* emerge not as manifestations of illiberal constitutional theories – valuing or defending slavery for its own sake – but

[101] Letter from Thomas Jefferson to John Holmes (April 22, 1820) in Library of Congress, http://www.loc.gov/exhibits/jefferson/159.html (accessed October 14, 2008).
[102] Noonan, *The Antelope*, 76.
[103] Robert Cover, *Justice Accused* (New Haven, CT: Yale University Press, 1975), 103.

as conservative judicial attempts to preserve increasingly weakened constitutional orders.

In a letter to Joseph Story, which was written as a sort of apology for his opinion in *The Slave Grace*, Lord Stowell explained that English politics were "in a very uncomfortable state, our revenue deficient, our people discontented, and a strong spirit of insubordination prevailing in the country, and the sense of religious obligation very much diminished."[104] While Stowell proclaimed himself to be a "friend of abolition generally," he emphasized practical considerations in effecting abolition. The principles behind the argument that would have Grace declared free, Stowell worried, might have induced other slaves "to try the success of various combinations to procure a conveyance to England for such purpose; and, by returning to the colony in their newly acquired state of freedom, if permitted, might establish a numerous population of free persons, not only extremely burdensome to the colony, but, from their sudden transition from slavery to freedom, highly dangerous to its peace and security."[105] As Stowell rightly recognized, the logic of a Court's opinion – whatever that opinion may be – will rest on principles that ultimately travel far beyond the particular case at hand.

Although these decisions demonstrate the limitations of abstract constitutional principles in overcoming concrete, practical considerations, they also demonstrate the importance of the ways in which interpreters construct those very constitutional principles. In his response to Berrien's accusation that slavery was at the very foundation of the American Constitution, Key asserted:

Free America did not introduce it. She led the way in measures for prohibiting the slave trade. The revolution which made us an independent nation, found slavery existing among us. It is a calamity entailed upon us, by the commercial policy of the parent country. There is no nation which has a right to reproach us with the supposed inconsistency of our endeavoring to extirpate the slave trade as carried on between Africa

[104] Letter from Stowell to Story (May 17, 1828) in Story, *Life and Letters of Joseph Story*, 571.
[105] *The Slave Grace*, 116.

and America, whilst at the same time we are compelled to tolerate the existence of domestic slavery under our own municipal laws.[106]

America's relationship with slavery was more convoluted than Key admitted, but by recognizing competing forces within the American constitutional tradition, Key was able to emphasize those constitutional principles working against the slave interest.

It may have been ill-conceived for a nineteenth-century jurist to let the heavens fall for the sake of justice, but judges did serve as guardians and tutors in the constitutional order, and, insofar as those principles working against the slave interest coincided with the fundamental principles of Anglo-American constitutional thought, a judicial posture tending toward the establishment and preservation of universal liberty was necessary for the maintenance of that particular constitutional heritage that finds its expression in the rule of law. As the conservative decisions in the 1820s confirm, however, there was a deep tension, first noted by Mansfield, between the universal principle of liberty and the institution of slavery, and this tension emerged after the 1820s with a more nuanced character. The election of Andrew Jackson in 1828 precipitated the increased democratization of American institutions while, perhaps paradoxically, an invigorated and unashamedly proslavery constitutionalism gained prominence on the national scene. The ranks of northern abolitionists grew, as well, as William Garrison and other antislavery activists expounded proslavery interpretations of the American Constitution, which they summarily denounced as "the most bloody and heaven-daring arrangement ever made by men for the continuance and protection of a system of the most atrocious villainy ever exhibited on earth."[107]

Within this milieu, John Quincy Adams – that "Favored Son of the Revolution" – emerged as an ideological defender of the antislavery constitutional tradition during his postpresidential career in the U.S. House of Representatives. In a case remarkably similar

---

[106] *The Antelope*, 112.
[107] William Garrison, "On the Constitution and the Union," *Liberator*, December 29, 1832.

to *The Antelope*, Adams was called on in 1841 to serve as counsel for a group of Africans who had come under the protection of the federal court system. Critically engaging John Marshall's *Antelope* opinion, Adams laid out a theory of constitutional disharmony that pitted "fact against right" while nonetheless maintaining an antislavery reading of the American Constitution. In Adams's struggle to introduce greater harmony between the principles undergirding American constitutionalism and the actual practices of American institutions, one can see, moreover, both the influence of the theoretical framework bequeathed by the English common law and the seeds of the antislavery arguments that would be taken up and defended, a generation later, by Abraham Lincoln and the burgeoning Republican Party.[108]

---

[108] See David Brion Davis, *Inhuman Bondage: The Rise and Fall of Slavery in the New World* (New York: Oxford University Press, 2006). Davis comments on Adams's *Amistad* argument: "Certainly anyone who reads the full text of Adams's powerful indictment of slavery can understand why he became in all likelihood the statesman who passed on to Abraham Lincoln, via Charles Sumner, the conviction that a president, as commander in chief during war or civil war, had the power to emancipate America's slaves" (26). Adams's first made the argument that the constitutional war power extended to slavery in a speech in the House of Representatives on May 25, 1836. See *Congressional Globe*, House of Representatives, 24th Congress, 1st Session, 447–450 (1836). Beyond the war power argument, Adams's influence on Lincoln is seen also in Adams's emphasis on the Declaration of Independence and in his natural law reading of the Constitution.

3

Constitutional Disharmony in *The Antelope* and *La Amistad*

In Jacksonian America, the debate over the relationship between slavery and American constitutionalism grew particularly divisive, and the floor of the U.S. House of Representatives emerged as one of the principal fronts in this rhetorical battle. Beginning in 1836, House Democrats employed a procedural "gag rule" against the presentation of antislavery petitions, which often agitated for the abolition of slavery in the District of Columbia. As William Freehling notes, the conflict and crisis that ensued, albeit bloodless, was the "Pearl Harbor" of the controversy that eventually culminated in the Civil War.[1] During this epoch, John Quincy Adams took a leading role in arguing against the congressional gag rule, and in the process developed and refined several arguments concerning the theoretical foundations of American constitutionalism and the price of neglecting or discarding those foundations.[2] Adams's arguments – emphasizing the disparity between natural law and positive law and hailing the self-evident truths in the Declaration of Independence as fundamental to the American regime – constitute a link in the chain from the *Somerset*

[1] William W. Freehling, *The Road to Disunion: Secessionists at Bay, 1776–1854* (New York: Oxford University Press, 1991), 308.
[2] For a historical overview of John Quincy Adams's role in the fight against the congressional gag rule, see William Lee Miller, *Arguing About Slavery: The Great Battle in the United States Congress* (New York: Alfred Knopf, 1996).

case through the antislavery arguments of some of the principal American Founders and on to the antebellum Republican Party.

When Adams was asked in 1841 to provide legal representation for a group of Africans who had been found aboard the slaving ship *La Amistad*, the Massachusetts Congressman then had the opportunity to articulate and summarize his antislavery arguments against the backdrop of John Marshall's *Antelope* opinion.[3] Chief Justice John Marshall had declared in his opinion for *The Antelope* (1825) that slavery's repugnance to the law of nature was "*scarcely* to be denied. That every man has a natural right to the fruits of his own labor," Marshall continued, "is generally *admitted*; and that no other person can rightfully deprive him of those fruits, and appropriate them against his will *seems* to be the necessary result of this admission."[4] Sixteen years later, during his oral argument before the Supreme Court in the case of *La Amistad* (1841), John Quincy Adams reflected on this aspect of Marshall's opinion: "Surely never was this exclamation more suitable than on this occasion; but the cautious and wary manner of stating the moral principle, proclaimed in the Declaration of Independence, as a *self-evident truth*, is because the argument is obliged to encounter it with matter of fact. To the moral principle the Chief Justice opposes general usage – *fact against right*."[5] Adams's summary of the *Antelope* opinion thus

---

[3] *La Amistad* (1841), 40 U.S. 518. During a voyage from Havana to Puerto Príncipe, Cuba, African captives on board the slave ship *La Amistad* freed themselves, killed the captain of the ship, and held two members of the crew hostage. The ship was later found off the coast of New York by a U.S. brig and brought into U.S. district court for adjudication. Spanish claimants libeled the court for return of the Africans as slave property under the same treaty provision that was operative in *The Antelope*. In contrast to *The Antelope*, however, the slave trade was illegal according to Spanish law when the Africans were taken captive. Joseph Story declared for the majority of the Court that the Africans were entitled to their freedom both by the laws of Spain and by the "eternal principles of justice." For a history of the case, see Howard Jones, *Mutiny on the Amistad: The Saga of a Slave Revolt and its Impact on American Abolition, Law, and Diplomacy* (New York: Oxford University Press, 1987).

[4] *The Antelope* (1825), 23 U.S. 66.

[5] John Quincy Adams, *Argument of John Quincy Adams, Before the Supreme Court of the United States, in the case of the United States, Appellants,*

highlighted a tension between the existential fact of slavery and the natural right to liberty, a tension implicit in what historian David Brion Davis describes as the "irreconcilable contradictions between American slavery and the principles of America's Revolutionary heritage."[6]

Such irreconcilable contradictions were part of the very constitutional fabric woven by the Founders. The "bargain between freedom and slavery contained in the Constitution of the United States," Adams had written some twenty years earlier,

> ... is morally and politically vicious, inconsistent with the principles upon which alone our Revolution can be justified; cruel and oppressive, by riveting the chains of slavery, by pledging the faith of freedom to maintain and perpetuate the tyranny of the master; and grossly unequal and impolitic, by admitting that slaves are at once enemies to be kept in subjection, property to be secured or restored to their owners, and persons not to be represented themselves, but for whom their masters are privileged with double share of representation.[7]

Still, while granting that America's fundamental law contained this "bargain between freedom and slavery," Adams insisted that the principles undergirding American constitutionalism were fundamentally inconsistent with the rights of mastery or conquest.

Indeed, the proclaimed theoretical foundations of American government in documents such as the Declaration of Independence seem to stand in marked contrast to the institution of chattel slavery. Twentieth-century observers of American politics – from Gunnar Myrdal and Louis Hartz to Derrick Bell and Rogers Smith – have offered competing interpretations as to why a system of chattel slavery continued to exist in a constitutional regime founded, as it were, on the inalienable rights

---

vs. Cinque, and others, Africans, Captured in the Schooner Amistad ... (New York: S.W. Benedict, 1841), 117.

[6] David Brion Davis, *Inhuman Bondage* (Oxford: Oxford University Press, 2006), 22.

[7] *Memoirs of John Quincy Adams Comprising Portions of His Diary From 1795 to 1848*, ed. Charles Francis Adams, 5 vols. (Philadelphia: J.B. Lippincott & Co., 1875), 5: 11 (March 3, 1820).

of man.[8] What many of these modern interpretations have in common, however, is a rejection of the philosophical validity of natural-law theories, which were prevalent in the late eighteenth and nineteenth centuries but are generally out of vogue today. As a result, the range of modern interpretations of the problem of slavery in American political development often excludes an explicitly natural-law perspective. In contrast, Adams's celebrated argument before the Supreme Court in the case of *La Amistad* (1841) – which emphasized the tragic disharmony of human nature and the disparity between natural law and positive law – offered an insightful and coherent natural-law diagnosis of the relationship between slavery and American ideals.

Fact against Right

Central to Adams's interpretation of American constitutionalism was the conflict between "fact and right" that he perceived at work in John Marshall's *Antelope* opinion. That is to say, there was a conflict between normative constitutional principles and existential realities – a constitutional *disharmony* – that complicated and constrained constitutional politics.[9] In what may be garnered from his speeches and writings, Adams's thought regarding the character of this disharmony was nuanced. On one level, there was a disharmony internal to the constitutional text

---

[8] See Gunnar Myrdal, *An American Dilemma: The Negro Problem and Modern Democracy*, Vol. I (New Brunswick, NJ: Transaction Publishers, 1996); Louis Hartz, *The Liberal Tradition in American Politics* (Orlando, FL: Harcourt Books, 1991); Derrick Bell, *The Derrick Bell Reader*, ed. Richard Delgado and Jean Stefancic (New York: New York University Press, 2005); Rogers Smith, *Civic Ideals* (New Haven, CT: Yale University Press, 1997). Three general interpretations of the relationship between slavery and liberalism in American politics include the anomaly thesis (i.e., slavery is anomalous to the dominant liberal strain in American politics), the symbiosis thesis (i.e., slavery and liberalism are mutually reinforcing), and the multiple traditions thesis (i.e., slavery represents one illiberal tradition in competition with other equally constitutive liberal and illiberal traditions).

[9] For similar discussions of the problem of constitutional disharmony, see Gary Jacobsohn, *The Disharmonic Constitution* (Cambridge, MA: Harvard University Press, 2010).

itself, inherent in the "bargain between freedom and slavery" made by constitutional framers. On another level, there was a historically contingent disharmony between the natural-law principles invoked by American revolutionaries and subsequent political practice.[10] Still on another level, there was a philosophical conundrum arising from the attempt to regard and treat men as property. Whereas the first two aspects of American constitutional disharmony were rooted in historical development (i.e., inconsistencies in the constitutional text itself or inconsistencies between political rhetoric and political action), the philosophical problem, for Adams, had as its referent a transhistorical basis of right against which the historical practice of slavery was thought to be antithetical.[11]

A harmonization of the discordant elements in the constitutional text could have been accomplished either through the abolition of slavery or through the abandonment or reinterpretation of those principles seemingly inconsistent with slavery. Similarly, the inconsistency between the natural-law principles invoked by the revolutionaries and the institution of slavery could have been reconciled either through the logical extension of liberty to slaves or through a reinterpretation of those principles of liberty that limited them to certain segments of humanity. The late Southern strategy generally seems to be of the latter variety, exemplified by the rise of the "positive good" defense of slavery and the Confederate Constitution's guarantee that no "law denying or impairing the right to negro slaves shall be passed."[12]

---

[10] This second type of disharmony between professed ideals and actual practice is explored at some length in Samuel Huntington, *American Politics: The Promise of Disharmony* (Cambridge, MA: Harvard University Press, 1981).

[11] Slavery posed a philosophical problem because men were thought to be an illegitimate species of property even when they were treated as such by the law of the state. The appeal, in other words, was beyond the law of the state to a transhistorical moral law, rooted in human nature. For a debate concerning the influence of nature and history as foundational concepts in American political development, see James W. Ceaser, *Nature and History in American Political Development: A Debate* (Cambridge, MA: Harvard University Press, 2006).

[12] *Constitution of the Confederate States of America* (1861), 9§4.

Although Adams did painstakingly argue that the defense of slavery as a positive good and a constitutional right was a radical departure from the theoretical foundations of American politics, his primary argument against slavery in the *Amistad* case was based on a standard transcending American history. A man who claimed another man as his property, Adams insisted, had, from the moral basis of human nature, claimed a "thing that is not."[13] But even this distinction between nature and history was convoluted inasmuch as Adams treated the Declaration's natural-law principles as true while treating the Declaration itself as a constitutive document of the American regime relevant to constitutional adjudication. In other words, principles of natural law and natural rights, according to Adams, had a metaphysical basis in reality while also having a historical basis in America's founding documents.[14]

The core political problem attending American constitutional disharmony arose from the existential and systematic denial of natural rights through the perpetuation of institutionalized slavery and the perverted enlistment of the ideals of liberty and equality in support of that institution. But slavery was perceived as a *problem* only insofar as it was measured against the fundamental political teaching of the Declaration of Independence – that all men are created equal and endowed by their Creator with certain inalienable rights. As Davis argues, the primary problem of slavery arose not from a historical incongruence

[13] Adams, *Amistad Argument*, 12.
[14] In his study of the Declaration of Independence, the historian Carl Becker famously asserted that "To ask whether the natural rights philosophy of the Declaration is true or false is essentially a meaningless question." For political participants who appeal away from the law of the state to a transcendent law or principle, Becker contended, the higher law "is 'true' because it brings their actions into harmony with a rightly ordered universe, and enables them to think of themselves as having chosen the nobler part, as having withdrawn from a corrupt world in order to serve God or Humanity or a force for the highest good." See Carl Becker, *The Declaration of Independence* (New York: Harcourt, Brace, and Co., 1922), 277–278. The assertion that it is essentially meaningless to ask whether the appeal to a higher law actually did bring the participants' actions more in line with a rightly ordered universe is an assertion with which Adams would have vigorously disagreed.

between professed ideals and actual practice, but rather from the "irreducible human dignity of the slave."[15] And the problem of reconciling slavery and human dignity became, in Adams's view, a multidimensional problem, creating a disharmony between existential and normative realities both within the larger constitutional order and within the heart of each individual master.

Greg Russell observes that Adams's anthropology began with a fundamental contradiction where there was "on the one hand, man's aspiration to the law of love as the true essence of *humanitas* and, on the other hand, the tragedy of his consistent betrayal of that law."[16] Similarly, Adams's constitutional interpretation began with the discord between the polity's aspiration to the natural-law principles invoked by the Declaration of Independence and the polity's consistent and tragic betrayal of those principles. At once a link to the founding generation and an intellectual precursor to later antislavery constitutional thought, Adams's reflections on American constitutionalism offer a unique perspective on the perplexing coexistence of liberalism and slavery in antebellum America. As a political actor – Ambassador, Secretary of State, President, Congressman, and finally legal counsel at the bar of the Supreme Court – Adams also operated within specific historical and political contexts, and he often commented on the disparity between constitutional principle and political practice.[17] At the heart of Adams's concept of constitutional disharmony, moreover, was the inherent disharmony of human nature.

Perverted Sentiment and the Disharmony of Human Nature

In the home of John and Abigail Adams, John Quincy enjoyed a classical education, and early in life he grappled with competing Greek and Roman views of human nature. Rather than

---

[15] Davis, *Inhuman Bondage*, 35.

[16] Greg Russell, *John Quincy Adams and the Public Virtues of Diplomacy* (Columbia: University of Missouri Press, 1995), 78–79.

[17] Some of these political contexts, involving international and domestic politics, are described in Michael Daly Hawkins, "John Quincy Adams and the

being nourished by the classics, however, Adams's emphasis on the fundamental condition of human nature as essentially fallen emerged from within the biblical orbit. As Russell explains, Adams "thought that Greek and Roman perspectives on human nature overly accentuated the uniqueness of man's rational faculties (*nous*). The Bible said nothing of a good mind and evil body; the dualism of the classical philosophers identifies the body with evil and assumes the essential goodness of mind or spirit."[18] In the biblical view, however, man suffered from a certain defect of mind and will as well as body. Man's condition thus could not be rectified merely by rightly ordering reason over passion through education, for reason itself was suspect. "Warned of the imperfections of my own reason," Adams confided to his diary, "I discount its conclusions, as I do those of others; and when I consider what man is, whence he comes, and where he goes, physically, I wonder only *at the degree* in which he does possess the power of linking cause and effect."[19]

Adams's relative pessimism concerning man's rational faculties was tempered by his equally firm insistence that the common inheritance of mankind was a knowledge of the natural law. Man saw dimly, but he was not blind. Thus, at the center of man was a certain paradox inherent in his very nature. "What I would, that I do not," St. Paul had written, in a scriptural passage familiar to Adams. "But what I hate, that I do."[20] Imperfect knowledge and imperfect will combined to create an internal disharmony, a division in the heart of man. Alluding to the same Pauline epistle in his *Amistad* argument, within a discussion of the wrong of arbitrary detention, Adams assured members of the Supreme Court, "I will not recur to the Declaration of Independence – your honors have it implanted in your hearts."[21] The natural law was, according

Antebellum Maritime Slave Trade: The Politics of Slavery and the Slavery of Politics," *Oklahoma City University Law Review* 25 (2000): 1–61.
[18] Greg Russell, *John Quincy Adams and the Public Virtues of Diplomacy*, 79–80.
[19] *Memoirs of John Quincy Adams*, 8: 140 (April 19, 1829).
[20] Romans 7:15.
[21] Adams, *Amistad Argument*, 16. Cf. Romans 2:15.

to Adams, known to all, and although susceptible to perversion in the minds of men by the influences of carnal passions or self-interested rationalizations, it could not be completely obfuscated. Conflicting visions of right, therefore, did not simply represent a Manichean struggle between two mutually exclusive principles or subjective passions. Rather, in the Augustinian theology of Adams's Puritan New England, evil was always a perversion of good that retained some element of its original goodness. "Good may exist on its own," Augustine asserted, "but evil cannot."[22] Similarly, Adams described the theoretical defense of slavery as something that was parasitic on true principles.

Adams's dual affirmation of (1) man's knowledge of the natural law and (2) the defect in man's mind and will in understanding and obeying that law in its particulars is relevant to the theory of constitutional disharmony both directly and by way of analogy. In *Dred Scott and the Problem of Constitutional Evil*, Mark Graber describes as "silly" the "proposition that Southerners fought to the death to preserve what they knew in their hearts was a necessary evil."[23] This precisely is what Adams suggested, however, when he wrote that in the South, the slavery question was "a perpetual agony of conscious guilt and terror attempting to disguise itself under sophistical argumentation and braggart menaces."[24] In other words, the defense of slavery in the abstract required a suppression of moral knowledge and a prevarication of conscience.[25] In a similar vein, Adams insisted that the defense of

---

[22] Augustine, *City of God*, trans. Henry Bettenson (New York: Penguin Books, 2003), Book XII, ch. 3., Para. 3.

[23] Graber, *Dred Scott and the Problem of Constitutional Evil*, 83.

[24] *Memoirs of John Quincy Adams* 9: 349 (April 19, 1837).

[25] Peter Myers has made a similar observation with respect to Frederick Douglass's moral psychology. "At some level," Myers writes, "... natural law informs the moral sense or conscience of virtually all persons. Even within the slaveholder, Douglass insisted, 'deep down in his own guilty soul, God has planted an abolitionist lecturer.' ... At the same time, he readily conceded that the liberty-affirming voice of conscience can be stifled or perverted. Our natural moral sentiment also coexists with contrary motivations that are also natural to humans." See Peter C. Myers, "'A Good Work for Our Race To-Day': Interests, Virtue, and the Achievement of Justice in Frederick Douglass's Freedman's Monument Speech," *American Political Science Review* 104 (2010): 220.

slavery as a positive good stemmed from a "perverted sentiment" that tainted "the very sources of moral principle."[26]

Reflecting on a conversation with John Calhoun during the crisis leading to the Missouri Compromise in 1820, Adams wrote: "[he] said that the [egalitarian] principles which I avowed were just and noble; but that in the Southern country, whenever they were mentioned, they were always understood as applying to white men." Calhoun then went on to insist that black slavery "was the best guarantee to equality among the whites. It produced an unvarying level among them. It not only did not excite, but did not even admit of inequalities, by which one white man could domineer over another."[27] By clinging to the idea of equality while denying its necessary theoretical foundation in the laws of nature and nature's God, Adams suggested, Calhoun's theory of white equality reflected a perversion of the principle of equality proclaimed in the Declaration. As such, the defense of black slavery as a prerequisite to the freedom and equality of white society was a manifestation of a disorder in the American liberal tradition rather than a self-standing rival to it.

Calhoun's argument in defense of slavery, Adams reflected,

… establishes false estimates of virtue and vice; for what can be more false and heartless than this doctrine which makes the first and holiest rights of humanity to depend upon the color of the skin? It perverts human reason, and reduces man endowed with logical powers to maintain that slavery is sanctioned by the Christian religion, that slaves are happy and contented in their condition, that between master and slave there are ties of mutual attachment and affection, that the virtues of the master are refined and exalted by the degradation of the slave; while at the same time they vent execrations upon the slave-trade, curse Britain for having given them slaves, burn at the stake negroes convicted of crimes for the terror of the example, and writhe in agonies over fear at the mention of human rights as applicable to men of color.[28]

According to Adams, the tradition of slavery – if that is what it is to be called – remained aberrational to the founding principles

---

[26] Ibid., 5:10–11 (March 3, 1820).
[27] Ibid., 5:10 (March 3, 1820).
[28] Ibid., 5: 11 (March 3, 1820).

of the American regime even at those times, such as during the Jacksonian era, when "the democracy of the country [was] supported chiefly, if not entirely, by slavery."[29] In other words, the normative principles that informed the very logic of American constitutionalism were in tension with certain existential realities. In the face of such constitutional disharmony, Adams argued that the task of the statesman was to bring constitutional practice in line with constitutional principle, and this duty was precisely the ground on which rested his argument against Marshall's deference to custom or usage in the *Antelope* opinion.

The Antelope and *La Amistad*

Although Marshall did concede in *The Antelope* that slavery was contrary to the law of nature, he nonetheless maintained that the case was to be decided by "those principles of action which are sanctioned by the usages, the national acts, and general assent, of that portion of the world in which he considers himself as a part, and to whose law the appeal is made." The Chief Justice further argued that the legal foundation of slavery had long been established by the international law of war. The right of the victor to enslave the vanquished was at one time recognized by all civilized nations as a "legitimate use of force, [and] the state of things which is thus produced by general assent cannot be pronounced unlawful." Even though there had been a growing trend among Western nations to criminalize the slave trade through domestic legislation and bilateral treaties, the trade was carried on legally according to the laws of Spain when the Antelope was captured, and the Chief Justice was reluctant to declare an action sanctioned by the laws of another nation to be contrary to international law. "Whatever might be the answer of a moralist to this question," Marshall asserted that, as a jurist, he was bound "by the path of duty" to deliver the slaves to their Spanish claimants.[30]

---

[29] Ibid., 9: 255 (August 18, 1835).
[30] *The Antelope* (1825), 23 U.S. 66.

In his *Amistad* argument, Adams insisted that the fallacy in Marshall's opinion was his recognition of the right of slavery as founded on the right of conquest. To hold this position, Marshall had either to maintain that slavery was a morally legitimate consequence of war or, recognizing slavery's moral illegitimacy, he had to insist that the Court ought nevertheless to recognize a legal right that contradicts moral right. The English judge Lord Stowell had put forth the latter argument in *Le Louis* (1817), holding that a jurist must be guided by a "legal standard of morality" that superintends considerations of abstract justice.[31] According to Adams, however, in American constitutional theory, as exemplified by those principles in "the Declaration of Independence the Laws of Nature are announced and appealed to as identical with the laws of nature's God, and as the foundation of all obligatory laws."[32] Contrasting the principles of the Declaration with Lord Stowell's proclamation in *Le Louis*, Adams charged that a *merely* legal standard of morality served only "to supersede the laws of God, and justify, before the tribunals of man, the most atrocious crimes in the eyes of God."[33]

In Adams's constitutional theory, the principles of the Declaration of Independence provided the normative foundation for subsequent constitutional politics. Those natural-law principles served to circumscribe executive power (which along with "*all* exercise of human authority must be under the limitation of right and wrong") while simultaneously requiring public authority to protect the natural rights of individuals.[34] Like Lincoln, Adams maintained that the Constitution drew its aspirational content from the founding document of the American regime, and, as George Anastaplo notes, Adams considered "the Constitution of 1787 the natural implementation of the principles of the

[31] *Le Louis* (1817), 2 Dodson 210.
[32] Adams, *Amistad Argument*, 126.
[33] Ibid.
[34] John Quincy Adams, *The Social Compact, Exemplified in the Constitution of the Commonwealth of Massachusetts* ... (Providence: Knowles and Vose, 1842), 31.

Declaration."[35] Nonetheless, the seasoned statesman qualified this connection between the normative and existential orders with an acknowledgment that the constitutions of the American states and nation were the "work, not of eternal justice ruling through the people, but of man, – frail, fallen, imperfect man, following the dictates of his nature and aspiring to perfection."[36]

Throughout his *Amistad* argument, Adams maintained that there existed a certain tension between normative principles and the realities of political praxis, a tension that was inherent in man's fallen and imperfect state. This tension was saliently expressed in those compromises struck at the constitutional convention over the institution of slavery. Yet, morally and politically vicious as those compromises were, the "words slave and slavery [were] studiously excluded from the Constitution," decently concealing with circumlocutions an institution that was fundamentally inconsistent with the principles undergirding American constitutionalism.[37] Slavery existed under the authority of the various state constitutions, but it was not recognized by the authority of the Federal Government, which was granted neither the power to establish nor to prohibit slavery in the states. At the same time, the moral legitimacy of both the state constitutions and the Federal Constitution rested on their congruence with the principles of the Declaration of Independence, which, according to Adams, were both true in principle *and* constitutionally relevant.

The Declaration of Independence provided the central ground on which Adams based his *Amistad* argument. Pointing to two copies of the Declaration, "which [we]re ever before the eyes" of the justices, Adams declared: "I know of no other law that reaches the case of my clients, but the law of Nature and Nature's God on which our fathers placed our own national existence. The circumstances are so peculiar, that no code or treaty has provided for such a case. That law, in its application to my clients, I trust will be the law on which the case will be decided by

---

[35] George Anastaplo, "John Quincy Adams Revisited," *Oklahoma City University Law Review* 25 (2000): 134.

[36] Adams, *The Social Compact*, 32.

[37] Adams, *Amistad Argument*, 39.

this Court."[38] In the absence of some expressed provision of the positive law, Adams suggested, the law of nature would become *solely* operative, and, as Davis notes, "What made the Amistad case so distinctive [e.g., in contrast to *The Antelope*] was the fact that the slave trade to Cuba was illegal after 1820, a violation of Spanish law as well as treaties.... Since there was no Spanish or American law that authorized the slavery in the Amistad blacks, they were entitled to fall back on natural law even if that meant revolution."[39]

The natural right to revolution in the Declaration was in fact a teaching concomitant with the doctrine of man's natural equality, and Adams insisted that such a doctrine be entertained by the highest judicial tribunal in the United States. In making this plea, Adams rested his argument squarely on the side of right, urging reconciliation between America's founding principles and the administration of her government, not by disobedience to law but through the securement of law in favor of those "unfortunate Africans, seized, imprisoned, helpless, friendless, [and] without language to complain."[40]

La Amistad and the Disharmonic Constitution

The story of how the Africans came to America under these unfortunate circumstances began a few years earlier in the Mende region of Sierra Leone. As Davis recounts, Joseph Cinqué, the principal defendant in the *Amistad* case, was in early 1839 "seized by four black strangers from his own tribe," chained by the neck to other captives, and forced to march for several days to the western coast of Africa. There he was sold, along with some 500 other Africans, to merchants working for a prominent slaving family out of Havana, Cuba.[41] Even though the Cuban slave trade had been declared a form of piracy by Spanish law in

---

[38] Ibid., 9.
[39] Davis, *Inhuman Bondage*, 20.
[40] Adams, *Amistad Argument*, 52.
[41] Davis, *Inhuman Bondage*, 12.

1820, the early "nineteenth-century Spanish government reaped enormous profits from Cuba's relatively sudden emergence as the world's greatest producer of sugar," and African slave labor was the engine that drove such sugar production.[42] The increased demand for Cuban sugar exports led to an increased demand for the illicit importation of slave labor, and, to cloak the flourishing underground slave trade in a pretense of legality, Spanish officials often issued documents certifying that newly captured slaves had been imported into Cuba *before* the criminalization of the trade in 1820.[43]

Such was the case when Cinqué and fifty-three others of the surviving Africans, along with papers falsely certifying their legal statuses, were sold in Cuba to Spanish slavers chartering the schooner *La Amistad*. The drama that eventually saw these individuals pleading for their freedom before the highest judicial tribunal in the United States began when the Africans, chained below decks and sailing for Puerto Príncipe a few hundred miles east of Havana, managed to free themselves before killing the ship's captain and cook, forcing some of the crew overboard, and overtaking their two remaining Spanish captors. After sailing for nearly two months in this condition, the Africans of the *Amistad* were then found by a U.S. brig off the coast of Long Island, and the vessel, along with its cargo and personnel, was taken into U.S. custody. As Joseph Story later recounted in his opinion for the Supreme Court, the legal controversy began when the two surviving Spaniards "filed claims [in U.S. federal courts] and asserted their ownership of the Negroes as slaves and parts of the cargo."[44]

Under the ninth article of a 1795 treaty with Spain, the United States had agreed

… that all ships and merchandise, of what nature soever, which shall be rescued out of the hands of any pirates or robbers, on the high seas,

[42] Ibid., 13.
[43] Or, in the case of children, the documents would certify that they had been born in Cuba to a slave legally imported before 1820.
[44] *The Amistad* (1841), 40 U.S. 518.

shall be brought into some port of either state, and shall be delivered to the custody of the officers of that port, in order to be taken care of and restored entire to the true proprietor, as soon as due and sufficient proof shall be made concerning the property thereof.[45]

As no one involved in the case of the *Amistad* disputed that the ship and its cargo were legally Spanish property that fell within the relevant treaty provision, the main legal controversy, Story pointed out, was "whether these negroes are the property" of the Spaniards and thus "ought to be delivered up."[46] Or, more specifically, the question was whether *men* might be included under the general title of merchandise, and, if so, whether these particular men should be so included when interpreting the treaty.

Story answered the first question in the affirmative, making clear that had the Africans been held legally as slaves under the laws of Spain, as was the case in *The Antelope*, then the Court could find "no reason why they may not justly be deemed within the intent of the treaty, to be included under the denomination of merchandise, and, as such, ought to be restored to the claimants: for, upon that point, the laws of Spain would seem to furnish the proper rule of interpretation."[47] The case, in other words, hinged, like *The Antelope*, on custom or usage, and, while relying on "the eternal principles of justice" for his final verdict that the Africans should be free, Story maintained the primacy of positive law over natural law in constitutional adjudication.[48] As Howard Jones writes, by declaring "that in the absence of positive law the eternal principles of justice had to prevail," Story had "implicitly legitimized the principle's corollary – namely, that with the *existence* of positive law, the same eternal principles became secondary."[49]

The possible tension alluded to by Story between positive law and the "eternal principles of justice" epitomized the conflict

[45] "Treaty of Friendship, and Navigation between Spain and the United States" (October 27, 1795). Quoted by Story in *The Amistad* (1841).
[46] *The Amistad* (1841).
[47] Ibid.
[48] Ibid.
[49] Howard Jones, *Mutiny on the Amistad*, 192.

between fact and right confronted by antislavery jurists in slaveholding societies. At least since the *Somerset* decision in 1772, judges in England and the United States had often conceded that slavery ran counter to the law of nature even while maintaining that courts lacked any formal authority to overturn legislatively enacted statutes. In his influential study of nineteenth-century antislavery jurisprudence, Robert Cover explains that "where positive law provided for slavery, the natural law idiom became a way of expressing the disparity between law and morality. It told of what law should be, but wasn't."[50] Perhaps fatigued by the extent to which slavery had been consistently denounced in the abstract and yet protected in fact, Adams's argument in the *Amistad* attempted to bridge this gap between law as it was and law as it ought to have been by emphasizing the convergence of fact and right in the case of the *Amistad* Africans.

Adams's *Amistad* argument, he later recounted, was "perfectly simple and comprehensive ... admitting the steady and undeviating pursuit of one fundamental principle, the ministration of *justice*."[51] The former president and sitting Massachusetts Congressman pursued this principle primarily through an examination of the logical foundations of American constitutionalism, which included an examination of the extent and scope of executive power and the natural-law foundations of the writ of *habeas corpus*. Throughout the argument there was a general amalgamation of ideas, as he linked together a theory of natural rights, the Declaration of Independence, the Constitution, and limitations on arbitrary executive power. Noting, for example, that the Van Buren administration had originally acquiesced in the demand of the Spanish ambassador to return at once the Africans to Cuba, Adams reflected:

Is it possible that a President of the United States should be ignorant that the right to personal liberty is individual. That the right to it of every one, is *his own* – JUS SUUM; and that no greater violation of

---

[50] Robert Cover, *Justice Accused: Antislavery and the Judicial Process* (New Haven, CT: Yale University Press, 1975), 17.
[51] *Memoirs of John Quincy Adams*, 10: 431 (February 24, 1841).

his official oath to protect and defend the Constitution of the United States, could be committed, than by an order to seize and deliver up at a foreign minister's demand, thirty-six persons, in a mass, under the general denomination of *all*, the negroes, late of the Amistad. That he was ignorant, profoundly ignorant of this self-evident truth, inextinguishable till yonder gilt framed Declarations of Independence shall perish in the general conflagration of the great globe itself. I am constrained to believe – for to that ignorance, the only alternative to account for this order to the Marshal of the District of Connecticut, is wilful and corrupt perjury to his official presidential oath.[52]

Adams thus assumed that an oath to protect and defend the Constitution was concomitantly an oath to protect and defend the right to individual liberty, a right founded on those self-evident truths embraced by the "gilt framed Declarations of Independence" on display in the Supreme Court chambers.

Adams was not, however, naïve about the difficulty of his argument, and he assumed no consensus about the principles he avowed. To the contrary, he acknowledged that nearly all of the parties involved in the case had "perverted their minds with regard to all the most sacred principles of law and right, on which the liberties of the United States are founded."[53] Those principles of law and right, and the "combined powers and dominions" struggling against them in favor of the continuance of the African slave trade, revealed the extent of the disharmony between fact and right in American constitutionalism. The character of this constitutional disharmony in Adams's argument took on several dimensions as he moved between the compromises in the

---

[52] Adams, *Amistad Argument*, 82. Davis explains, "When the trial began in the federal district court in New Haven ... the president diverted a small naval vessel, the USS Grampus, to New Haven harbor. He issued secret orders to the district attorney to have the captives smuggled to the ship, presumably in the wholly expected even of a court decision favorable to the president and to Spain. Such action would immediately cut off any right of an appeal to the Supreme Court. But as John Quincy Adams ... would later point out to the Supreme Court, Van Buren's order was 'not conditional, to be executed only in the event of a decision by the court against the Africans, but positive and unqualified to deliver up all the Africans in his custody ... while the trial was pending.'" See Davis, *Inhuman Bondage*, 18.

[53] Adams, *Amistad Argument*, 95.

constitutional text, the disparity between principles and action in historical practice, and the metaphysical or philosophical problem engendered by the enslavement of a rational being endowed with a natural right to liberty.

The constitutional text, Adams argued in a formula that became prominent in later antislavery constitutional thought,

> ... recognizes the slaves, held within some of the States of the Union, only in their capacity of *persons* – *persons* held to labor or service in a State under the laws thereof – *persons* constituting elements of representation in the popular branch of the National Legislature – *persons*, the migration or importation of whom should not be prohibited by Congress prior to the year 1808. The Constitution no where recognizes them as property.... Slaves, therefore, in the Constitution of the United States are recognized only as *persons*, enjoying rights and held to the performance of duties.[54]

Certainly the historical situation was more complicated – as Adams himself admitted in other places – but the point remained that the inconsistency of slavery with the principles of government avowed in America's founding documents was recognized by most of the constitutional framers even as they made constitutional provisions for the protection of slavery from federal interference. One of the New York delegates to the convention, for example, writing under the anti-federalist pseudonym Brutus, observed during debates over the Constitution's ratification: "If we collect the sentiments of the people of America, from their own most solemn declarations, they hold this truth as self-evident, that all men are by nature free. No one man, then, or any class of men, have a right, by the laws of nature, or of God, to assume or exercise authority over their fellows."[55] Brutus later pointed to the inconsistency of the doctrine of man's natural equality with the constitutional compromises struck concerning "their fellow men, who are held in bondage ... contrary to all the principles of liberty, which have been publickly avowed in

---

[54] Adams, *Amistad Argument*, 39.
[55] Herbert Storing, *The Complete Anti-Federalist*, 2.9.24. The letters of Brutus were probably written by New York delegate Robert Yates.

the late glorious revolution."[56] It was this inconsistency that led to the sentiment, voice by the slaveholder Madison, that it would be "wrong to admit in the constitution the idea that there could be property in men."[57]

The inconsistency between the publicly avowed principles of the American Revolution and the subsequent history of political practice constituted the second prong of Adams's attack on the legitimacy of slavery in America. Particularly important to Adams's argument was the principle behind *habeas corpus*. If the logic of that Great Writ, which the Constitution assumed to be operative in the new federal regime, hinged on the proposition that arbitrary detention is inconsistent with the requirements of justice, how then, Adams wondered, might the President of the United States, upon his own authority and without a judicial hearing, ship the *Amistad* Africans back to Cuba? The adverb used by the Spanish ambassador in his request that the Van Buren administration return the Africans to Cuba was *gubernativamente*, and, as Adams reflected, "[i]t means, by the simple will or absolute *fiat* of the Executive ... that is what the Spaniard means by *gubernativamente*, when he asks the Executive of the United States, by its own *fiat*, to seize these MEN, wrest them from the power and protection of the courts, and send them beyond the seas!"[58]

Adams attributed this demand by the Spanish ambassador to a fundamental misapprehension of the principles of American government. Rhetorically, Adams asked: "Is it possible to speak of this demand in language of decency and moderation? Is there a law of Habeas Corpus in the land? Has the expunging process of black lines passed upon these two Declarations of Independence in their gilded frames? Has the 4th of July, '76, become a day of ignominy and reproach?"[59] Thus, in Adams's interpretation, the principles of *habeas corpus* and the principles of the

---

[56] Storing, *The Anti-Federalist*, 2.9.39.
[57] James Madison, *Notes of Debates in the Federal Convention of 1787* (New York: W.W. Norton & Company, 1987), 532.
[58] Adams, *Amistad Argument*, 38.
[59] Ibid., 43.

Declaration – "deep principles, involving the very foundation of the liberties of this country"[60] – coalesced in their circumscription of arbitrary executive power.

The moral right not to be subject to arbitrary force was, moreover, a right that was not dependent on one's status as an Englishman or an American, but rather was dependent on one's status as a man. Appealing to "common humanity, independent all law," Adams insisted that the Africans be afforded certain protections that were due to them simply by virtue of the kind of beings they were.[61] Thus the rights of human nature provided the foundation for Adams's third, and perhaps most penetrating, assault on the disparity between fact and right in the American constitutional order. Moving beyond the tensions in the constitutional text and the gross contradiction between American ideals and the history of American practice, Adams appealed finally to simple justice.

In his *Antelope* opinion, Marshall had suggested that the right to slavery, recognized by international law, was founded on the right of conquest in war. In his review of the case, Adams insisted, "with all possible reverence for the memory" of the esteemed Chief Justice, that Marshall had both misinterpreted the requirements of the positive law of nations and perniciously discarded natural-law reasoning as irrelevant to the construction of the positive legal rules at play. It was an "error of the first concoction," Adams later asserted, to proclaim a "*legal standard of morality*, different from, opposed to, and transcending the standard of nature and of nature's God."[62]

A similar error was provided by an article published in the *Executive Journal of Administration*, likely by John Calhoun, which competently rehearsed several of the proslavery arguments fashionable among intellectuals in the antebellum south. "The truth is," the author proclaimed,

... that property in man has existed in all ages of the world, and results from the *natural* state of man, *which is war*. When God created the

[60] Ibid., 69.
[61] Ibid., 89.
[62] Ibid., 126.

first family and gave them fields of the earth as an inheritance, one of the number, in obedience to the impulses and passions that had been implanted in the human heart, rose and slew his brother. This universal nature of man is alone modified by civilization and law. War, conquest, and force, have produced slavery, and it is state necessity and the internal law of self preservation, that will ever perpetuate and defend it.[63]

In rebuttal, Adams insisted that such a principle would reduce all of the rights of man to violence or force. Like the position espoused by Thrasymachus in Plato's *Republic*, justice would merely connote the interest of the stronger. "No man has a right to life or liberty, if he has an enemy able to take them from him," Adams summarized. "There is the principle. There is the whole argument of this paper. Now I do not deny that the only principle upon which a color of right can be attributed to the condition of slavery is by assuming that the natural state of man is War. The bright intellect of the South, clearly saw, that without this principle for a corner stone, he had no foundation for his argument."[64] Adams asserted that such an argument was "utterly incompatible with any theory of human rights, and especially the rights which the Declaration of Independence proclaims as self-evident truths."[65]

Those self-evident truths led to theoretical absurdities when trying to classify men as the property of other men. As the ancient Roman jurist Justinian had pointed out in his *Institutes* – a work quoted by Adams in his opening salvo – the law of slavery "makes man the property of another, contrary to natural right,"[66] and this tension led to certain existential contradictions or inconsistencies in the positive law. In his application of the relevant treaty provision to the *Amistad* case, for example, Story had suggested that the Africans would have been considered as property if they had been so deemed by the laws of Spain. But, as Adams pointed out, his "clients [were] claimed under the treaty as merchandize, rescued from pirates and robbers," and this situation

[63] Ibid., 88.
[64] Ibid., 89.
[65] Ibid., 89.
[66] Justinian, *Institutes of Justinian*, trans. Thomas Collett Sandars (Chicago: Callaghan, 1876) Book I, chapter 3.

begged the question, "Who were the merchandise and who were the robbers?"[67] The Africans, in other words, were being considered in one and the same breath as inanimate chattel and as rational and moral beings capable of piracy and theft. They were the robbers even as they were the merchandise. "Can a greater absurdity be imagined in construction than this," Adams asked, "which applies the double character of robbers and merchandise to human beings?"[68]

A similar problem had emerged in *Federalist* No. 54 as Madison attempted, in the character of the "Southern Gentleman," to offer a coherent account of the ways in which slaves were treated in American law as both property and persons. "The slave may appear," the Southern Gentleman conceded, "to be degraded from the human rank, and classed with those irrational animals which fall under the legal denomination of property." But, in other ways – chiefly in being held accountable for wrongs committed by him against others – "the slave is no less evidently regarded by the law as a member of the society, not as a part of the irrational creation; as a moral person, not as a mere article of property."[69] This contradiction between the true nature of the slaves as moral persons and the attempt through law to place them under what the Southern Gentleman deemed the "unnatural light of property" led to the curious situation, in the application of the 1795 Treaty, of considering the Africans both as chattel and as moral agents responsible for pirating themselves.

A second line of argument advanced by Spanish claimants was that if the Africans were not slaves to be returned as property, then they were assassins to be delivered as a matter of justice. But in the absence of a ruling provision providing for such a remedy, Adams insisted that the Africans be considered according to their humanity, along with concomitant the rights of humanity, including the right of revolution. For once they were considered in their status "as men – as infant females, with flesh, and blood,

---

[67] Adams, *Amistad Argument*, 23.

[68] Ibid., 23.

[69] *Federalist* no. 54 (ed. Rossiter), para. 4.

and nerves, and sinews" – then the demand for their return, either as merchandise or as assassins, descended into absurdity, hinging not on *justice* but on *sympathy* for one of the parties in the case.[70] When considering them as men, the principles of the American Revolution became determinative: "The moment you come, to the Declaration of Independence," Adams asserted, "that every man has a right to life and liberty, an inalienable right, this case is decided. I ask nothing more in behalf of these unfortunate men than this Declaration."[71]

The Law of Nature in a Nation of Laws

It would be inaccurate to conclude from Adams's explicit appeal to the natural-law principles of the Declaration of Independence that he was ignorant of the practical difficulties – perhaps impossibilities – of fully realizing those principles on the ground. The disharmony of fallen human nature itself prohibited such Utopian speculations, and Adams suggested that prudential politics must take account of both the possibilities and limits of statesmanship. Within the context of a prohibition measure in the Massachusetts state legislature, Adams previously observed:

There is no duty more impressive upon the legislature than that of accommodating the exercise of its power to the spirit of those over whom it is to operate. Abstract right, deserving as it is of the profound reverence of every ruler over men, is yet not the principle which must guide and govern its conduct; and whoever undertakes to make it exclusively his guide will soon find in the community a resistance that will overrule him and his principles.[72]

---

[70] Adams, *Amistad Argument*, 40. See also page 6: "The charge I make against the present Executive administration is that in all their proceedings relating to these unfortunate men, instead of *Justice*, which they were bound not less than this honorable Court itself to observe, they have substituted *Sympathy!* – sympathy with one of the parties in this conflict of justice, *Antipathy* to the other. Sympathy with the white, antipathy to the black."

[71] Ibid., 89.

[72] Quoted in Bennett Champ Clark, *John Quincy Adams: "Old Man Eloquent"* (Boston: Little, Brown and Company, 1933), 379–380.

The same might have been said for the duty of the courts, as there were certainly dangers in making abstract right the exclusive guide to adjudication. Yet, Adams seemed to do precisely this, emphasizing the peculiarity of the *Amistad* case and suggesting that no other law than the law of nature could be invoked to decide the rights of his clients.

A clue to the motivation behind Adams's emphasis on the Declaration in the *Amistad* case perhaps is provided by his journal entry twenty-two years earlier, as he contemplated, in the midst of the controversy leading to the Missouri Compromise, the historical trajectory of the axioms of the Declaration. Those natural-law principles, Adams wrote, "laid open a precipice into which the slave-holding planters of this country sooner or later must fall."[73] The disharmonic state of the American constitutional order was tided over for time by Henry Clay's legislation, but Adams saw clearly that the compromise was temporary, that there would come a time when the constitutional disharmony created by the bargain between freedom and slavery could no longer be maintained.

In his later reflections on the Missouri Compromise, Adams presciently proclaimed that "if slavery be the destined sword in the hand of the destroying angel, which is to sever the ties of this Union, the same sword will cut asunder the bonds of slavery itself."[74] As early as February 1820, a fifty-two-year-old Adams had contemplated such a dissolution, declaring that

Slavery is the great and foul stain upon the North American Union, and it is a contemplation worthy of the most exalted soul whether its total abolition is or is not practicable: if practicable, by what means would accomplish it at the smallest cost of human sufferance. A dissolution, at least temporary, of the Union, as now constituted, would be certainly necessary, and the dissolution must be upon a point involving the question of slavery, and no other. The Union might then be reorganized on the fundamental principle of emancipation. This object is vast in its compass, awful in its prospects, sublime and beautiful in its issue. A life devoted to it would be nobly spent or sacrificed.[75]

[73] *Memoirs of John Quincy Adams* (December 27, 1819) 4:492–493.
[74] Quoted in Josiah Quincy, *Memoir of the Life of John Quincy Adams* (Boston: Phillip, Sampson & Co., 1858), 114.
[75] *Memoirs of John Quincy Adams*, 4: 531 (February 24, 1820).

By the time he was called on to represent the Africans in the *Amistad* case, an older Adams had grown weary. His decade-long battle with the congressional gag rule against antislavery petitions in the House of Representatives had hardened him to the spirit of compromise, and he no longer had the patience to acquiesce in the maintenance of American constitutional disharmony.[76] Comparing the *Amistad* case to the *Antelope*, Adams insisted that he did not question the propriety, in 1825, of "postponing the discussion," but, Adams demanded, it was "no longer a time for this course, the question must be met, and judicially decided."[77]

In Adams's concluding remarks before the Court, he declared, in an untranslated verse from Virgi's *Aeneid*, "*hic caestrus artemque repono*."[78] Adams's Latin quotation, taken from the legendary but aged boxer Entellus's post-fight oration, after his defeat of the brazen and much younger challenger Dares, translated: "In this place I, the victor, put down my gloves and my training." As Michele Valerie Ronnick points out, however, Adams edited out the word *victor*.[79] He could not know if victory lay on the horizon, but he did indeed view himself as an old fighter nobly confronting a new challenge. That new challenge was provided by the rising defense of slavery as something good to be preserved and protected rather than a necessary evil to be tolerated; the cornerstone of American democracy rather than the rock on which it must break. Because of this new challenge, American constitutional disharmony might have found its resolution in *favor* of slavery as a perpetual and fundamental institution, and the Declaration of Independence was the final obstacle, the last stumbling block, to those forces working toward such a resolution.

[76] For an account of this part of Adams's career, see William Lee Miller, *Arguing Against Slavery: The Great Battle in the United States Congress* (New York: A. Knopf, 1996).

[77] Adams, *Amistad Argument*, 94.

[78] Ibid., 135.

[79] Michele Valerie Ronnick, "Virgil's *Aeneid* and John Quincy Adams's Speech on Behalf of the *Amistad* Africans," *The New England Quarterly* 71 (1998): 473–477.

In the year of his death, 1848, Adams's old colleague John Calhoun declared during congressional debates on the Oregon Bill that the cause of the crisis in American constitutionalism was found in "the most false and dangerous of all political errors," expressed in the proposition that "all men are born free and equal" and in the "not less erroneous" version of that proposition found in the Declaration.[80] As Adams predicted, the veracity of the Declaration's principles had to be denied before slavery could be defended as a positive good and a constitutional value to be enlarged and protected. The proper resolution of the disharmony between fact and right, in all of its various dimensions, was precisely the point on which the American house became divided, and, although Adams did not live to see the resolution of this conflict, his mark and influence was easily recognized, a decade later, in the arguments put forward by antislavery constitutionalists associated with a new political party, founded expressly for "the maintenance of the principles promulgated in the Declaration of Independence."[81]

In a climate of heightened ideological contestation over constitutional identity and constitutional meaning, however, the Court's decision in the *Amistad* case was subsequently followed by decisions in *Prigg* v. *Pennsylvania* (1842) and *Dred Scott* v. *Sandford* (1857) that entrenched constitutional protections for domestic slavery. In connecting these cases, Davis goes so far as to conjecture that the Court's "affirmation of freedom [in the *Amistad*] may well have helped to motivate Chief Justice Roger Taney to issue his later defense of slavery and official racism in his infamous Dred Scott decision of 1857."[82] Whatever the private impetus for these opinions may have been, the new and grave challenge they posed to America's revolutionary principles did

---

[80] See John C. Calhoun, "Speech on the Oregon Bill" (June 27, 1848) in H. Lee Clark, Jr., ed., *John C. Calhoun: Selected Writings and Speeches* (Washington, DC: Regnery, 2003), 661–684.

[81] "Republican Party Platform" (1856) in *National Party Platforms: Volume I, 1840–1956*, compiled by Donald Bruce Johnson (Champaign: University of Illinois Press, 1978), 27–28.

[82] Davis, *Inhuman Bondage*, 26.

give occasion for the historically marginalized Supreme Court justice John McLean, in his spirited dissents in *Prigg* and *Dred Scott*, to take up the mantle, alongside Abraham Lincoln, as defender of an antislavery constitutional tradition whose spirit was preserved, for a time, by John Quincy Adams.

4

Constitutional Construction in *Prigg* and *Dred Scott*

The Supreme Court's decision in favor of the Mende Africans in the *Amistad* case proved to be a transitory victory for opponents of slavery in America. Although Joseph Story had based his decision, at least nominally and in part, on the "eternal principles of justice," the positive laws of Spain and the United States were also arrayed against the claims of the Spanish slavers.[1] Story was clear, however, that had the laws of Spain been different, the decision of the Court would have been different as well. When the requirements of eternal justice come in tension with the law, it is the law, Story suggested, that commands a judge's allegiance. Indeed, although employing a natural-law idiom to express the disparity between law and morality, antislavery jurists often sided *against* morality.

In no instance was this more apparent than in the application of the Constitution's fugitive-slave clause. As Robert Cover noted, the crisis of conscience faced by antislavery judges in fugitive-slave cases finds a particularly apt analogy in Melville's *Billy Budd*, where the protagonist is a man innocent of wrongdoing in some fundamental sense whom, within the technicalities of the law, is nevertheless charged with violating a legislative act against mutiny. In a dramatic scene, the captain of the ship articulates

[1] *La Amistad* (1841) 40 U.S. 518.

the fundamental tension between law as it is and law as it ought to be: "How can we adjudge to summary and shameful death a fellow creature innocent before God, and whom we feel to be so? – Does that state it aright? You sigh sad assent. Well, I too feel that, the full force of that. It is Nature. But do these buttons that we wear attest that our allegiance is to Nature? No, to the King."[2] Like the reluctant captain who dutifully executed the sailor, Cover writes, antislavery judges in antebellum America paraded their "helplessness before the law; lamented harsh results; intimated that in a more perfect world, or at the end of days, a better law would emerge, but almost uniformly, marched to the music, steeled themselves, and hung Billy Budd."[3]

One such judge was Joseph Story, who, despite of his own antislavery inclinations, gave the most ardent protections to slave catchers in his decision in *Prigg v. Pennsylvania* (1842). In the mid-1820s, the state of Pennsylvania had passed a statute that "provided that if any person shall, by force and violence, take and carry away, or shall by fraud or false pretense to take, carry away, or seduce any negro or mulatto from any part of the Commonwealth," then such person would be guilty of felony kidnapping.[4] After the Maryland slave catcher Edward Prigg was indicted in Pennsylvania under the statute for forcibly carrying a runaway slave and her children back to Maryland, Prigg initiated a suit against the state. The Constitutional question hinged on the ambiguously worded fugitive-slave clause, which required "a Person held to Service or Labour in one state" to be "delivered up on Claim of the Party to whom such Service or Labour may be due."[5] But whether it was a state or federal function to deliver up the fugitive from labor, and whether state laws protecting free blacks against kidnapping were unconstitutional preemptions of federal law, the text did not make explicit.

---

[2] Herman Melville, *Billy Budd*, ed., Hayford and Sealts (Chicago: University of Chicago Press, 1962). Quoted in Robert Cover, *Justice Accused: Antislavery and the Judicial Process* (New Haven, CT: Yale University Press, 1975), 2.
[3] Cover, *Justice Accused*, 6.
[4] *Prigg v. Pennsylvania* (1842) 41 U.S. 539, 550.
[5] U.S. Constitution Art. IV§2.

Story thus wrote a self-styled pragmatic opinion, declaring that "no uniform rule of interpretation" could be applied that did not attain the ends for which the clause was written. And it was "historically well known," Story insisted, that the fugitive-slave clause was written "to secure to the citizens of the slave-holding States the complete right and title of ownership in their slaves as property in every State in the Union which they might escape from the State where they were held in servitude." The judicial interpretation, then, had to reflect that reality, and the Constitution guaranteed a "positive unqualified right on the part of the owner of the slave which no state law or regulation can in any way qualify, regulate, control, or restrain."[6] As the national government was "clothed with the appropriate authority and functions to enforce it," moreover, federal law necessarily super-seded any state law to the contrary.

In an odd way, Story paid homage to the antislavery tradition, citing the principle posited in *Somerset* – that the "state of slavery is deemed to be a mere municipal regulation" contrary to natural law – as the *reason* why the fugitive slave clause was historically necessary. For "if the Constitution had not contained this clause, every non-slaveholding State in the Union would have been at liberty to have declared free all runaway slaves coming within its limits, and to have given them entire immunity and protection against the claims of their masters – a course which would have created the most bitter animosities and engendered perpetual strife between the different States."[7] By this reasoning, a practice contrary to natural law was sanctioned and protected to secure the Constitution's very existence. The act by the Pennsylvania legislature, Story argued, was thus "unconstitutional and void" because it purported "to punish as a public offense against the State the very act of seizing and removing a slave by his master which the Constitution of the United States was designed to jus-tify and uphold."[8]

---

[6]   *Prigg v. Pennsylvania* (1842) 41 U.S. 539, 540 (Story, J.).
[7]   Ibid., 612.
[8]   Ibid., 543.

There were, however, other avenues open to Story in his construction of the constitutional principles. John McLean, for instance, dissented from Story's opinion, arguing that there was "no conflict between the law of the state and the law of Congress" written to enforce the fugitive-slave clause.[9] The runaway slave, McLean noted, was found "in a State where every man, black or white, is presumed to be free, and this State, to preserve the peace of its citizens, and its soil and jurisdiction from acts of violence, has prohibited the forcible abduction of persons of color." On its face, the state statute did "not include slaves, as every man within the State is presumed to be free, and there is no provision in the act which embraces slaves."[10] If, after an alleged slave had been brought before a federal judicial officer and had been determined to owe service or labor to a citizen of another state under the laws of another state, then the federal remedy would stand. But, McLean insisted, such a remedy was not inconsistent with state protections against arbitrary force.

McLean particularly took issue with Story's claim that the slave was to be subject, without qualification, to the common-law rights of "seizure and recaption." Quoting Blackstone, Story asserted that "when anyone hath deprived another of his property in goods or chattels personal" or wrongfully detained "one's wife, child, or servant," then that person might "lawfully claim and retake them wherever he happens to find them."[11] To this McLean replied:

Can the master seize his slave and remove him out of the State, in disregard of its laws, as he might his horse which is running at large? This ground is taken in the argument. Is there no difference in principle in these cases?

The slave, as a sensible and human being, is subject to the local authority into whatsoever jurisdiction he may go; he is answerable under the laws for his acts, and he may claim their protection; the State may protect him against all the world except the claim of his master. Should anyone

[9] Ibid., 669 (McLean, J., dissenting). See Fugitive Slave Act of 1793 in *Annals of Congress*, 2nd Congress, 2nd Session, 1414–1415.
[10] Ibid., 671 (McLean, J., dissenting).
[11] Ibid., 613 (Story, J.).

commit murder, he may be detained and punished for it by the State in disregard of the master. Being within the jurisdiction of a State, a slave bears a very different relation to it from that of mere property.[12]

In light of McLean's dissent, which tried, at a minimum, to ameliorate the severity of the constitutional remedy provided to masters for the reclamation of fugitive slaves, Story's opinion is notable for its unbending affirmation of the absolute right of a master to seize and recapture his slave and for its assertion that state laws against kidnapping blacks and carrying them across state lines were therefore unconstitutional.

The severity of Story's opinion is puzzling, as well, given his public assertions that the "existence of slavery, under any shape," was "so repugnant to the natural rights of man and the dictates of justice, that it seem[ed] difficult to find for it any adequate justification."[13] Neither is there reason to suppose Story's estimate of the evils of slavery had changed by the time *Prigg* was decided. To the contrary, according to Story's son, the eminent jurist considered his opinion in *Prigg* to be a great "triumph of freedom."[14] But a triumph of freedom in what sense? The younger Story suggested that his father's opinion promoted the cause of liberty principally in two ways: (1) by resting power over fugitive slaves exclusively in the hands of the "whole people" (i.e., the federal government) rather than a section (i.e., state governments), it allowed national debate such that Congress could "remodel the law and establish ... a legislation in favor of freedom"; and (2) by limiting the *national* constitutional protections (as opposed to municipal or local protections) for slavery only to masters of runaway slaves, it implied that "the authority of a master does not extend to those whom he voluntarily takes with him into a free State where slavery is prohibited."[15]

---

[12] Ibid., 668–669 (McLean, J., dissenting).

[13] William W. Story, ed., *Miscellaneous Writings of Joseph Story* (Boston: Little & Brown, 1852), 136.

[14] William W. Story, ed., *Life and Letters of Joseph Story*, 2 vols. (Boston 1851), 2:392. For an overview of the scholarly treatment of *Prigg*, see Leslie Feidman Goldstein, "A 'Triumph of Freedom' After All? *Prigg v. Pennsylvania* Re-examined," *Law and History Review* 29 (2011): 763–796.

[15] Ibid., 2: 398–400.

If this is, in fact, a sufficient explanation of his father's reasoning, then the federal Fugitive Slave Law of 1850 and the *Dred Scott* case of 1857 surely cast doubt on how much of Story's decision in *Prigg* was actually a boon to liberty. Granting exclusive claim to the federal legislature to implement the relevant constitutional provision certainly did not engender national legislation in "favor of freedom," and, as Lincoln maintained, the logic of Roger Taney's subsequent opinion in *Dred Scott* seemed to protect the rights of a master who took his slave *voluntarily* "into a free state where slavery is prohibited."[16] Story's opinion has thus understandably been the subject of much critical commentary. In an attempt to rehabilitate Story's opinion in the midst of modern criticism, Christopher Eisgruber has offered this explanation:

[A]ccording to Story, the Constitution aimed to create not merely a free North, or a collection of states partly free and partly slave, but rather a free Union. In order to effectuate this purpose, the Constitution had to accommodate and include both the recognition that slavery was immoral and also the means sufficient to keep the Union together until the federal government could eliminate slavery. As such, the Constitution reflected both a natural law judgment and a pragmatic concession to the exigencies of power and interest. This dual character of the Constitution is itself entirely consistent with, and perhaps even demanded by, natural law. As a result, any sound interpretation of the Constitution must attend both to its ethical purposes and to its practical compromises.[17]

Yet even if we grant Eisgruber's interpretation of Story's judicial reasoning, subsequent political events in the decades preceding the Civil War belied Story's hope that *Prigg* would spur national legislative and judicial activity in favor of freedom. *Prigg* v. *Pennsylvania* – along with the plethora of cases in which antislavery men steeled themselves to hang Billy Budd – thus

[16] See Abraham Lincoln, "First Debate with Stephen Douglas" (August 21, 1858) in Roy Basler, ed., *Collected Works of Abraham Lincoln*, 9 vols. (New Brunswick, NJ: Rutgers University Press, 1953), 3:24. Lincoln warned of "another *Dred Scott* decision ... holding that they cannot exclude [slavery] from a state."

[17] Christopher L.M. Eisgruber, "Justice Story, Slavery, and the Natural Law Foundations of American Constitutionalism," *The University of Chicago Law Review* 55 (1998): 298.

brings up difficult questions pertinent to our assessment of the antislavery constitutional tradition.

The Slavery of Politics

In fact, it seems that none of the moderate antislavery jurists and statesmen was completely immune from the practical necessities of compromise. In his eulogy of John Quincy Adams, for example, the antislavery theologian and preacher Theodore Parker declared of Adams that there was "one sentiment that [ran] through all his life – an intense love of freedom for all men; one idea, the idea that each man has Unalienable Rights."[18] Even so, Parker reluctantly catalogued the ways in which Adams aided the cause of slavery during his political career:

> It must be confessed that Mr. Adams, while Secretary of State, and again while President, showed no hostility to the institution of slavery. His influence all went the other way. He would repress the freedom of the blacks in the West Indies, lest American slavery should be disturbed and its fetters broke; he would not acknowledge the independence of Hayti, he would urge Spain to make peace with her descendents for the same reason – "not for those new republics," but lest the negroes in Cuba and Porto Rico should secure their freedom. He negotiated with England, and she paid the United States more than a million of dollars for the fugitive slaves who took refuge under her flag during the late war. Mr. Adams had no scruples about receiving the money during the administration.... Nay, he negotiated a treaty with Mexico, which bound her to deliver up fugitive slaves escaping from the United States – a treaty which the Mexican Congress refused to ratify![19]

Concessions to slavery by antislavery men were not, therefore, unique to the Court, due perhaps to the limited role of the judiciary in a constitutional republic and the emphasis in the nineteenth century on a judicial separation of law and morality. In this vein, what is to be made of a man like Adams, who professed his hatred

---

[18] Theodore Parker, *Discourse Occasioned by the Death of John Quincy Adams: Delivered at the Melodron in Boston, March 5, 1848* (Boston: Bela Marsh, 1848), 18–19.

[19] Ibid., 32–33.

for slavery and nevertheless fought for its protection, in various ways, during his tenure as Secretary of State and president?

Perhaps part of the answer is to be found in the recognition that to leave an imprint on the law, politicians, as much or even more than judges, must take account of political constraints, popular prejudices and fears, and the priority of issues demanding their attention. Exploring the constraints of the political environment in which Adams operated, Michael Hawkins writes, therefore, not only of the "politics of slavery" but also of the "slavery of politics."[20] Within the convoluted political environment of the day, many antislavery politicians in the nineteenth century, like many of the Founders of the Republic, "gave the [antislavery] movement their sympathy and formal endorsement but always had other more pressing claims on their sustained attention." Don Fehrenbacher observes of the generation of 1776 that they "were inhibited by their desire for continental unity, by a tender concern for the rights of private property, and, in the South, by racial fears that made universal emancipation difficult to visualize. In the end, there was a strong disposition to settle for moral gesture and a reliance on the benevolence of history."[21] History, of course, was not so benevolent, and the political calculation that a strong national union would lead eventually to a free national union was proved false by the increasing militancy and fervor of the slave interest in the mid-nineteenth century.

This perhaps is why, as Joshua Giddings later recounted, a disillusioned seventy-seven-year-old Adams declared to a group of free blacks in 1844: "We know that the day of your redemption must come: The time and manner of its coming we know not; but *whether in peace or in blood*, LET IT COME." When publicly challenged about the implications of his speech on the floor of the House of Representatives, Adams then repeated, emphatically, "though it cost the blood of MILLIONS OF WHITE MEN,

[20] Michael Daly Hawkins, "John Quincy Adams and the Maritime Slave Trade: The Politics of Slavery and the Slavery of Politics," *Oklahoma City University Law Review* 25 (2000): 1–61.

[21] Don Fehrenbacher, *Slavery, Law, & Politics: The Dred Scott Case in Historical Perspective* (New York: Oxford University Press, 1981), 9.

LET IT COME. *Let justice be done, though the heavens may fall.*"²² Adams's father had early on acknowledged, however, that adopting the maxim *fiat justitia ruat caelum* could never settle the myriad practical moral and political questions surrounding slavery. "If we should agree with him in this maxim," the elder Adams wrote in response to St. George Tucker, who had reiterated the maxim that justice should be done without regard to consequences, "the question would still remain, what is justice? Justice to the Negroes would require that they should not be abandoned by their masters and turned loose upon a world in which they have no capacity to procure even a subsistence. What would become of the old? the young? the infirm? Justice to the world, too, would forbid that such numbers should be turned out to live by violence, by theft, or by fraud."²³ The answer to the question of what justice required was thus never unidimensional and the antislavery movement was divided over the appropriate role of judges in bringing about social reformation.

Still, the fact remained that the antebellum Supreme Court inevitably played an important role in interpreting and constructing the ambiguous constitutional rules governing slavery in America, and the constitutional debate after *Prigg* centered on the expansion of slavery in the federal territories. Within this context, a case involving an obscure slave named *Dred Scott* ignited the nation and thrust Abraham Lincoln into the political spotlight. Like *Prigg*, the case gave the moderate antislavery constitutionalist John McLean occasion to write a spirited dissenting opinion.

The *Dred Scott* Case

After residing in the free state of Illinois and at Fort Snelling in the Wisconsin Territory, Dred Scott returned with his master

²² Joshua Giddings, *History of the Rebellion* (New York: Follett, Foster & Company, 1864), 217–218.

²³ John Adams to Jeremy Belknap (October 22, 1795), *Massachusetts Historical Society.* http://www.masshist.org/database/onview_full.cfm?queryID=639 (accessed May 29, 2009).

to the state of Missouri (under whose laws he was originally held in slavery). When his master died, Scott then sued for his own freedom, alleging that his residence in a free state and free territory had, consistent with the *Somerset* principle, worked to manumit him from his former state of servitude. Through a convoluted series of events, his case entered the federal court system and was heard by the Supreme Court in the mid-1850s. On the preliminary question of jurisdiction, the Court considered whether Scott was a citizen such that his case could enter the federal court system under the diversity of citizenship requirement for federal cases (U.S. Const. Art. 3§2). Because part of Scott's claim to the status of citizen rested on his prior claim that he was made free by his residence in free federal territories, the Court also took up the question of whether the piece of legislation (i.e., the Missouri Compromise of 1820) that barred slavery from the territories was constitutional. When considering the constitutionality of the Missouri Compromise, moreover, the Court inquired into whether the Fifth Amendment's protection against deprivation of property without due process of law prevented the national government from prohibiting slave property in the federal territories.[24]

In what has now come to be considered the majority opinion, Chief Justice Taney sought, initially, to demonstrate "too clear[ly] for dispute" the prevailing animus toward members of the African race during the founding era, the intent of the constitutional framers to exclude members of that "unfortunate" race from political society, and the acquiescence of the Founders to – and their participation in – a system of race-based chattel slavery that was already well established in the states by 1776 and was left untouched by the events of 1787. Conceding that the "Government was not made especially for the colored race," John McLean, dissenting in *Dred Scott* as he had in *Prigg*, nonetheless noted that as a matter of historical fact "many of

---

[24] For a history of the case, see Don E. Fehrenbacher, *Slavery, Law, & Politics: The Dred Scott Case in Historical Perspective* (New York: Oxford University Press, 1981).

them were citizens of the New England States, and exercised the rights of suffrage when the Constitution was adopted." Yet quite independent of any historical squabble over the intentions and motivations of those men who wrote the document, McLean asserted that "[a]ll slavery has its origin in power, and is against right."[25]

Perhaps the moral indignation evident in McLean's dissent has rendered it less serious to scholars, who nearly universally have considered it the weaker of the case's two dissenting opinions. McLean's presidential ambitions were well known, and, as a consequence, much of the moral language employed in his opinion has been interpreted as *obiter dicta* directed at placating the abolitionist sentiment of the emerging Republican Party. A brief survey of some of the relevant literature uncovers assertions that McLean's dissent "was not an impressive legal document," that it contained "more emphasis than logic," exhibited "more bluster than sound reasoning," and marshaled arguments that were both "erroneous and beside the point." Scholars have identified the impetus behind McLean's second-rate judicial opinion – with its "seemingly gratuitous assaults on the institution of slavery" – as the Ohio justice's "blind[ing] ... political ambition," which compelled him always to keep "one eye on the Constitution and another on political fortune."[26]

Such criticism fails to appreciate the depth and importance of the constitutional principles articulated by McLean in his *Dred Scott* dissent. There was, additionally, a great affinity

---

[25] *Dred Scott v. Sandford*, 60 U.S. 393 (1857), 537 (McLean, J., dissenting).

[26] James F. Simon, *Lincoln and Chief Justice Taney: Slavery, Secession, and the President's War Powers* (New York: Simon and Schuster, 2006), 127; David M. Potter, *The Impending Crisis: 1846–1861*, ed. Don Fehrenbacher (New York: Harper and Row, 1976), 278.; David P. Currie, *The Constitution in the Supreme Court: The First Hundred Years, 1789–1888* (Chicago: University of Chicago Press, 1985), 279; Edward S. Corwin, "Dred Scott," in *The Doctrine of Judicial Review* (Princeton, NJ: Princeton University Press, 1914), 145; Earl Maltz, *Dred Scott and the Politics of Slavery* (Lawrence: University of Kansas Press, 2007), 132; Frank H. Hodder, "Some Phases of the *Dred Scott* Case," *Mississippi Valley Historical Review* 16 (1929), 22; Donald Lively, *Foreshadows of the Law: Supreme Court Dissents and Constitutional Development* (Westport, CT: Praeger Publishers, 1992), 441.

between several aspects of McLean's opinion and Lincoln's later (and widely celebrated) constitutional arguments against the *Dred Scott* decision. In particular, McLean shared in common with Lincoln an aspirational theory of the Constitution and an understanding of natural justice that were absent from the Court's other opinions, including that of McLean's fellow dissenter Benjamin Curtis. McLean (and Lincoln after him), in turn, offered a construction of the meaning of the Fifth Amendment that differed, in important ways, from both Taney and Curtis. To consider the merits of the McLean-Lincoln position, a brief consideration of the jurisprudential issues implicated by the *Dred Scott* case is necessary, and for this task, John Finnis's analytic framework for discussing legal injustice is particularly helpful.[27] Within the context of the arguments made by Taney and Curtis, Finnis's natural-law framework for analyzing legal injustice brings into clearer focus the construction of the Fifth Amendment put forward by McLean and Lincoln, respectively.

Constitutional Construction and Legal Injustice

It is a famous caricature of natural-law theory that the theory itself may be summed up by the words of Augustine, given force by Aquinas, that "an unjust law seems to be no law at all."[28] Yet a sympathetic stance toward the theory of natural law coupled with a careful examination of concrete examples of legal injustice reveals that this phrase represents the way in which one and the same grammatical form (e.g., "law") may assume different meanings in different contexts. Perhaps the inadequacy of understanding natural law theory simply as the phrase "*lex injusta non est lex*" lies in the tendency of such an understanding to collapse the necessary distinction between the various senses of the word "legal," thus collapsing the necessary

---

[27] See John Finnis, *Natural Law and Natural Rights* (Oxford: Oxford University Press, 1980), 351–367.
[28] See Thomas Aquinas, *S.T.*, I-II, Q.95, Art. 2.

distinction between what is, in some sense, "legal" and what is "just."[29]

In his discussion of natural law and legal injustice, Finnis distinguishes analytically between various types of normative statements, such as the statement that some laws are not laws at all. For example, one who makes a normative statement about law may intend to assert one of three meanings within one and the same grammatical form: "(S[1]) what is justified or required by practical reasonableness *simpliciter* [i.e., what is 'just'], or (S[2]) what is treated as justified or required in the belief or practice of some group, or (S[3]) what is justified or required *if* certain principles or rules are justified (but without taking any position on the question whether those principles or rules *are* so justified)."[30] With these distinctions in mind, the proposition "an unjust law is not law" becomes less enigmatic: The statement is asserting that (S[2]/S[3]) rule has the status of law in a given community; that the community's law is judged to be unjust by a source collateral to the legal system itself; and, therefore, that an unjust law is not (S[1]) law in the focal sense of the word because it commands what is unjustified by practical reasonableness (i.e., it commands one to do what one ought not to do). In other words, the statement is asserting that some (S[2]) law has obtained force in the community through the administration of the municipal law and/or that a such a (S[3]) law is justified or required according to some set of intrasystemic legal rules or principles, even as the (S[1]) law is without foundation in justice or natural right.

The different possible connotations of the same grammatical form "law" – and the application of this distinction to the classical formula "*lex injusta non est lex*" – open up a broader way of thinking about law that permeates McLean's dissenting opinion. When McLean asserted in protest to Taney's Due Process

---

[29] See Finnis, *Natural Law and Natural Rights*, 364. "For the statement is either pure nonsense, flatly self-contradictory, or else it is a dramatization of the point more literally made by Aquinas when he says that an unjust law is not law in the focal sense of the term 'law' [i.e., *simpliciter*] notwithstanding that it is law in a secondary sense of that term [i.e., *secundum quid*]."

[30] Finnis, *Natural Law and Natural Rights*, 365.

argument that "[t]he slave is not mere chattel," he was making an (S^1) assertion without regard to whether or not the slave, from one (S^2/S^3) legal perspective, was merely chattel. McLean recognized, for instance, that fugitive slave laws had force according to the Constitution and that the municipal laws of various communities under the Constitution sanctioned systems of chattel slavery; yet, McLean's statement that the slave was more than just property was not in any way inconsistent with Justice Curtis' assertion that whether or not "the slave is known to the law simply as chattel, with no civil rights" was determined by the municipal law in force. As it happened, McLean also agreed with Curtis against Taney that the right to property in a slave was neither distinctly nor expressly affirmed in the Constitution and that Congress in its regulation of the federal territories had never considered any such property right to be so enshrined.[31] It is important to keep in mind that McLean, while considering the requirements of the law, frequently shifted from one of these three viewpoints to another, often asserting multiple types of normative statements within the same discussion.

It is precisely because McLean thought the intrasystemic legal rules laid down by the Constitution did not sanction and enforce a right to own property in slaves that he assented to the justness of the legal order itself. As Cover notes in a somewhat Lincolnian allusion: "A judge like John McLean respected the formal structure of his role because of a faith in the ultimate necessity and utility of a legal system with integrity. But that respect was founded in large part on a firm conviction that the Constitution – the ultimate source of formalism – was not itself committed to slavery, and that conviction was at the heart of his dissent in *Dred Scott*."[32] In a certain respect, then, McLean shared an important premise with Lon Fuller: "If laws, even bad laws, have a claim to

---

[31] To demonstrate the analytical separation of these perspectives, consider that Chief Justice Taney and the Garrisonian abolitionists *both* considered (S^2) the right to property in a slave to be "distinctly and expressly affirmed in the Constitution" while disagreeing on the (S^1) reasonableness or justness of slavery itself.

[32] Cover, *Justice Accused*, 209.

our respect, then law must represent some general direction of human effort that we can understand and describe, and that we can approve in principle even at the moment when it seems to us to miss the mark."[33] For McLean, no less than Lincoln, the general direction of human effort represented by the Constitution was toward liberty; slavery was anomalous to the liberal aspirations of the constitutional order and, as such, was illegitimate in principle even as it obtained force through local legislation.

As the various opinions in *Dred Scott* make clear, however, there were ambiguities and even injustices codified in varying degrees in the Constitution. The interpretive difficulty was compounded by the existence of competing liberal and illiberal constitutional commitments. Still, the aspirational claims of a jurist like McLean were, first, that one need not remain neutral with respect to competing and even disparate aspects of the constitutional order and, second, that the constitutional text was predominantly committed to true principles of right. The most famous exposition of this position is found in the celebrated debates between Abraham Lincoln and Stephen Douglas. In his exchange with Douglas, Lincoln argued that the Supreme Court's ruling in *Dred Scott* did not fully settle the constitutional question, in part, because the Court rejected true principles of natural right, which served to undergird the logic of the constitutional text.

Constitutional Aspirations in Dred Scott

The positions taken by Taney and McLean (and, to a lesser extent, Curtis) concerning the meaning and purpose of certain preconstitutional principles with respect to American citizenship and slavery were precursors to those great senatorial debates between Lincoln and Douglas. According to Taney, colonial laws regarding the status of the African race supported, and the intent and practice of the signers of the Declaration of Independence affirmed, the claim that the sovereign political body created by the Constitution of 1787 did not – nor could it ever – include

---

[33] Lon Fuller, "Positivism and Fidelity to Law – A Reply to Professor Hart," *Harvard Law Review* 71 (1958), 632.

Africans held in slavery. Moreover, members of this class of persons did not constitute foreigners such that they might have been naturalized by congressional legislation. Rather, they were an altogether separate class, neither members of the sovereign body nor members of a foreign nation. Being esteemed by the colonists to be "so far inferior, that they had no rights which the white man was bound to respect ... [Africans] were bought and sold, and treated as an ordinary article of merchandise and traffic, whenever a profit could be made by it."[34] Given that the system of race-based chattel slavery continued throughout the revolutionary era, it was inconceivable to Taney that the Founders intended to declare – or even to entertain the possibility of – the equality (political or otherwise) of members of the African race, who lived in a state of perpetual subordination and bondage to the continent's white inhabitants.

Conceding that the Declaration's language "would seem to embrace the whole human family," Taney nonetheless insisted that "it is too clear for dispute, that the enslaved African race were not intended to be included, and formed no part of the people who framed and adopted this declaration."[35] The inconsistency between the conduct of the authors of the Declaration and the great principle that "all men are created equal" was, for Taney, enough to prove that the Founders could not have meant what the plain construction of the language seemed to imply.

Curtis, I think, offered an adequate rejoinder to Taney's charge of inconsistency, although there are, no doubt, conflicting and convoluted historical sources:

My own opinion is, that a calm comparison of these assertions of universal abstract truths, and of their individual opinions and acts, would not leave these men under any reproach of inconsistency; that the great truths they asserted on that solemn occasion, they were ready and anxious to make effectual, wherever a necessary regard to circumstances, which no statesman can disregard without producing more evil than good, would allow; and that it would not be just to them, nor true in itself, to allege that they intended to say that the Creator of all men had

[34] *Dred Scott*, 407 (Taney, J.).
[35] Ibid., 407 (Taney, J.).

endowed the white race, exclusively, with the great natural rights which the Declaration of Independence asserts.[36]

Yet what is perhaps more important for this inquiry is that Curtis disavowed the relevance to the *Dred Scott* case of any such speculation over the intent of the authors of the Declaration. "As I conceive," Curtis wrote, "we should deal here not with such disputes ... but with those substantial facts evinced by the written Constitution of States, and by the notorious practice under them." Curtis's complaint against Taney was primarily that the Declaration was irrelevant to the construction of the legal rules at play in *Dred Scott*. If one was to inquire into whether Africans were meant, without exception, to be excluded from national citizenship, one needed only examine the constitutions and practices of the original thirteen states. "And they show," Curtis claimed, "in a manner which no argument can obscure, that in some of the original thirteen States, free colored persons, before and at the time of the formation of the Constitution were citizens of those states."[37]

McLean agreed with Curtis' historical claim that "free colored persons" were admitted to citizenship in some states at the time of the Founding, but he did not treat the historical question of state policy as solely relevant. Responding to Taney's review of pre-revolutionary state policies enacted to enlarge and protect the slave trade, McLean declared, "We need not refer to the mercenary spirit which introduced the infamous traffic in slaves, to show the degradation of negro slavery in our country." Although acknowledging the operation of illiberal principles in colonial America, McLean declined to afford such principles interpretive authority. Rather, when interpreting the Constitution, McLean wrote, "I prefer the lights of Madison, Hamilton and Jay ... than to look behind that period, into a traffic which is now declared to be piracy, and punished with death by Christian nations." And the lights of Madison, Hamilton, and Jay, McLean seemed to suggest, would show that the Constitution itself was antislavery in

[36] Ibid., 575 (Curtis, J. dissenting).
[37] Ibid., 575 (Curtis, J. dissenting).

its tendencies. "James Madison," he asserted, "... was solicitous to guard the language of that instrument so as not to convey the idea that there could be property in man." Moreover, McLean observed, "In the provision respecting the slave trade, in fixing the ratio of representation, and providing for the reclamation of fugitives from labor, slaves were referred to as persons, and in no other respect are they considered in the Constitution."[38]

Within this discussion, McLean was largely silent regarding the meaning of the Declaration of Independence and its insistence that "all men are created equal." Whereas Taney and Curtis engaged in a short dialectic concerning the intent of the Founders with respect to those Jeffersonian principles, McLean simply declared that "our independence was a great epoch in the history of freedom." In his judicial opinion, McLean did not treat the text of the Declaration as determinative of the Founders' moral understanding. Rather, he limited himself to the era surrounding the Constitution's ratification, and he took for granted what Hadley Arkes has described as "the principles of natural right that stood behind the Constitution, and guided even its compromises."[39] McLean found evidence of the Founders' moral understanding in the "well-known fact that a belief was cherished by leading men, South as well as North, that the institution of slavery would gradually decline until it would become extinct."[40] Although there were certainly historical elements at

---

[38] Ibid., 537 (McLean, J. dissenting).

[39] Hadley Arkes, "Natural Law and the Law: An Exchange," *First Things*, May 1992, 48.

[40] Cf. Lincoln's argument that behind the constitutional compromises with the slave interest was the intention of the framers to place slavery on a path toward ultimate extinction: "I entertain the opinion upon evidence sufficient to my mind, that the fathers of this government placed that institution where the public mind did rest in the belief that it was in the course of ultimate extinction. Let me ask why they made provision that the source of slavery – the African slave trade – should be cut off at the end of twenty years? Why did they make the provision that in all the new territory we owned at that time slavery should be forever inhibited? Why stop its spread in one direction and cut off its source in another, if they did not look to its being placed in the course of ultimate extinction?" Basler, ed., *Collected Works of Abraham Lincoln*, 3: 307.

work during and before the Founding era that were opposed to the liberal principles championed by McLean, he insisted that a principled preference for historical sources that embody true principles of right was hermeneutically legitimate: "[I]f we are to turn our attention to the dark ages of the world, why confine our view to colored slavery? On the same principles, white men were made slaves. All slavery has its origin in power, and is against right."[41]

Within McLean's opinion, the *telos* of the American regime, in opposition to the opinions of both Taney and Curtis, was to be understood in terms of justice. Yet McLean was the inheritor of an American legal tradition that discounted "[t]he notion that out beyond [the posited law] lay a higher law to which the judge *qua* judge was responsible."[42] As a matter of social fact, McLean conceded, slavery was sanctioned by the laws of the states, and the right to own property in a slave was protected by the municipal regulations of various jurisdictions within the United States. The Court, therefore, ought not to have pronounced illegal what was "unquestionably" a legally established institution. But where there was a conflict of law situation or where the applicable legal rules were ambiguous, McLean's opinion seemed to suggest that a judge might properly maintain a preference for what is just. Viewed within the "intellectual milieu that accepted the natural law tradition on slavery," McLean's jurisprudence may fitly be described as insisting that "[s]lavery has no source in right, and the ultimate end (*telos*) of the law ought to be liberty."[43] When coupled with a commitment to judicial positivism, such a jurisprudence could not, by itself, decide any particular point of law; but such a jurisprudence, anchored in the tradition of natural law, nevertheless did breathe life into the judicial enterprise by recognizing an end or aspiration toward which it could strive. Soon after the *Dred Scott* ruling, such a theory of constitutional aspiration was taken up by Lincoln in the Senate campaign of

---

[41] *Dred Scott*, 538 (McLean, J. dissenting).
[42] Cover, *Justice Accused*, 29.
[43] Ibid., 30.

1858, where the principle issue in contention was slavery in the territories and the soundness of the *Dred Scott* decision.

Constitutional Aspirations in the Lincoln-Douglas Debates

"The long political duel between Stephen A. Douglas and Abraham Lincoln," observes Harry Jaffa, "was above all a struggle to determine the nature of the opinion which should form the doctrinal foundation of American government."[44] This struggle was principally concerned with the meaning and purpose of the proposition "all men are created equal," and Lincoln, no less than Douglas, centered the debate on the opinions expressed in *Dred Scott*. As Jaffa notes, "For Lincoln there was, indeed, 'only one issue,' but that issue was whether or not the American people should believe that 'all men are created equal' in the full extent and true significance of that proposition."[45] For Douglas, however, the central issue in the debate with Lincoln concerned the right of the people to maintain popular sovereignty over their own domestic institutions, including the institution of slavery: Douglas famously asserted his own indifference to whether or not slavery was voted up or down in a given community. But in so making popular sovereignty the central issue, Douglas was forced to deny explicitly the Lincolnian interpretation of the Declaration's meaning and significance.

The *telos* of the American regime was, for Douglas, the "great principle of self-government, which asserts the right of every people to decide for themselves the nature and character of the domestic institutions and fundamental law under which they are to live."[46] David Zarefsky aptly notes that "Douglas . . . was not an amoral man. Rather, his highest moral value was procedural: the principle of local self-government, the right of each community

---

44 Harry V. Jaffa, *Crisis of the House Divided: An Interpretation of the Issues in the Lincoln-Douglas Debates*, 2nd ed. (Chicago: University of Chicago Press, 1982), 308.

45 Jaffa, *Crisis of the House Divided*, 309.

46 Basler, ed., *Collected Works of Abraham Lincoln*, 3: 210.

to make its own decisions about its domestic affairs."[47] Yet in conceding that slavery was a matter reasonably resolved by the democratic process – and in expressing his "don't care" policy as to whether or not slavery was voted up or down – Douglas had to deny the full extent of the Declaration's insistence on human equality. "The signers of the Declaration of Independence," declared Douglas, "never dreamed of the negro when they were writing that document. They referred to white men, to men of European birth and European decent, when they declared the equality of all men."[48] Douglas did not go so far as to defend slavery as morally right, but he did find refuge for his position in asserting that neither the Declaration of Independence nor the great principle of self-governance declared it to be wrong. For Douglas, "[m]oral judgment of the slaveholders was not a subject for political debate but was a matter for their consciences and their God."[49]

Lincoln accused Douglas of inconsistently claiming that slavery could rightfully be voted up or down in a community, regardless of the moral status of slavery itself: "When Judge Douglas says that whoever, or whatever community, wants slaves, they have a right to have them, he is perfectly logical if there is nothing wrong in the institution; but if you admit that it is wrong, he cannot logically say that anybody has a right to do wrong."[50]

---

[47] David Zarefsky, foreword to Paul M. Angle, ed., *The Complete Lincoln-Douglas Debates of 1858* (Chicago: University Press of Chicago, 1958 [1991]), xv.

[48] Basler, ed., *Collected Works of Abraham Lincoln*, 3: 216.

[49] Zarefsky, foreword to *Complete Lincoln-Douglas Debates*, xvi. See, for example, Douglas' speech at Quincy: "I hold that the people of the slaveholding states are civilized men as well as ourselves, that they bear consciences as well as we, and that they are accountable to God and their posterity and not to us. It is for them to decide therefore the moral and religious right of the slavery question for themselves within their own limits ... I repeat that the principle is the right of each state, each territory, to decide this slavery question for itself, to have slavery or not, as it chooses, and it does not become Mr. Lincoln, or anybody else, to tell the people of Kentucky that they have no consciences, that they are living in a state of iniquity, and that they are cherishing an institution to their bosoms in violation of the law of God. Better for him to adopt the policy 'judge not lest ye be judged.'" Basler, ed., *Collected Works of Abraham Lincoln*, 3: 274.

[50] Basler, ed., *Collected Works of Abraham Lincoln*, 3: 257. Cf. ibid. 3: 226 and 3: 315.

Conceding that democratic self-governance was one of the great principles of the American regime, Lincoln nonetheless declared that the principles of the Declaration anteceded the Constitution and were "the principles and axioms of a free society."[51] And yet, Lincoln later reflected, the principles of the Declaration were "denied and evaded, with small show of success. One dashingly calls them 'glittering generalities'; another bluntly calls them 'self-evident lies'; and still others insidiously argue that they apply only to 'superior races.'"[52]

In the Lincolnian interpretation, the Declaration declared that all men, without exception, were created equal, and the Founders intended to assert that proposition in its most expansive meaning and significance. Nonetheless, for Lincoln, the real issue at stake in the debate over territorial expansion and slavery – a debate centered on the opinions in the *Dred Scott* case – was whether or not slavery was intrinsically right:

You may turn over everything in the Democratic policy from beginning to end, whether in the shape it takes on the statute book, in the shape it takes in the *Dred Scott* decision, in the shape it takes in conversation or the shape it takes in short maxim-like arguments – it everywhere carefully excludes the idea that there is anything wrong in it.

That is the real issue. That is the issue that will continue in this country when these poor tongues of Judge Douglas and myself shall be silent. It is the eternal struggle between these two principles – right and wrong – throughout the world. They are the two principles that have stood face to face from the beginning of time; and will ever continue to struggle.[53]

Even though slavery was legally established by local legislation, still it was contrary to right, and it was contrary to the Jeffersonian axioms declared by the Declaration of Independence, which undergirded the logic of the constitutional text.[54] "Let us turn

---

[51] Abraham Lincoln, "The Principles of Jefferson: Letter to Henry L. Pierce and Others," April 6, 1859. In *Abraham Lincoln: A Documentary Portrait Through His Speeches and Writings*, ed., Don E. Fehrenbacher (Stanford, CA: Stanford University Press, 1964), 120.

[52] Lincoln, "The Principles of Jefferson," 120.

[53] Basler, ed., *Collected Works of Abraham Lincoln*, 3: 315.

[54] Lincoln on the relevant clauses in the Constitution: "Again; the institution of slavery is only mentioned in the Constitution of the United States two or

slavery from its claims of 'moral right,'" declared Lincoln, "back
upon its existing legal rights, and its arguments of 'necessity.' Let
us return it to the position our fathers gave it; and there let it rest
in peace. Let us readopt the Declaration of Independence, and
with it, the practices, and the policy, which harmonize with it."[55]
In Lincoln's interpretation, the Declaration of Independence and
the Constitution of the United States – that "great charter of
liberty" – were understood as incorporating enduring principles
of justice that were substantively true even when they were existentially denied.[56] Or, to bring the point back to the *Dred Scott*
case, the reason why the "judges were tragically mistaken," as
Gary Jacobsohn argues, "... [was] precisely because they did not
take the Constitution seriously; that is, they failed to acknowledge the moral dimensions of American constitutionalism."[57]
The failure of the judges in this regard became most explicit
within the discussion of property rights and the requirements of
the Fifth Amendment.

> three times, and in neither of these cases does the word 'slavery' or 'negro
> race' occur; but covert language is used each time, and for a purpose full of
> significance ..." [Lincoln goes on to discuss the language used in the 1808
> Clause, the 3/5 Clause, and the Fugitive Slave Clause] "... And I understand
> the contemporaneous history of those times to be that covert language was
> used with a purpose, and that purpose was that in our Constitution, which it
> was hoped and is still hoped will endure forever – when it should be read by
> intelligent and patriotic men, after the institution of slavery had passed from
> among us – there should be nothing on the face of the great charter of liberty
> suggesting that such a thing as negro slavery had ever existed among us."
> Basler, ed., *Collected Works of Abraham Lincoln*, 3: 307
> [55] Basler, ed., *Collected Works of Abraham Lincoln*, 2: 276.
> [56] Ibid., 2: 405–406. "I think the authors of that notable instrument intended to
> include all men, but they did not mean to declare all men equal in all respects.
> They did not mean to say all men were equal in color, size, intellect, moral
> development or social capacity. They defined with tolerable distinctness in
> what they did consider men created equal – equal in certain inalienable rights,
> among which are life, liberty and the pursuit of happiness. This they said, and
> this they meant. They did not mean to assert the obvious untruth, that all
> men were then actually enjoying that equality, nor yet, that they were about
> to confer it immediately upon them. In fact they had no power to confer such
> a boon. They meant simply to declare the right so that the enforcement of it
> might follow as fast as circumstances should permit."
> [57] Gary J. Jacobsohn, *The Supreme Court and the Decline of Constitutional
> Aspiration* (Totowa, NJ: Rowan & Littlefield Publishers, 1986), 8.

The Fifth Amendment stipulates that the Federal Government shall not deprive anyone of "life, liberty, or property without due process of law." In his opinion, Chief Justice Taney argued that the due process clause contained a substantive component, which ensured that a man may not be deprived of his property in slaves while entering the federal territories. McLean and Lincoln both interpreted this provision as including a substantive component as well, yet the emphasis in their exegesis was not on the words *due process* so much as it is on the word *property*. According to both McLean and Lincoln, the Constitution presupposed a distinction between species of things that could be held *rightfully* as property and species of things – including rational beings – that could not be held *rightfully* as property and which might only be held as such under a regime of local positive legislation.[58] In other words, the substantive nature of the property being claimed for protection under the Fifth Amendment mattered immensely.

Nature and Property in *Dred Scott*

After discussing the nature of the federal government as a government of limited and enumerated powers, Chief Justice Taney declared:

These powers, and others, in relation to rights of person, which it is not necessary to enumerate here, are, in express and positive terms, denied to the General Government; and the rights of private property have been guarded with equal care. Thus the rights of property are united with the rights of person, and placed on the same ground by the fifth amendment to the Constitution, which provides that no person shall be deprived of life, liberty, and property, without due process of law. And an act of Congress which deprives a citizen of the United States of his liberty or property, merely because he came himself or brought his property into a particular Territory of the United States, and who had committed no offence against the laws, could hardly be dignified with the name of due process of law.[59]

---

[58] Cf. U.S. Constitution, Art. 4 §2: "No person held to service or labor in one State *under the laws thereof* ..." [emphasis mine].

[59] *Dred Scott*, 450 (Taney, J.).

In his treatment of Taney's Fifth Amendment argument, Curtis took the position that the Constitution granted to the Federal Government the authority to enact general legislation respecting the territories. Because the Constitution was devoid of any specific provisions *protecting* slavery in the territories, it was reasonable to conclude that Congress had the power under the "needful rules and regulations" clause to limit or sanction slavery rights as it saw fit. The legal issue for Curtis, then, was whether

... it can be shown, by anything in the Constitution itself, that when it confers on Congress the power to make all needful rules and regulations respecting the territory belonging to the United States, the exclusion or the allowance of slavery was excepted; or if anything in the history of this provision tends to show that such an exception was intended by those who framed and adopted the Constitution to be introduced into it; [and if it can] I hold it to be my duty carefully to consider, and to allow just weight to such considerations in interpreting the positive text of the Constitution. But where the Constitution has said all needful rules and regulations, I must find something more than theoretical reasoning to induce me to say it did not mean all.[60]

Concerning the guarantee against deprivation of property without due process of law, Curtis noted that this guarantee was based on the Magna Carta and that prohibitions and restrictions on rights to certain species of property had been entertained by England as well as by all of the state legislatures (whose state constitutions also incorporated provisions of the Magna Carta) and by the national legislature through the passage of the Northwest Ordinance and the Missouri Compromise. If the Founders intended to declare through the Fifth Amendment such a vested right to property in a slave, it was the first time that their intention has been so declared, and, if nothing else, custom had abolished whatever theoretical protection the Constitution gave to an individual's right to bring slaves into the territories.[61]

---

[60] *Dred Scott*, 621 (Curtis, J. dissenting).

[61] Ibid., 627 (Curtis, J. dissenting). Curtis: "I think I may at least say, if the Congress then did violate Magna Charta by the ordinance, no one discovered that violation. Besides, if the prohibition upon all persons, citizens as well as others, to bring slaves into a Territory, and a declaration that if brought they shall be free, deprives citizens of their property without due process of law,

As Mark Graber notes, Curtis "implicitly denied the constitutional right to bring personal property into the territories by treating persons seeking to bring slaves into the territories as demanding a special 'exception.'"[62] McLean, however, disagreed with Curtis over "whether persons had a constitutional right to bring personal property into the territories"; and, according to Graber, McLean "disputed Taney's conclusion only because the Ohio justice maintained that 'a slave is not mere chattel.'"[63] Graber's characterization of McLean's position on this point is perhaps uncharitable; McLean certainly did maintain that "a slave is not mere chattel," but he also based his argument against slavery in the territories on a nuanced understanding of the nature of the powers of the federal government and the nature of the right in question. "By virtue of what law is it," McLean asked, "that a master may take his slave into free territory, and exact from him the duties of a slave? The law of the Territory does not sanction it. No authority can be claimed under the Constitution of the United States, or any law of Congress."[64] In making this argument, McLean implicitly sided with Taney that the federal government did not possess the authority to wantonly prohibit any property whatever from entering into the federal territories, and, as Graber suggests, part of the reason for his disagreement with Taney was his conviction that there was no rightful claim to property in another man because a man, by nature, was not "mere chattel." But McLean also appealed to the Constitution, to the state policies of Missouri and Illinois, to the common law, to international law, and to legal precedent in Britain and America, before he asked, "Will it be said that the slave is taken as property, the same as other property which the master may own? To this I answer, that colored persons are property by the law of the State, and no such power has been given to Congress."[65]

what shall we say of the legislation of many of the slaveholding States which have enacted the same prohibition?"

[62] Graber, *Dred Scott and the Problem of Constitutional Evil*, 61.

[63] Ibid., 62.

[64] *Dred Scott*, 548 (McLean, J. dissenting).

[65] Ibid., 548 (McLean, J. dissenting). Cf. Lincoln at Charleston in *Lincoln-Douglas Debates*, echoing McLean's argument that a slave is not to be regarded in the

On this point, Curtis agreed: "The constitution refers to slaves as 'persons held to service in one State, under the laws thereof.' Nothing can more clearly describe a *status* created by municipal law ... [and this court has declared in *Prigg v. Pennsylvania* that] 'The state of slavery is deemed to be a mere municipal regulation, founded on and limited to the range of territorial laws.'"[66] In their characterizations of the legal status of slavery, Curtis and McLean drew on "the understandings that ran back to the classic teachers of jurisprudence, on the difference between the natural law and the 'municipal,' or the positive law (the law that was posited, or set down, in a particular place)."[67] McLean's dispute with Curtis, then, was a dispute over the breadth and scope of the positive grant of power to the federal government. As a government of limited and enumerated powers, McLean argued, the federal government no more had the authority to prohibit slavery in local jurisdictions than it did to introduce slavery into federal jurisdictions. The "needful rules and regulations" clause did not abolish other constitutional restrictions that might be placed on the federal government by the text and design of the Constitution. According to McLean, it was the locality and artificiality of slavery ordinances – rather than the general power of the federal government – that legitimized the Northwest Ordinance and the Missouri Compromise.[68]

---

same class as other "common matters of property": "The other way is for us to surrender and let Judge Douglas and his friends have their way and plant slavery over all the state – cease speaking of it as in any way a wrong – regard slavery as one of the common matters of property, and speak of negroes as we do of our horses and cattle" (270). Cf. Lincoln's argument against Douglas' characterization of the nature of this property: "When he says that slave property and horse and hog property are alike to be allowed to go into the territories, upon the principles of equality, he is reasoning truly, if there is no difference between them as property; but if the one is property, held rightfully, and the other is wrong, then there is no equality between the right and the wrong; so that, turn it any way you can, in all the arguments sustaining the Democratic policy, and in that policy itself, there is a careful, studied exclusion of the idea that there is anything wrong in slavery." Basler, ed., *Collected Works of Abraham Lincoln*, 2: 357.

[66] Ibid., 624 (Curtis, J. dissenting).

[67] Hadley Arkes, *Beyond the Constitution* (Princeton, NJ: Princeton University Press, 1990), 44.

[68] See Michael Zuckert, "Legality and Legitimacy in *Dred Scott*: The Crisis of the Incomplete Constitution," *Chicago-Kent Law Review* 82 (2007): 291–328.

To claim for the federal government such a sweeping grant of power over property rights would have, for McLean, ran counter to his understanding of the limited nature of the power conferred on the federal government and would have frustrated the design and spirit of the Constitution. In the majority opinion, it was "said [that] the Territories are common property of the States, and that every man has a right to go there with his property." In McLean's dissent, "This is not controverted."[69] At the same time, McLean suggested that failure to discriminate between legitimate and illegitimate property would equally frustrate the design and spirit of the Constitution, for "property in a human being does not arise from nature or from the common law"; and the "Constitution, in express terms, recognizes the status of slavery as founded on the municipal law."[70] However, according to McLean, the majority opinion in *Dred Scott* asserted to the contrary that a slave was a common article of chattel – the same as "a horse, or any other kind of property" – and that each citizen had a right to bring his slave into the federal territories. McLean disagreed, but if a jurist was to discriminate between legitimate and illegitimate species of property, the question properly arose how one is to make such a distinction. Inasmuch as there was any ambiguity or conflict in what the law might require, the answer for McLean, like Hamilton in a different context, was to be found in the "nature and reason of the thing."[71]

As previously noted, Graber asserted that McLean disagreed with Taney's due process argument "only" because McLean

Zuckert argues that McLean's denial of the constitutional authority of the federal government to make slaves was an implicit denial of the constitutionality of the Missouri Compromise. I do not think this is McLean's claim, but Zuckert raises a strong point: If slavery can be established only by local law – and if Congress makes all "needful rules and regulations" for the territories – then it seems to follow that Congress has no authority to strike a compromise that would maintain a system of slavery in *some* of the federal territories.

[69] *Dred Scott*, 549 (McLean, J. dissenting).

[70] Ibid., 549 (McLean, J. dissenting). McLean, referring to the U.S. Constitution, Art. 4 § 3: "'No person held to service or labor in one State, under the laws thereof, escaping into another, shall' &c."

[71] *Federalist* no. 78 (ed. Rossiter), para. 14. Hamilton speaking of the Federal Judiciary: "The exercise of judicial discretion, in determining between two

"maintained that 'a slave is not mere chattel.'"[72] Graber is dismissive of this argument; but, like Lincoln, McLean thought it mattered immensely "whether a negro is *not* or *is* a man." Lincoln declared in his speech at Peoria, within the context of the debate over popular sovereignty in the territories, that "[i]f [the slave] is not a man, why in that case, he who is a man may, as a matter of self-government, do just as he pleases with him. But if the negro *is* a man, is it not to that extent, a total destruction of self-government, to say that he too shall not govern *himself*?"[73] McLean asked this same question within the context of *Dred Scott*: If there was some property right that attached to a man *as* man (i.e., in the absence of local legislation), then was it not a total destruction of property rights if the property itself was a man? For McLean, there could be no doubt as to the humanity of the slave, for "He bears the impress of his Maker, and is amenable to the laws of God and man; and he is destined to an endless existence."[74] Within the natural-law tradition that McLean so heavily drew on, Arkes rightly notes, it was a common understanding that "human beings did not deserve to be ruled in the way that humans ruled dogs, horses, and monkeys. Creatures who could give and understand reasons deserved to be ruled through the giving of reasons, by a government that would seek the consent of the governed."[75] It was part of the nature and

contradictory laws, is exemplified in a familiar instance. It not uncommonly happens, that there are two statutes existing at one time, clashing in whole or in part with each other, and neither of them containing any repealing clause or expression. In such a case, it is the province of the courts to liquidate and fix their meaning and operation. So far as they can, by any fair construction, be reconciled to each other, reason and law conspire to dictate that this should be done; where this is impracticable, it becomes a matter of necessity to give effect to one, in exclusion of the other. The rule which has obtained in the courts for determining their relative validity is, that the last in order of time shall be preferred to the first. But this is a mere rule of construction, not derived from any positive law, but from the nature and reason of the thing."

[72] Graber, *Dred Scott and the Problem of Constitutional Evil*, 62.

[73] Roy P. Basler, ed., *The Collected Works of Abraham Lincoln*, 9 vols. (New Brunswick, NJ: Rutgers University Press, 1953), 2: 265–66. Quoted in Arkes, *Beyond the Constitution*, 43.

[74] *Dred Scott*, 549 (McLean, J. dissenting).

[75] Arkes, *Beyond the Constitution*, 43.

reason of the thing that a being "amenable to the laws of God and man" – a creature, in other words, that could give and understand reasons – was not "merely chattel." Whatever abstract property rights were presupposed by the Fifth Amendment, the right to own another man could not, by its very nature, have been among them.

Nature and Property in the Lincoln-Douglas Debates

On the question of vested property rights is perhaps where there was the greatest divergence between Douglas' insistence on the principle of popular sovereignty and Taney's declared "right to property in a slave." For if the Constitution protected slave property in the federal territories, slavery would have ceased to be a local institution. Douglas's solution to this problem was to declare the right of local communities to nullify the Court's decision by failing to provide legislation that would protect this particular type of property. When recast in this light, Lincoln charged, Douglas' interpretation of the *Dred Scott* decision became "the strongest abolition argument ever made."[76] If one was to argue that a right, enshrined in the Constitution, could be disregarded by local communities, then one could not "avoid furnishing an argument by which Abolitionists may deny the obligation to return fugitives, and claim the power to pass laws unfriendly to the right of the slaveholder to reclaim his fugitive."[77] When the principles of Douglas' argument were applied in this way, Lincoln asserted, there had "never been as outlandish or lawless a doctrine from the mouth of any respectable man on earth."[78]

For Lincoln, the relevant question was whether or not the Court had decided *correctly* in *Dred Scott*; whether or not there was, in fact, a constitutional right to own another man. Lincoln intended to exploit the contradictory principles championed by Douglas (i.e., popular sovereignty in the territories *and* adherence to the Supreme Court's decision in *Dred Scott*), and he did so by

[76] Basler, ed., *Collected Works of Abraham Lincoln*, 3: 317.
[77] Ibid., 3: 318.
[78] Ibid., 3: 317.

emphasizing the nature of the right in question and by denying the persuasiveness of the Supreme Court's reasoning in the case. As Lincoln made clear, he believed "that the Supreme Court and the advocates of that decision might search in vain for the place in the Constitution where the right of property in a slave is distinctly and expressly affirmed."[79] On the question of the federal government's general power to curtail property rights in the territories, however, Lincoln sided with McLean over Curtis. The federal government did not possess an unlimited grant of power under the "needful rules and regulations" clause, and the nature of the property in question was wholly relevant to the legal discussion in *Dred Scott*: "When [Judge Douglas] says that a slave property and horse and hog property are alike to be allowed to go into the territories, upon the principles of equality, he is reasoning truly, if there is no difference between them as property; but if the one is property, held rightfully, and the other is wrong, then there is no equality between the right and wrong."[80]

Like McLean, the reason Lincoln declared that a slave was not among that species of property "held rightfully" was because of his consideration of the nature and reason of the thing in question. The spirit that said to another man, "You work and toil and earn bread, and I'll eat it," Lincoln argued, was based on a tyrannical principle "[n]o matter in what shape it comes, whether from the mouth of a king who seeks to bestride the people of his own nation and live by the fruit of their labor, or from one race of men as an apology for enslaving another race."[81] Whereas the Founders of the American government intended to place slavery on a course toward ultimate extinction and the Constitution itself neither distinctly nor expressly affirmed the right to hold property in men, the "real issue in this controversy – the one pressing upon every mind – is the sentiment on the part of one class that does look upon [slavery] *as a wrong*, and another class that *does not* look upon it as a wrong."[82] Such

[79] Basler, ed., *Collected Works of Abraham Lincoln*, 3: 231.
[80] Ibid., 3: 257.
[81] Ibid., 3: 315.
[82] Ibid., 3: 312.

moral considerations were subject to the charge of "abstract reasoning," but the thing at stake in this controversy, according to Lincoln, was "rather *concrete* than *abstract*."[83] Lincoln, no less than McLean, would have agreed with the assessment made by Jaffa a century later that the "attempt to legitimize the extension of slavery was impossible without denying the Negro's humanity or without denying the moral right of humanity or both."[84] And McLean, no less than Lincoln, thought that the illiberal principles behind the slave interest were too heavy for the Constitution to bear.

Dred Scott and the Jurisprudence of John McLean

The reason McLean supported fidelity to the Constitution, even when the law was unambiguous in its accommodation of what was unjust, such as in the fugitive-slave clause, was because of his conviction that the Constitution was essentially antislavery. In other words, fidelity to law was, for McLean, a moral consideration; the reason it was his duty to support the Constitution was because the Constitution incorporated moral understandings that were substantively just. McLean found evidence for this in the text of the document, but his reading of that text was informed by a moral understanding that anteceded the Constitution; an understanding, shared by Lincoln, that

[t]he ground of right and wrong ... in regard to slavery, could not depend on any moral judgments stipulated in the Constitution. The wrongness of slavery was rooted in the understandings of right and wrong that *preceded* the Constitution. Indeed, as Lincoln recognized, the right of human beings to be ruled only with their own consent was a necessary part of that moral ground on which the Constitution was founded.[85]

McLean, like Lincoln, withheld his support from the majority's decision in *Dred Scott* partly because he perceived that the

---

[83] Ibid., 2: 518.
[84] Jaffa, *Crisis of the House Divided*, 313.
[85] Arkes, *Beyond the Constitution*, 44.

decision ran counter to the moral understandings that undergirded American constitutionalism.

Nonetheless, the legal issues at stake in the *Dred Scott* decision were multitiered, and McLean did not reduce the legal question (merely) to a question of justice or injustice, policy or impolicy. The authority and jurisdiction of the Supreme Court, considerations of federalism and the separation of government powers, the legal and moral obligation of fidelity to law, constitutional design and the ground of constitutional rights, the scope of congressional power, the status of the federal territories, and the intent of the Framers with regard to territorial expansion all brought up questions that could not be answered merely by an appeal to simple justice. Yet while substantially agreeing with Curtis on many of the legal questions at issue in *Dred Scott*, McLean's jurisprudence was unique in that it undertook a serious consideration of the nature of law, constitutional aspirations, and property rights within the context of the humanity of the slave. Curtis tendered a powerful dissent in *Dred Scott*, particularly with respect to the historical materials put forward by Taney, but McLean challenged Curtis' opinion by incorporating a style of legal reasoning that was seemingly out of vogue on the High Court in 1857.

Contemporary constitutional jurisprudence suffers from a dilemma that was foreshadowed by the *Dred Scott* case. In this vein, Jacobsohn questions what modern relevance is to be found in the eighteenth-century idea of "inalienable rights" once the intellectual status of that doctrine is held in disrepute.[86] Similarly, Jaffa observed at the centennial of the Lincoln-Douglas debates that "[m]odern social science appears to know neither God nor nature. The articulation of the world, in virtue of which it is a world and not undifferentiated substratum, has disappeared from view. The abolition of God and nature has therefore been accompanied by the abolition of that correlative concept, man, from this same world."[87] Modern commentary on the *Dred Scott*

---

[86] Jacobsohn, *The Supreme Court and the Decline of Constitutional Aspiration*, 2.
[87] Jaffa, *Crisis of the House Divided*, 11.

decision is particularly affected by this dilemma. For if man is a non-teleological being, then the nature of man ceases to bear any jurisprudential relevance. The law is not made for man, because man himself is not made for anything. There is a radical cognitive separation between what the law requires and what the law *ought* to require, because, strictly speaking, the realm of *ought* exists as mere feeling or value and not as fact.

The contemporary legal community has ever felt the holding of *Dred Scott* to be odious, but modern commentators seek to ground their opposition in something more concrete than personal distaste. This may explain, in part, why modern schools of jurisprudence are quick to claim Curtis – who devoted much of his opinion to debunking Taney's history – as their legitimate precursor. Keith Whittington laments that the road not taken in *Dred Scott* was the road offered by Justice Curtis's dissent.[88] Jack Balkin asserts, "The appropriate rejoinder [to Taney's substantive due process argument] is Justice Curtis's in his dissent in *Dred Scott*."[89] Robert Bork writes that "Justice Benjamin Curtis of Massachusetts dissented in *Dred Scott*, destroyed Taney's reasoning, and rested his own conclusions upon the original understanding of those who made the Constitution."[90] Christopher Eisgruber, responding to Bork's claim that Curtis is the original originalist, attempts to claim Curtis as a "fundamental values" jurist.[91] Yet all of these appeals to Curtis' dissent

---

[88] See Keith E. Whittington, "The Road Not Taken: Dred Scott, Judicial Authority and Political Questions," *The Journal of Politics* 63 (2001): 365–391.

[89] J. M. Balkin, "*Dred Scott* and *Kelo*" (August 11, 2005). http://www.balkiniz ation.com (accessed May 14, 2008).

[90] Robert H. Bork, *The Tempting of America: The Political Seduction of the Law* (New York: Free Press, 1990), 33.

[91] See Christopher L. Eisgruber, "Dred Again: Originalism's Forgotten Past," *Constitutional Commentary* 10 (1993). Eisgruber is sympathetic to arguments based on natural law, and he attributes more natural-law legal reasoning to Curtis's opinion than I do. Nonetheless, within a discussion of Joseph Story on natural law and property rights, Eisgruber indicates that the "out-moded language of natural law," the "rhetoric of natural rights," and "the Declaration's references to a 'Creator'" are superfluous and unnecessary to a modern aspirational and justice-seeking constitutionalism (44).

have in common a rejection of the eighteenth-century natural-rights tradition.[92]

McLean's dissent in *Dred Scott* can at least be viewed as one instantiation of an older understanding. Instead of drawing such a stark distinction between what is "political rather than legal," as many of McLean's detractors have been tempted to do, perhaps his dissent is better perceived in light of Lincoln's subsequent arguments on this very subject. For in the debates between Lincoln and Douglas, Lincoln insisted that the "real issue" with the democratic policy "in the shape it takes in the *Dred Scott* decision ... [is that it] carefully excludes the idea that there is anything wrong in [slavery]."[93] As Jaffa argues, the question at the heart of *Dred Scott* was the question "which took precedence when a slave owner entered a Territory with his slave, the Negro slave's human personality, under 'the laws of nature and nature's God,' or his chatteldom, under the laws of the slave state whence he came."[94] Speaking to that issue, McLean responded relevantly that the slave, by his very nature, was not "mere chattel."

There is another modern challenge to McLean's jurisprudence, however, that consists in an accusation that, whether right or wrong about the Constitution, McLean imprudently exacerbated the sectional conflict brewing over the expansion of slavery in the territories. An early version of this thesis was proffered in the 1920s by the historian Frank Hodder and has been repeated, in various forms, in modern literature. According to Hodder, the question of the constitutionality of the Missouri

---

[92] See Sanford Levinson, "Slavery in the Canon of Constitutional Law," in *Slavery and the Law*, ed., Paul Finkelman (Madison, WI: Madison House, 1992). "If one wishes to attack *Dred Scott*, therefore, an obvious question is whether one must go after Taney's originalist modality or, instead, after his specific historical analysis. Many students, for example, endorse Justice's Curtis's dissent, which attacks Taney's history. I ask them if this means they would in fact support Taney if further historical research called Curtis's assertion into question and supported Taney's account instead" (103).

[93] Basler, ed., *Collected Works of Abraham Lincoln*, 3: 315.

[94] Harry V. Jaffa, *Original Intent and the Framers of the Constitution: A Disputed Question* (Washington, DC: Regnery Gateway, 1994), 68.

Compromise was a question that the Court did not originally intend to answer.[95] Rather, Hodder maintained, the Court was forced into a discussion of that piece of congressional legislation by the dissenters, and particularly McLean, who was "blinded by political ambition."[96]

Regarding the Court's original intention to leave the Missouri Compromise unaddressed, Robert McCloskey similarly argued:

[A]t least one judge, McLean, was dissatisfied with this prudent arrangement. It became known that he, an ambitious politician and a firm abolitionist, intended to dissent, arguing that Scott became free when he entered the free territory of the Louisiana Purchase. This necessarily involved the contention that Congress had the power to enact the Missouri Compromise which had made that area free. A majority of his fellow judges believed in fact that the Compromise was invalid, and they were unwilling to let McLean go unanswered, if the question was to be posed at all.[97]

The controversial *Dred Scott* decision, it has accordingly been suggested, paved the way for the subsequent split in the Democratic Party that allowed the election of Lincoln and hastened the coming of the Civil War. Under this assumption, Hodder maintained, for example, that "the only chance of averting [war] lay in the election of [Stephen] Douglas by a united party and the adoption of a new compromise which would have tided over the crisis until a larger degree of intercommunication and a better understanding between the sections had rendered possible a peaceful solution to the problem of slavery."[98]

More recently, Graber has argued that a better constitutional choice for men of antislavery sentiments may have been to "accommodate more evil than constitutionally necessary in order to maintain constitutional conversations, however truncated, that over time *might* have realized a more just society."[99] Graber,

---

[95] F. H. Hodder, "Some Phases of the *Dred Scott* Case," *The Mississippi Valley Historical Review* 16 (1929): 3–22.

[96] Ibid., 22.

[97] Robert McCloskey, *The American Supreme Court*, 62.

[98] Hodder, "Some Phases of the *Dred Scott* Case," 21.

[99] Graber, *Dred Scott and the Problem of Constitutional Evil*, 253.

however, identifies John Bell, rather than Stephen Douglas, as the likely candidate of constitutional peace.[100] According to each account, the antislavery jurist McLean, like the antislavery politician Lincoln – albeit well-meaning and perhaps correct as a matter of simple justice – was woefully misguided as a matter of statesmanship, desiring a just peace in theory while in fact hastening the scourge of war. A serious reconsideration of McLean's opinion amid these contemporary challenges, then, points also to a reconsideration of the theoretical grounds of Lincoln's antislavery constitutionalism and his subsequent reflections on both the necessity and limits of extrajudicial constitutional statesmanship. Within the context of Lincoln's opposition to the *Dred Scott* opinion and his moral engagement with the costs of the Civil War, the natural law and providential aspects of Lincoln's thought shed light on the massive gulf between the underlying premises of modern constitutional theory and the tradition of American antislavery constitutionalism.

---

[100] Douglas is problematic as a candidate for constitutional peace, according to Graber, because his approval of the theory of Manifest Destiny would have led to a foreign "war for the immediate purpose of expanding slavery." See Graber, ibid., 240.

5

Natural Law, Providence, and Lincoln's Constitutional Statesmanship

Even before the *Dred Scott* decision was handed down, the Court garnered vocal support from the executive and legislative branches. Two days before Taney's opinion was read from the bench, President Buchanan asserted in his inaugural address that the territorial question regarding slavery was a "judicial question, which legitimately belongs to the Supreme Court of the United States, before whom it is now pending, and will, it is understood, be speedily and finally settled." Indeed, Buchanan proclaimed that to the Court's "decision, in common with all good citizens, I shall cheerfully submit, whatever this may be."[1] Senator Douglas similarly praised the Court's decision and insisted that the Supreme Court was the final and authoritative interpreter of the meaning of the Constitution. Yet Douglas's past insistence on the principle of popular sovereignty for territorial legislatures was difficult to square with the Court's declaration in *Dred Scott* that (1) Congress had no power to limit slavery in the territories and (2) Congress could not delegate to territorial legislatures power that it did not itself possess. Douglas had seemingly developed an opinion about the constitutional legitimacy of the

[1] James Buchanan, "Inaugural Address" (March 4, 1857) in Jonathan French, ed., *The True Republican: Containing the Inaugural Addresses ... of All the Presidents of the United States from 1789 to 1857* (Philadelphia: J.B. & Smith Company, 1857), 292.

Kansas-Nebraska Act that was independent of (and contrary to) the Supreme Court's opinion, but he went out of his way to reconcile his popular sovereignty principle with his equally firm insistence on the doctrine of judicial supremacy.[2]

Lincoln as well had to square his previous political teachings with his reaction to the Court's decision. A younger Lincoln had taught that respect for law – even bad law – was the central doctrine in American political religion. In his famous Lyceum Speech in 1838, Lincoln declared, "Let every American, every lover of liberty, every well wisher to his posterity, swear by the blood of the Revolution, never to violate in the least particular, the laws of the country; and never to tolerate their violation by others." But, Lincoln went on:

When I so pressingly urge a strict observance of all the laws, let me not be understood as saying there are no bad laws, nor that grievances may not arise, for the redress of which, no legal provisions have been made. – I mean to say no such thing. But I do mean to say, that, although bad laws, if they exist, should be repealed as soon as possible, still while they continue in force, for the sake of example, they should be religiously observed.[3]

---

[2] Douglas presented his mature argument on the reconcilability of the ruling in *Dred Scott* with the principle of popular sovereignty in an article printed by *Harper's* magazine in 1859. See "The Dividing Line between Federal and Local Authority: Popular Sovereignty in the Territories." *Harper's Magazine*, September 1859, 519–537. Reprinted in Harry Jaffa and Robert Johannsen, eds., *In the Name of the People* (Columbus: The Ohio State University Press, 1959). Douglas's argument rests on an analytic distinction between, on the one hand, powers that Congress can *exercise* but not *confer* and, on the other hand, powers that Congress can *confer* and not *exercise*. The enumerated powers in Article I are powers that Congress may exercise but not confer. The power to craft a policy for the domestic institutions of a territory is a power that Congress may confer but not exercise. As such, Douglas argued, regulations affecting slavery – as a domestic institution – are within the authority conferred on the territorial legislatures by Congress and such regulations are not inconsistent with the *Dred Scott* decision, even though Congress may not exercise this power under the Court's ruling. Even if this distinction is granted, it still is very difficult to square Douglas's position with the Court's insistence that Congress "can confer no power on any local Government, established by its authority, to violate the provisions of the Constitution," when it is also considered that "the right to property in a slave is distinctly and expressly affirmed in the Constitution" (see *Dred Scott* at 451).

[3] Lincoln, "The Perpetuation of our Political Institutions: Address Before the Young Men's Lyceum of Springfield, Illinois" (January 27, 1838) in Basler, ed., *Collected Works of Abraham Lincoln*, 1: 108–115.

While nothing in Lincoln's previous teaching is necessarily inconsistent with his opposition to the *Dred Scott* ruling, the ruling did provide the impetus for Lincoln to articulate (and perhaps develop) a nuanced understanding of the appropriate role of judicial authority in upholding the rule of law. If a strict observance of law was the central doctrine in America's political religion – and if the Taney Court was wrong in its *Dred Scott* ruling – then the Court could not play the role of the magisterium in American political life.

On the question of judicial authority, moreover, Lincoln had to defend himself against the charge of waging "warfare upon the Supreme Court of the United States" and uttering a proposition that "carries with it the demoralization and degradation destructive of the judicial department of the federal government."[4] Senator Douglas's criticism of Lincoln on this point was particularly strong. In a part of his speech that was reminiscent of Lincoln's warning in the "Lyceum Address," Douglas asked, "When we refuse to abide by judicial decisions what protection is there left for life and property? To whom shall you appeal? To mob law, to partisan caucuses, to town meetings, to revolution?"[5] Douglas thus thrust on Lincoln the burden of providing a coherent theory of judicial authority that respected the rule of law while denying the concept of judicial supremacy. Additionally, Douglas charged Lincoln with attempting to usher in the very thing many of the nineteenth-century opponents of the Constitution had feared would be the tendency of the federal government. Lincoln's fundamental principle, Douglas asserted, was "for consolidation, for uniformity in our local institutions, for blotting out state rights and state sovereignty, and consolidating all the power in the federal government, for converting these thirty-two sovereign states into one empire, and making uniformity throughout the length and breadth of the land."[6] From Lincoln's perspective, however, the *Dred Scott* decision portended a different kind of consolidation – a consolidation of proslavery principles and the

---

[4] Angle, ed., *The Complete Lincoln-Douglas Debates*, 57–58.
[5] Ibid., 58.
[6] Ibid., 55.

nationalization of slavery throughout the Union. Viewed in this light, Lincoln attempted to refute Douglas's charge by drawing out the logic of the principles posited by the Court, principles Lincoln pledged to disregard as "rules of political action for the people and all the departments of the government."[7]

Lincoln the Statesman

A pivotal moment in Lincoln's public campaign against the *Dred Scott* decision occurred at the 1858 Illinois State Republican Convention, where Lincoln led off his address to the delegates with the following observation: "If we could first know *where* we are, and *whither* we are tending, we could then better judge *what* to do, and *how* to do it."[8] He had just been unanimously selected as the Republican candidate for the senatorial campaign against the Democratic incumbent, and the *Dred Scott* decision weighed heavily on his mind. The Kansas-Nebraska Act did not end the slavery agitation; in fact, Lincoln argued, conflict "*will* not cease, until a *crisis* shall have been reached, and passed." Quoting from the Gospels, Lincoln famously exhorted, "a house divided against itself cannot stand."[9] The Union would cease to be divided over the slavery question by becoming entirely slave or entirely free, and the engine in the machinery tending toward the resolution of that crisis in favor of slavery had been provided by Taney's opinion in *Dred Scott*.

"The several points of the Dred Scott decision," Lincoln asserted, "... constitute the piece of machinery, in its *present* state of advancement."[10] According to the logic of the decision, "what

---

[7] Ibid., 78.

[8] Basler, ed., *Collected Works of Abraham Lincoln*, 3: 86.

[9] Ibid., 3: 86.

[10] Ibid., 2: 464. The antecedent states of this machinery, according to Lincoln, were: (1) the repeal of the Missouri Compromise by the Kansas-Nebraska act; (2) the exclusion from the Kansas-Nebraska act of the amendment proposed on the floor by Samuel Chase to expressly declare that slavery could in fact be prohibited by territorial legislatures; (3) the declaration of the author of the Kansas-Nebraska act on the floor of the Senate that whether or not slavery could be prohibited by territorial legislatures was "a question for the Supreme

Dred Scott's master might lawfully do with Dred Scott, in the free state of Illinois, every other master may lawfully do with any other *one*, or one *thousand* slaves, in Illinois, or in any other free state."[11] The logic of the decision, in other words, tended toward the resolution of the slavery question through the nationalization of slavery *via* the judiciary. Given the acquiescence of the current president and Congress in the Supreme Court's decision, and their declared commitment to the supremacy of the Court's interpretation of the Constitution, it would only take "another Supreme Court decision, declaring that the Constitution of the United States does not permit a *state* to exclude slavery from its limits" for this nationalization to be complete. Whether or not it was the result of "preconcert," the alliance between Senator Douglas, President Buchanan, and Chief Justice Taney represented the "present political dynasty" that "shall be met and overthrown."[12]

Lincoln's call for the overthrow of the "present political dynasty" and his opposition to the *Dred Scott* decision did not constitute a call for force or violence, however. Rather, they constituted a call for the development of independent perspectives on constitutional meaning by the legislative and executive branches, and part of Lincoln's work in the Republican Party was to encourage candidates for office who would act on political principles that were formed independent of the Court's tutelage. Regarding legitimate judicial authority, Lincoln maintained that Supreme Court decisions were authoritative and final for the parties involved in the suit. Whomever the Court declared to be a slave, Lincoln assured, would not through private force or mob rule be declared free. But the principles of the Court's decision would not become binding and authoritative as "political rules" for the coordinate branches of government. "If I were in Congress," Lincoln explained, "and a vote should come up on a question whether slavery should be prohibited in a new

Court"; and (4) the endorsement by President Buchanan of the Supreme Court's forthcoming decision in *Dred Scott*.

[11] Ibid., 2: 464–465.
[12] Ibid., 2: 467.

territory, in spite of that Dred Scott decision, I would vote that it should."[13]

It is not enough to presume that Lincoln's departmentalist view of constitutional interpretation and his opposition to *Dred Scott* were based simply on an exegesis of the constitutional text. Lincoln's articulation of the constitutional wrong of the *Dred Scott* decision cannot be understood apart from his view that the Constitution was informed by moral principles, grounded in human nature, which provided the logical basis for republican government. Lincoln maintained that these principles were corroborated by the opening lines of the Declaration of Independence, and he managed to get a lot of mileage out of those "Jeffersonian axioms" during his debates with Douglas. Nevertheless, Lincoln's argument was not historicist, and it would be wrong to assume that the egalitarian principles he trumpeted were relevant only *because* they were acknowledged in the Declaration or *because* the Declaration somehow was bound up with the Constitution.

The reason Lincoln declared that a slave was not among that species of property "held rightfully" under Taney's reading of the Fifth Amendment was based on his consideration of the nature of the thing in question. The spirit that says to another man, "You work and toil and earn bread, and I'll eat it," Lincoln

---

[13] Ibid., 2: 495. We also know from the very first days of the Lincoln administration that he had to decide whether or not he, as president, would obey the principles of *Dred Scott* in his actions as an executive officer. In separate instances, one free black man was denied a passport to study in France, and another free black man was denied a patent for his invention. Both of these denials were premised on the ground that black people could not be citizens of the United States per the ruling in *Dred Scott*. Lincoln's Attorney General, Edward Bates, disputed the legitimacy of the Court's ruling by declaring that free blacks born in the United States were citizens of the United States and were thus entitled to the benefits of national citizenship. Accordingly, the administration issued both the passport and the patent. Moving beyond these specific instances within the executive branch, the Republican Congress also passed legislation banning slavery in the territories while extending that prohibition to all territories that might be added in the future. As James Randall noted, "Congress passed and Lincoln signed a bill, which, by ruling law according to the Supreme Court interpretation was unconstitutional." James Randall, *The Civil War and Reconstruction* (Boston: D.C. Heath & Company, 1937), 136.

argued, is based upon a tyrannical principle "[n]o matter in what shape it comes, whether from the mouth of a king who seeks to bestride the people of his own nation and live by the fruit of their labor, or from one race of men as an apology for enslaving another race."[14] While Lincoln declared – in opposition to Taney's originalist proslavery argument – that the Founders of the American government intended to place slavery on a course toward ultimate extinction and that the Constitution itself neither distinctly nor expressly affirmed the right to hold property in men, he insisted that the "real issue in this controversy" could be boiled down to the morality or immorality of slavery.[15] Additionally, the wrongness of the *Dred Scott* opinion inhered not in its substantive interpretation of the Fifth Amendment, but rather in its failure to extend the substantive protections of the Fifth Amendment to all men residing in the federal territories. But the answer to the constitutional question of whether or not the protections of the Fifth Amendment ought to be extended to any particular man depended on the answer to the antecedent question of whether that man is a man who is in full possession of those natural rights that are afforded by nature to man as such. Lincoln's answer was that there is no relevant difference between the white man and the black man that would constitute the possession of different natural rights.

In order consistently to support the principles posited by Taney in *Dred Scott*, one had either to deny the humanity of black men or deny the moral relevance of human status to the constitutional rules governing property in the federal territories. For Lincoln, both of those denials were false. Equally – and perhaps more – problematic, according to Lincoln, however, was the possibility that such a sweeping denial of natural rights for one class of people would destroy the logical foundation of the rights of the oppressing class. Lincoln expounded his argument in the following syllogism:

If A. can prove, however conclusively, that he may, of right, enslave B. – why may not B. snatch the same argument, and prove equally, that he

---

[14] Ibid., 3: 315.
[15] Ibid., 3: 314.

may enslave A.? – You say A. is white and B. is black. It is *color*, then; the lighter, having the right to enslave the darker? Take care. By this rule, you are to be slave to the first man you meet, with a fairer skin than your own. You do not mean color exactly? – You mean the whites are *intellectually* the superior of blacks, and, therefore have the right to enslave them? Take care again. By this rule, you are to be slave to the first man you meet, with an intellect superior to your own. But, say you, it is a question of *interest*; and, if you can make it your interest, you have the right to enslave another. Very well. And if he can make it his interest, he has the right to enslave you.[16]

The true basis of one's own freedom, Lincoln suggested, was a recognition that the *rightful* claim to freedom is not something won by convention or superior strength; this recognition carried with it the concomitant denial that the freedom of another might *rightfully* be taken merely on the basis of convention or strength. The primary evil of the *Dred Scott* decision was its denial of this fundamental truth. Lincoln foresaw what he thought would have been the devastating effect of this principle being adopted by the legislative and executive branches, and he combated the Court's rhetoric in an attempt to prevent this principle from capturing the imagination of the public mind.

The Constitution in the Public Mind

One of the chief criticisms of the Constitution made during ratification debates in the late 1780s was that federal judges – through the adoption of their principles as rules of action for the legislative and executive branches – would "mould the government, into almost any shape they please."[17] Lincoln's opposition to *Dred Scott* had less to do with his concern for Mr. Scott and the particular case at hand than with the way it would mold the government and shape the public mind on the issue of slavery. Douglas's

---

[16] *Abraham Lincoln: A Documentary Portrait Through His Speeches and Writings*, ed., Don Fehrenbacher (Stanford, CA: Stanford University Press, 1977), 70.

[17] Brutus, "Letter XI" (January 31, 1788) in Herbert Storing and Murray Dry, eds., *The Anti-Federalist: An Abridgement* (Chicago: University of Chicago Press, 1985), 167.

"don't care" policy with respect to slavery and popular sovereignty
in the territories was mistaken precisely because the policy excluded
"the thought that there is anything whatever wrong in slavery."[18]
Lincoln feared that Douglas's policy, coupled with the principles at
work in Taney's *Dred Scott* opinion, would "gain upon the public mind sufficiently to give promise" to another judicial decision
drawing out the logical implications of Taney's reasoning, which
would extend and protect slavery in every state of the Union.

In his critique of the *Dred Scott* opinion, Lincoln endeavored
not just to represent politically those citizens who carried antislavery sentiments, but also to educate the citizens about constitutional realities and to help form and develop those very
sentiments. In his judgment of "what to do and how to do it,"
Lincoln surveyed the political landscape and offered a solution
within the confines of real constitutional limitations, having a
"due regard for [slavery's] actual existence ... and the difficulties
of getting rid of it in any satisfactory way, and to all the constitutional obligations which have been thrown about it; but, nevertheless, desir[ing] a policy that looks to the prevention of it as a
wrong, and looks hopefully to the time when as a wrong it may
come to an end."[19] Lincoln's preferred constitutional policy was
predicated on his understanding that "there is no just rule other
than that of moral and abstract right,"[20] and the reason Lincoln
so emphasized the Declaration of Independence was because he
saw that, to be consistent, the defenders of slavery had to reject
the self-evident truths spoken of in the Declaration and instead
insist "that there is no right principle of action but *self-interest*."[21]
Once the repudiation of the principles of the Declaration had
been complete, there would be no firm basis upon which republican government could rest.

Lincoln's solution to the problem posed by a wayward
judiciary was not, as it was in the tradition of many of the
Constitution's opponents, to declare the legislature superior to

[18] Basler, ed., *Collected Works of Abraham Lincoln*, 2: 225.
[19] Ibid., 3: 226.
[20] Ibid., 3: 222
[21] Ibid., 3: 14.

the Court. Rather, Lincoln explicitly acknowledged the power of judicial review of legislative enactments, as this "is a duty from which [judges] may not shrink." Still, Lincoln's views on judicial authority became more nuanced through his political duel with Stephen Douglas over the territorial question, and in his First Inaugural Address, with the impending sectional crisis on his mind, Lincoln went on to lay out the danger of political acquiescence in the principles of the *Dred Scott* decision:

> I do not forget the position assumed by some, that constitutional questions are to be decided by the Supreme Court; nor do I deny that such decisions must be binding in any case, upon the parties to a suit; as to the object of that suit, while they are also entitled to very high respect and consideration in all parallel cases by all other departments of the government ... At the same time, a candid citizen must confess that if the policy of the government upon vital questions, affecting the whole people, is to be irrevocably fixed by decisions of the Supreme Court, the instant they are made, in ordinary litigation between parties, in personal actions, the people will have ceased to be their own rulers, having to that extent practically resigned their government into the hands of that eminent tribunal.[22]

The departmentalist view of constitutional interpretation that Lincoln articulated offered a separation-of-powers solution to the problem brought on by the potential for judicial pronouncements on the meaning of the Constitution to mold the government into any shape it pleased. Yet, Lincoln's solution was not merely procedural. It also required the work of statesmen, who would identify the tendency of constitutional politics, measure that tendency against the only just rule of action, and then propose "what to do and how to do it" within the exigencies of the contemporary political and constitutional landscape.

Contemporary Challenges to Lincoln's Statesmanship

From a certain vantage point, however, Lincoln misapprehended entirely the project of modern constitutionalism. The challenge of "twentieth-century Hobbesians" to the old paradigm of

[22] Ibid., 4: 268.

natural-law constitutionalism, Mark Brandon asserts, is "that a constitution is largely incapable of making a world that is distinguishable from the imperatives of economics, morality, culture, or politics."[23] The problem confronted by constitutionalism is therefore how to "constrain and direct political power" in light of the inability of written words to assume meaning independent of these existential realities. In dealing with this problem, modern constitutional theory has rejected, *a priori*, the notion of a "metaphysical higher law," because invocation of such a higher law is riddled with practical difficulties, including the difficulty of engendering a consensus regarding (1) where such a law originates, (2) what makes it binding, (3) how its principles are to be discerned, and (4) how compliance is to be enforced.[24]

Hobbes, of course – like latter-day Hobbesians – was critical of the classical and scholastic natural lawyers for their ineptness at providing any quantifiable methodology for arriving at the content of the laws of nature. "For the most part," Hobbes asserted, "such writers as have occasion to affirm, that anything is against the law of nature, do allege no more than this, that it is against the consent of all nations, or the wisest and most civilized nations." The precepts of the laws of nature, Hobbes asserted in contrast, could be no more than "those which declare unto us the ways of peace, where the same may be obtained, and of defence where it may not."[25] In this, Hobbes's natural-law theory was founded on the most universal or shared human passion, which, he maintained, was the fear of violent death. The old moral codes, however, were problematic for Hobbes's theory, because traditional notions of duty and obligation were precisely what led men to willingly endure violence and even martyrdom for a good ostensibly higher than peace. Hobbes therefore attempted to reduce this threat (i.e., the threat of violence embraced for the sake of some contested notion of a higher good) by diminishing the force and sway

[23] Brandon, *Free in the World*, 7.
[24] Ibid., 9.
[25] Hobbes, *The Elements of Law* (ed. Gaskin), I.15.1. See also Hobbes, *Leviathan* (ed. Curley), 13–15.

of the traditional moral doctrines associated with classical and scholastic natural-law theories.[26]

Remnants of this Hobbesian framework are evident in Mark Graber's approach to modern constitutionalism as well. Deriving lessons from the constitutional problems posed by the institution of slavery in the nineteenth century, Graber suggests that constitutions should not be viewed as reflections or manifestations of transcendent realities, but rather as "vehicles for preserving the peace among persons who have very different visions of the good society, a robust democracy, and the rule of law."[27] In light of the problem of moral disagreement, in other words, the purpose of modern constitutionalism is to mediate controversies that arise between citizens with competing political aspirations rooted in competing conceptions of what is good. "The constitutional task," Graber asserts, "is better described as finding settlements that everyone perceives as 'not bad enough' to justify secession and civil war than as making the Constitution 'the best it can be' from some contestable normative perspective."[28]

In the American context, the failure of the original constitutional design consisted in its inefficiency at sustaining a national political community among people with deep and pervasive disagreements about the morality of slavery. Modern constitutional theory, Graber likewise maintains, vainly attempts to adjudicate constitutional disputes, and it employs some favored constitutional methodology to ascertain which party is right. Yet, past

---

[26] My interpretation of Hobbes here assumes that the Hobbesian laws of nature are, as Norberto Bobbio suggests, "not laws, but mere theorems" that lead men to covenant themselves to a sovereign lawgiver. "All that Hobbes manages to squeeze out of the traditional doctrine of natural law is thus an argument in favor of the state, and of our absolute obligation to obey positive law." Norberto Bobbio, *Thomas Hobbes and the Natural Law Tradition*, trans., Daniela Gobetti (Chicago: University of Chicago Press, 1993), 145; 148. See also Leo Strauss, *Natural Right and History* (Chicago: University of Chicago Press, [1950] 1963), 166–202. For a rival interpretation of Hobbes's natural-law theory as a deontic divine command theory, see A.P. Martinich, *The Two God's of Leviathan* (New York: Cambridge University Press, 2003), 100–134.

[27] Graber, *Dred Scott and the Problem of Constitutional Evil*, 253.

[28] Ibid., 2.

accommodations with evil provide resources for reasonable legal arguments to be made in favor of past injustices where there are remaining constitutional ambiguities. Constitutions, therefore, can only "successfully settle political conflicts in the long run by creating a constitutional politics that consistently resolves contested questions of constitutional law in ways that most crucial political actors find acceptable."[29]

Problems of constitutional evil are thus not simply about whether persons should respect explicit constitutional provisions that accommodate practices they believe to be unjust. Rather, Graber argues,

Political orders in divided societies survive only when opposing factions compromise when constitutions are created and when they are interpreted. The price of constitutional cooperation and union is a willingness to abide by clear constitutional rules protecting evil that were laid down in the past and a willingness to make additional concessions to evil when resolving constitutional ambiguities and silences in the present.[30]

Dred Scott emerges, in this context, as a centrist decision; a decision, in other words, that was at least as legitimate an interpretation of American constitutionalism as any other. After the American bi-sectional consensus broke down, the only remaining political branch that was controlled by a Southern majority was the Supreme Court, and "In *Dred Scott*," Graber suggests, "the Supreme Court fostered sectional moderation by replacing the original Constitution's failing political protections for slavery with legally enforceable protections acceptable to Jacksonians in the free and slave states."[31] Under these conditions, he maintains, slavery could only be eradicated by civil war – "not by judicial decree or the election of an anti-slavery coalition."[32] Graber's challenge, then, is this: Modern partisans of the antislavery cause ought to consider, with all of the benefits of hindsight, "whether antislavery Northerners should have provided more accommodations for slavery than were constitutionally strictly necessary

[29] Ibid., 3.
[30] Ibid., 3.
[31] Ibid., 13.
[32] Ibid., 4.

or risked the enormous destruction of life and property that pre-ceded Lincoln's 'new birth of freedom.'"[33]

In Brandon's similarly iconoclastic treatment of modern consti-tutionalism and American slavery, he has suggested an alternative theory that emphasizes the procedural and historically contingent character of the constitutional enterprise. On Brandon's account, the "new constitutionalism" ushered in by the 1787 Constitution jettisoned nature as a source of constitutionally relevant norms. Rather than being an attempt to secure rights that have a tran-scendent basis, the new constitutionalism is defined as a certain type of activity – "an experiment in a particular mode of estab-lishing, directing, and limiting political power" – that is itself historically contingent.[34] Accordingly, constitutional failure with respect to slavery is not understood in terms of a denial of nat-ural human rights, but rather as a failure to abide by the histor-ically contingent standards of modern constitutionalism. Those standards require that individuals be able to "construct their pol-itical identities" with reference to the regime's fundamental law. "Notice that this claim," Brandon points out, "does not rest on the notion that the Constitution violated the principle of 'human dignity.' It may well have done so, but within the assumptions of the new constitutionalism, invoking a standard of human dig-nity is problematic, not least because of its metaphysical roots. Human dignity evokes natural law and natural rights, which are off limits in the new constitutionalism."[35]

Yet on a different account – commonly associated with Lincoln, but having deep roots in the American political tradition – the failure of the antebellum constitutional order was understood precisely in terms of natural law and natural rights. It is not sur-prising, then, that antislavery constitutionalists in the nineteenth century, such as John Quincy Adams, quite consciously rejected the general premises of Hobbes's political science. Hobbes's doctrine, Adams asserted, was "utterly incompatible with any

[33] Ibid., 4.
[34] Brandon, "Constitutionalism and Constitutional Failure," in Barber and George, eds., *Constitutional Politics*, 304.
[35] Ibid., 306.

theory of human rights, and especially with the rights which the Declaration of Independence proclaims as self-evident truths."[36] In the founding generation, as well, Alexander Hamilton offered his own conventionalist interpretation of Hobbes's theory: "Moral obligation according to him, is derived from the introduction of civil society; and there is no virtue, but what is purely artificial, the mere contrivance of politicians, for the maintenance of social intercourse."[37] The ultimate reason for Hobbes's rejection of the classical natural-law paradigm, Hamilton conjectured, was because Hobbes "disbelieved the existence of an intelligent superintending principle, who is the governor, and will be the final judge of the universe."[38]

The ultimate grounding principle for the laws of nature was for Hamilton, as it was in the Declaration, a providential God who was at once a lawgiver and a judge for mankind. This was not mere window dressing. Diverse thinkers within the natural-law tradition have alike concluded that moral obligation makes sense only within a world ordered by a providential God. In Locke's natural-law theory, as interpreted by the Founders and amalgamated with American Protestant theology, a providential God provided the grounds of moral obligation to obey the laws of nature.[39] In his influential *Natural Right and History*,

[36] John Quincy Adams, *Argument of John Quincy Adams, Before the Supreme Court of the United States, in the Case of the United States, Appellants, vs. Cinque, and others, Africans, Captured in the Schooner Amistad ...* (New York: S.W. Benedict, 1841), 89. See also John Quincy Adams, *The Social Compact Exemplified in the Constitution of the Commonwealth of Massachusetts ...* (Providence, RI: Knowles and Vose, 1842), 24. Hobbes's theory, Adams asserted, "severs the Gordian knot with the sword, extinguishes all the rights of man, and makes force the corner stone of all human government. It is the only theory upon which slavery can be justified as conformable to the law of nature."

[37] Alexander Hamilton, "The Federal Farmer Refuted," in *The Works of Alexander Hamilton*, ed. Henry Cabot Lodge, 12 vols. (New York: G.P. Putnam's Sons, 1904), 1: 61–62. For an insightful essay on Hamilton's views of slavery, see Michael D. Chan, "Alexander Hamilton on Slavery," *Review of Politics* 66 (2004): 207–231.

[38] Hamilton, *The Works of Alexander Hamilton*, 1:62.

[39] See Steven Forde, "Natural Law, Theology, and Morality in Locke," *American Journal of Political Science* 45 (2001): 396–409.

Leo Strauss recognized this central place of God in Locke's natural-law theory but famously noted that Locke did not offer a rational argument for the existence of God. "This would mean," Strauss concluded, "that [according to Locke] there does not exist a law of nature in the strict sense."[40] Although most Americans regarded Locke as a pious philosopher in the mold of Hooker, rather than an atheist in the mold of Hobbes, the premise underlying Strauss's provocative suggestion was that divine providence was indeed necessary for any theory that purported to offer a defense and explanation of a system of natural moral laws.[41]

To put the matter differently: If an intelligent, creating and moralistic God has not imbued the natural order with discernible purposes, then it is senseless to talk about morally binding laws accessible to human reason. From a different angle, however, we might ask whether our intuitive grasp of human goods and the ubiquitous distinction we draw between right and wrong – indeed our ability to reason at all – is not itself evidence for the existence of such a providential God. As John Finnis notes: "The remarkable fact that there is an order of nature which, like the orders of human artefacts, actions, and thoughts, is amenable to human understanding calls for some explanation. Often it has been explained by attributing the order(s) to an ordering intelligence and will, creating or in some other way causing the whole-order."[42] What the classical natural lawyers would have called the Eternal Law – the meta-order of the universe in which the natural law allows us

---

[40] Leo Strauss, *Natural Right and History* (Chicago: University of Chicago Press, 1953), 204.

[41] Several proslavery professors in the late antebellum South provide an interesting exception to the American reception of Locke. See, for example, Robert Lewis Dabney, *A Defence of Virginia* (New York: E.J. Hale & Son, 1867), 242. "Notwithstanding Locke's amiable and pious spirit," Dabney wrote, "the history of philosophic opinion has shown that he is but a disguised follower of the philosopher of Malmesbury." See also Chad Vanderford, "Proslavery Professors: Classic Natural Right and the Positive Good Argument in Antebellum Virginia," *Civil War History* 55 (2009): 5–30.

[42] John Finnis, *Natural Law and Natural Rights* (Oxford: Oxford University Press, 1980), 380–381.

to participate – has been a central preoccupation of natural-law thinkers throughout the ages.

The challenge of neo-Hobbesians, I take it, is directed precisely at this foundational understanding, based, in part, on a perceived tendency for debates about theology and metaphysics – which inevitably bring into play contested notions of a higher good – to engender political violence and disrupt peaceful order. Inasmuch as Lincoln constantly appealed back to first principles to provide a foundation for the American regime, and an ultimate justification for prosecuting the Civil War, Lincoln's statesmanship has thus been the subject of revised interpretations in light of conventionalist or antifoundationalist constitutional theories that privilege peace over contested notions of the good.[43] In this vein, Brandon questions whether the cost in blood of the Civil War could possibly justify the end of preserving the Union (even if Lincoln was correct in maintaining that secession was itself unconstitutional), and Graber, within his discussion of constitutional evil, asserts forcefully: "*Dred Scott* was wrong and Lincoln right only if John Brown was correct when he insisted that slavery was sufficiently evil to warrant political actions that 'purge[d] this land in blood.'"[44] The historical causality of the Civil War is, of course, convoluted and deeply contested, and it would be anachronistic to assume that Lincoln, or any other participant, could have anticipated the level of devastation the war would bring. Yet, as the war progressed, Lincoln did wrestle with these questions, and as he did, he emphasized the practical limits of prudential statesmanship while his rhetoric became increasingly deferential to the mysterious workings of divine providence.

The Limits of Constitutional Statesmanship

The Civil War historian and Lincoln scholar Allen Guelzo notes that "[p]rudence was, for Lincoln, a means for balancing respect for a divine purpose in human affairs with the candid

---

[43] For a fuller sketch of what Brandon means by "new" and "old" constitutionalism, see Brandon, *Free in the World*, 3–33.

[44] Graber, *Dred Scott and the Problem of Constitutional Evil*, 8.

recognition that it was surpassingly difficult to know what purposes God might have."[45] To broach the issue of Lincoln's providentialism in connection with his constitutional statesmanship is, of course, to foray into the perennially contested issue of Lincoln's theology. In his own day, Lincoln was accused both of impiety and fanaticism, and debate over the true character of Lincoln's religion has continued unabated in contemporary scholarship. Given the pervasiveness of theological language and biblical imagery in Lincoln's political rhetoric, however, questions concerning the content and political implications of his theology cannot be avoided. As William Wolf argued, after his own study of the sixteenth president's political speeches and writings, "Lincoln's religion cannot be hermetically sealed off from his social, economic, and political attitudes. His political action, as revealed by his own words, was ultimately the social expression of an understanding of God and of man that demanded responsible activity."[46] Lincoln's political action, committed to certain ideals yet flexible in application, navigated between the Scylla of moral relativism and the Charybdis of unfettered moral idealism through the prudent application of moral principles to particular political circumstances. But in the application of principle to political reality, Lincoln constantly declared, his goal was to be the instrument of divine purposes.

Because of the prevalence of theological concepts in Lincoln's political rhetoric, observers often regard him, understandably, as "either 'the mere politician' or 'the pious man' of Washington's Farewell Address."[47] As Lucas Morel notes, however, "Lincoln transcends the mere politician and the pious man in a statecraft that is both politic and pious."[48] This, too, was the view

---

[45] Allen Guelzo, "The Prudence of Abraham Lincoln," *First Things*, January 2006, 13.

[46] William J. Wolf, *The Almost Chosen People: The Religion of Abraham Lincoln*, 2nd ed. (New York: Doubleday & Company, [1959] 1963), 91.

[47] Lucas Morel, *Lincoln's Sacred Effort: Defining Religion's Role in American Self-Government* (Lanham, MD: Lexington Books, 2000).

[48] Ibid. For utilitarian accounts of Lincoln's religious rhetoric, see, for example, Harry V. Jaffa, *Crisis of the House Divided: An Interpretation of the Issues*

advanced by Reinhold Niebuhr in his classic essay in *The Christian Century*. "Analysis of Abraham Lincoln's religion," Niebuhr wrote, "… in the context of the prevailing religion of his time and place and in the light of the polemical use of the slavery issue, which corrupted religious life in the days before and during the Civil War, must lead to the conclusion that Lincoln's religious convictions were superior in depth and purity to those held by the religious as well as by the political leaders of his day."[49] In this vein, Niebuhr maintained that "Lincoln's religious faith was informed primarily by a sense of providence … [and that] the chief evidence of the purity and profundity of Lincoln's sense of providence is the fact that he was able to resist the natural temptation to … identify providence with the cause to which he was committed."[50]

Because men did not agree in Lincoln's day, as they do not in our own, any association of one's own preferred policy with the good and right could have been met with a disparate contention and the association with the good and right of a diametrically opposed policy. Such a problem was certainly amplified by the tendency of each side to associate their own preferred policy with the will of God. In the face of such disagreement, then, the problem of constitutional evil emerged in an especially cogent way on the eve of civil war. Quoting Sanford Levinson's *Constitutional Faith*, Graber describes the universal condition of large, diverse polities as one in which "one person's notion of justice is often

---

in the *Lincoln-Douglas Debates*, 2nd edition (Chicago: University of Chicago Press, 1982); Harry V. Jaffa, *A New Birth of Freedom* (Lanham, MD: Rowman & Littlefield, 2000); Michael Zuckert, "Lincoln and the Problem of Civil Religion" in John A. Murley, et al., eds., *Law and Philosophy: The Practice of Theory: Essays in Honor of George Anastaplo*, 2 vols. (Athens: Ohio University Press, 1992), 2: 720–743. For more pious accounts (that also recognize the utility of religion), see, for example, Allen Guelzo, *Abraham Lincoln: Redeemer President* (Grand Rapids, MI: William B. Eerdmans, 1999); Joseph R. Fornieri, *Abraham Lincoln's Political Faith* (DeKalb: Northern Illinois University Press, 2003); Mark Noll, *The Civil War as a Theological Crisis* (Chapel Hill: The University of North Carolina Press, 2006).

[49] Reinhold Niebuhr, "The Religion of Abraham Lincoln," *The Christian Century* (February 10, 1965), 172.

[50] Niebuhr, "The Religion of Abraham Lincoln," 172–173.

perceived as manifest injustice by someone else."[51] Lincoln recognized this when he wrote to Alexander Stephens, "You think slavery is right and should be extended; while we think slavery is wrong and ought to be restricted. That I suppose is the rub."[52]

Although Lincoln desired peace, he was willing to accept war rather than compromise this principle, disavowing "those sophisticated contrivances such as groping for some middle ground between the right and the wrong."[53] His willingness to accept war also reflected his recognition that there were limits to what might be achieved through statesmanship, and in recognizing these limits, Lincoln sought to absolve himself of responsibility for the conflict. "In your hands," Lincoln told his southern brethren, "... and not in mine, is the momentous issue of civil war."[54] As the war progressed, Lincoln increasingly framed the contest in terms of providential history. Finally, in his Second Inaugural Address, Lincoln reflected:

The Almighty has His own purposes. "Woe unto the world because of offences! for it must needs be that offences come; but woe to that man by whom the offence cometh!" If we shall suppose that American Slavery is one of those offences which, in the providence of God, must needs come, but which, having continued through His appointed time, He now wills to remove, and that He gives to both North and South, this terrible war, as the woe due to those by whom the offence came, shall we discern therein any departure from those divine attributes which the believers in a Living God always ascribe to Him? Fondly do we hope – fervently do we pray – that this mighty scourge of war may speedily pass away. Yet, if God wills that it continue, until all the wealth piled by the bond-man's two hundred and fifty years of unrequited toil shall be sunk, and until every drop of blood drawn with the lash, shall be paid by another drawn with the sword, as was said three thousand years ago, so still it must be said "the judgments of the Lord, are true and righteous altogether."[55]

[51] Sanford Levinson, *Constitutional Faith* (Princeton, NJ: Princeton University Press, 1989), 72. Quoted in Graber, *Dred Scott and the Problem of Constitutional Evil*, 8.
[52] Basler, *Collected Works of Abraham Lincoln*, 4: 160.
[53] Ibid., 4: 29
[54] Ibid., 4: 268.
[55] Ibid., 8: 333.

Even before the conflict, however, Lincoln had constructed an overarching narrative of American constitutional development that was imbued with theological ideas. Of those lines in the Declaration of Independence proclaiming that "all men are created equal" and "endowed by their Creator with certain inalienable rights," Lincoln asserted that this was the Founders' "majestic interpretation of the economy of the Universe. This was their lofty and wise, and noble understanding of the justice of the Creator to His creatures ... In their enlightened belief, nothing stamped with the Divine image and likeness was sent into the world to be trodden on, and degraded, and imbruted by its fellows."[56] By wedding the self-evident truths in the Declaration to a providentially ordered universe and by making natural rights derivative from the image of God in man, the very logic of American constitutionalism was given a theological meaning. Lincoln perceived, in the words of David Trueblood, that "the Declaration of Independence makes sense in a theological context, but fails to make sense in any other."[57] That theological context was, admittedly, paradoxical, and there was a constant tension between providence and human action, moral knowledge and moral responsibility. "The will of God prevails," Lincoln later reflected in his private journal:

In great contests each party claims to act in accordance with the will of God. Both *may* be, and one *must* be wrong ... In the present civil war it is quite possible that God's purpose is something different from the purpose of either party – and yet the human instrumentalities, working just as they do, are of the best adaptation to affect His purpose. I am almost ready to say this is probably true – that God wills this contest, and wills that it shall not end yet. By his mere quiet power, on the minds of the now contestants, He could have either saved or destroyed the Union without a human contest. Yet the contest began. And having begun He could give the final victory to either side any day. Yet the contest proceeds.[58]

[56] Basler, ed., *Collected Works of Abraham Lincoln*, 2: 546.
[57] David Elton Trueblood, *Abraham Lincoln: Theologian of American Anguish* (New York: Harper & Row, 1973), 69.
[58] Basler, ed., *Collected Works of Abraham Lincoln*, 5: 403–404.

In his reflections on providence, Lincoln constantly qualified his remarks with a certain humility that evidenced the internal dynamic at work in "an anguished participant searching for ultimate meaning."[59] By grappling with these foundational questions, Lincoln came to view the tragic conflict within the context of a universe that made sense of ancient theological concepts such as collective guilt and collective punishment as well as a divine justice, which, however indiscernible in its particularities, did ultimately guide human events. The sins of the fathers truly were visited upon the third and fourth generations.

After the *Dred Scott* decision in 1857 and continuing throughout the Civil War, Lincoln interpreted his own public actions as motivated by principle and guided by prudence while nevertheless being limited by purposes beyond his control. Reevaluating Lincoln's statesmanship thus requires that we attend to the theological context in which Lincoln interpreted the conflict. In his discussion of constitutional justice and constitutional peace, Graber identifies today's John Bell voters – that is, voters who are always willing to compromise with evil to procure peace – as those who maintain that "peace ... is intrinsically more just than war."[60] Yet in his discussion of today's Lincoln voters, Graber is conspicuously silent about the notion that war could ever be an instrument of providential justice transcending, in some, the individual participants. In his account of constitutional failure, Brandon relatedly discounts the idea that the antebellum constitutional order rested "on *a priori* assumptions about the character, worth, or rights of human beings."[61] Lincoln, however, did conceive of constitutional failure and the impetus of the Civil War precisely in these metaphysical and theological terms.

Perhaps it is an implicit premise in modern scholarship that Lincoln could not have meant what he said in this respect or that what he said has been deemed irrelevant by the progression of the social sciences. That premise, however, needs to be made

[59] Fornieri, *Abraham Lincoln's Political Faith*, 40.
[60] Graber, *Dred Scott and the Problem of Constitutional Evil*, 253.
[61] Brandon, "Constitutional Failure," in *Constitutional Politics*, 306.

explicit and argued for before the old constitutionalism, which was conceived of in terms of a providential order and judged by its compatibility with the dignity of human nature, is jettisoned in our modern analysis of the lingering problems of constitutional evil and constitutional failure. For we must first grapple with those nineteenth-century arguments concerning natural rights, man's place in the divinely constituted cosmos, and the tragic and uncertain price of maintaining free government amid the contingencies of political life before we are adequately able to judge or even to consider whether there are political goods higher than peace and whether, after the avenues of prudent statesmanship have been exhausted, some principles are worth dying for. We must, in short, grapple with these enduring, fundamental questions before we can even begin to consider the contention of one observer – after reflecting on the massive cost of the war, including Lincoln's own violent death at the hand of an assassin – that "it was perhaps better for the country and for mankind that the good man could not know the end from the beginning."[62] For such could only have been the sentiment of a man who did not think peace was intrinsically more just than war.

Our inability, or unwillingness, to attend to the terms of debate over slavery in the nineteenth century has been fortified by a modern solution to the enduring problems posed by political and moral disagreement. Reasons that seek to provide ultimate justification for political actions, it has been suggested, ought to be abandoned in constitutional deliberation in favor of public reasons that can be mutually affirmed by citizens independent of their disparate philosophical and theological premises. In its most prominent form, the theory of public reason developed by John Rawls draws its sustenance from the public political culture of modern democratic societies. But the arguments of antislavery constitutionalists in the nineteenth century were notable precisely because they challenged, from foundational premises, important aspects of their own public political culture.

---

[62] Frederick Douglass, *Life and Times of Frederick Douglass* (Hartford, CT: Park Publishing Company, 1881), 409.

The types of arguments that were developed and sustained by the American antislavery constitutional tradition, extending, in its diverse manifestations, from the American Founders to the former slave and prolific public orator Frederick Douglass, highlight the incompatibility between this tradition and the general premises underlying the idea of public reason.

6

Public Reason and the Wrong of Slavery

The runaway slave-turned-abolitionist Frederick Douglass told a Boston crowd in 1855 that he found it "exceedingly difficult to suppose the existence of an honest difference of opinion with regard to the wrongfulness of slavery ... And yet," Douglass contended, "... it is proper for an anti-slavery man to assume that those who defend slavery are honest in their views of things. But it is difficult to see how any one can suppose that such an open, flagrant, enormous violation of right as is involved in the relation of master and slave, can exist without sin and wrong."[1] In a society deeply fractured by disagreement about the morality of slavery – an issue that called into question the foundational principles around which public life was ordered – what types of arguments, then, could a man such as Frederick Douglass have offered fellow citizens with whom he had honest, but deep, disagreements? What resources, in other words, could have legitimately been brought to bear on such a divisive question in an already divided society? The public arguments made by Douglass and his fellow abolitionists offer an answer to this question that

[1] Frederick Douglass, "An Inside View of Slavery: An Address Delivered in Boston, Massachusetts" (February 8, 1855) in John W. Blassingame, ed., *The Frederick Douglass Papers Series One: Speeches, Debates, and Interviews*, 5 vols. (New Haven, CT: Yale University Press, 1985), 3: 6.

diverges greatly from the peculiarly modern notion of "public reason," which seeks to ground public deliberation in a consensus found in the overlapping views of reasonable citizens irrespective of other disagreements concerning religious, moral, or philosophical questions.

Of course, many scholars and theorists have argued that the particular genius of American constitutionalism is precisely that it *does* cabin divisive religious and philosophical doctrines from public debate about political matters. Liberal societies such as the United States are able to achieve a large degree of consensus in politics, it is argued, in part because the state remains neutral with respect to competing notions of the good rooted in philosophical or religious doctrines. Accordingly, there is often a distinction drawn between the types of ultimate questions that require recourse to (essentially private) comprehensive doctrines about the nature and destiny of man and (essentially public) political questions about how we should divide and use political power in a modern liberal society. When discussing political questions, it is suggested, citizens should not appeal to reasons based on controversial religious or philosophical claims; rather, they should draw from the store of acceptable public reasons.

The late philosopher John Rawls put forward the most prominent version of this argument, and from it he developed a wide-ranging and influential theory of public reason. When deliberating on matters of constitutional essentials and basic justice, Rawls argues, the idea of public reason requires public actors to articulate reasons that can be mutually affirmed by citizens independent of any particular comprehensive religious, moral, or philosophical doctrine. And yet a particular controversy over the theory of public reason has emerged because of the prevalent public use of theological and philosophical arguments by both nineteenth-century abolitionists and twentieth-century civil rights leaders. Many influential abolitionists – from William Wilberforce to William Garrison – largely based their case against slavery on theological grounds, and civil rights leaders such as Martin Luther King, Jr. drew heavily from the Christian, natural law, and German idealist traditions while making their case against racial segregation.

Because contemporary liberals are partisans of the abolitionist and civil rights movements, a debate has emerged among scholars about whether the rhetoric of these movements is in fact compatible with public reason, and, if not, whether this inflicts a fatal blow on the liberal credentials of Rawls's theory.[2]

Rawls, however, did maintain that his theory of public reason could accommodate the religious rhetoric of the abolitionist and civil rights movements, and, as David A. J. Richards notes, "The thought must [have been]: if these forms of rights-based dissent were deemed illegitimate by a distinctively liberal political theory, such a theory would be fundamentally inadequate to its task."[3] In a Rawlsian defense of the religious rhetoric of American abolitionists such as Theodore Weld, William Ellery Channing, Sarah and Angela Grimke, and Frederick Douglass, Richards suggests that many of the abolitionists' arguments were theologically heterodox, anticlerical, and individualistic. Thus, even though abolitionist arguments in the nineteenth century assumed a religious form, Richards suggests that they were critical of established epistemological and religious orthodoxies and demonstrated a streak of antiracism and antisexism that could be affirmed independent of any particular religious doctrine. Within the context of the religious public culture of the nineteenth century, Richards argues that the distinctive feature of abolitionist dissent was its critique of orthodox religion (rather than its religious moorings), and he takes the heterodox and critical aspects of abolitionist dissent to be evidence that the core of abolitionism would have fallen within the bounds of public reason rather than within the idiosyncrasies of a particular sectarian doctrine.[4]

---

[2] See, for example, David A. J. Richards, "Public Reason and Abolitionist Dissent," *Chicago-Kent Law Review* 69 (1994): 787; Stephen Macedo, "In Defense of Liberal Public Reason: Are Slavery and Abortion Hard Cases?" 42 *American Journal of Jurisprudence* 42, no. 1 (1997): 1–29; Christopher Wolfe, *Natural Law Liberalism* (New York: Cambridge University Press, 2006), 9–43; David Lewis Schaefer, *Illiberal Justice: John Rawls vs. the American Political Tradition* (Columbia: University of Missouri Press, 2006), 287–289.

[3] David A. J. Richards, "Public Reason and Abolitionist Dissent," 787.

[4] Richards, "Public Reason and Abolitionist Dissent," 787. For Rawls's statements on abolitionism and public reason, see *Political Liberalism*, Expanded

The actual arguments made in the course of political debate in the nineteenth century, however, suggest that Rawlsian public reason is not only incompatible with abolitionism (however heterodox and critical), but also with much of the moderate antislavery constitutional tradition. Indeed, the constitutional arguments put forward even by moderate antislavery jurists and statesmen would have been illegitimate according to the standards for public reason. Public deliberation on the constitutionality of slavery in antebellum America provides a particularly cogent example of debate that centers on "constitutional essentials and questions of basic justice,"[5] to which the strictures of Rawlsian public reason ostensibly apply. Yet it is impossible to give an account, consistent with the "idea of public reason," of why Rawls would have sided with the antislavery constitutionalist Abraham Lincoln (to say nothing of the more radical abolitionists) over Stephen Douglas and his popular-sovereignty platform in 1858.[6]

Douglas, an avowed democrat and a defender of the *Dred Scott* decision, held that the cornerstone of the American regime was "the great principle of self-government, which asserts the right of every people to decide for themselves the nature and character of the domestic institutions and fundamental law under which they are to live."[7] For Douglas, the moral propriety of slavery was an inappropriate subject for national deliberation, and slave policy was a question legitimately determined by the local *demos*. The editor of one compilation of the debates summarizes Douglas's position: "Moral judgment of the slaveholders

---

Edition (New York: Columbia University Press, 2005), 250–251. See also John Rawls, *Justice as Fairness: A Restatement* (Cambridge, MA: Harvard University Press, 2001), 90, n. 12, and John Rawls, "The Idea of Public Reason Revisited," reprinted in *The Law of Peoples* (Cambridge, MA: Harvard University Press, 1999), 154, n. 54, and 174.

[5] John Rawls, *Justice as Fairness: A Restatement*, 89.

[6] On the difficulties of squaring public reason with Lincoln's political rhetoric, see Michael J. Sandel, "Political Liberalism," *Harvard Law Review* 107, no. 7 (1994). See also Michael J. Sandel, *Liberalism and the Limits of Justice* (New York: Cambridge University Press, 1982).

[7] Basler, *Collected Works*, 3: 210.

was not a subject for political debate but was a matter for their consciences and their God."[8] Lincoln, in response, attempted to exploit the inconsistency in Douglas's argument that slavery should be left to democratic majorities regardless of the moral status of slavery. "When Judge Douglas says that whoever, or whatever community, wants slaves, they have a right to have them," Lincoln asserted, "he is perfectly logical if there is nothing wrong in the institution; but if you admit that it is wrong, he cannot logically say that anybody has a right to do wrong."[9]

It was a "false philosophy" and "false statesmanship," Lincoln declared in his final debate with Douglas, to endeavor "to build up a system of policy on the basis of caring nothing about *the very thing that everybody does care the most about.*"[10] Conceding that self-governance was indeed one of the great principles of the American regime, Lincoln nonetheless held that the principles of the Declaration anteceded and undergirded the Constitution and were, as he later wrote, "the principles and axioms of a free society."[11] According to those principles, "nothing stamped with the Divine image and likeness" – a description that encompassed all of humanity – "was sent into the world to be trodden on, and degraded, and imbruted by its fellows."[12] Douglas, on the other hand, affirmed that the universal language in the Declaration of Independence was "intended to allude only to the people of the United States, to men of European birth or decent, being white men, that they were created equal, and hence that Great Britain had no right to deprive them of their political and religious privileges."[13] Thus, the liberties secured by the Constitution applied only to white men, according to

[8] David Zarefsky, foreword to Angle, ed., *The Complete Lincoln-Douglas Debates*, xvi.
[9] Basler, ed., *Collected Works of Abraham Lincoln*, 3: 257.
[10] Ibid., 3: 311.
[11] Abraham Lincoln, "The Principles of Jefferson: Letter to Henry L. Pierce and Others" (April 6, 1859) in *Abraham Lincoln: A Documentary Portrait Through His Speeches and Writings*, ed., Don E. Fehrenbacher (Stanford, CA: Stanford University Press, 1964), 120.
[12] Basler, ed., *Collected Works of Abraham Lincoln*, 2: 546.
[13] Angle, ed., *The Complete Lincoln-Douglas Debates*, 62–63.

Douglas, and the question of whether or not "inferior races" were to be enslaved was a question to be decided legitimately by the ballot.

Taking his cue from these debates between Lincoln and Douglas, Michael Sandel argues that the contested political question at the heart of the controversy over national slave policy in the nineteenth century was a question that could not have been settled merely by appealing to notions of citizenship implicit in American political culture, which is the starting point for Rawls's theory of public reason. Rawls had the advantage of writing in the late twentieth century, and he began with a public political culture that regarded it as a fact, as he continually affirmed, that we are all free and equal. But that fact certainly was not the subject of anything like a consensus in 1858, and, as Sandel argues, "To the extent that political liberalism refuses to invoke comprehensive moral ideals and relies instead on notions of citizenship implicit in the political culture, it would have a hard time explaining, in 1858, why Lincoln was right and Douglas was wrong."[14] What is often overlooked is that Lincoln's arguments against the moral and constitutional wrong of slavery emerged within a wider tradition in American politics, which consistently argued that the logic of American constitutionalism rested on a theological and philosophical foundation that was antithetical to chattel slavery. Within the context of various nineteenth-century accounts of the moral and constitutional wrong of the *Dred Scott* decision, however, Rawls's theory can neither account for the legitimacy of such arguments nor offer an adequate normative basis from which to critique the laws governing slavery in nineteenth-century America.

The Idea of Public Reason

The idea of public reason, according to Rawls, is "part of the idea of democracy itself."[15] That is to say, democracy engenders

---

[14] Sandel, "Political Liberalism," 1782.
[15] John Rawls, "The Idea of Public Reason Revisited," in *The Law of Peoples*, 131.

a culture of free institutions, and the "normal" result of such institutions is the existence of a "plurality of conflicting reasonable comprehensive doctrines, religious, philosophical, and moral."[16] Beginning with the "fact of reasonable pluralism," then, Rawls proposes that we "consider what kinds of reasons [democratic citizens] may reasonably give one another when fundamental political questions are at stake."[17] The answer is that citizens, as free and equal members of the political community, must give reasons that are part of an "overlapping consensus" between reasonable comprehensive doctrines. Because citizens in a democratic regime hold reasonable but mutually exclusive comprehensive doctrines, the idea of public reason bars arguments that are not part of this overlapping consensus (i.e., it excludes reasons based on particular comprehensive doctrines) from the "public political forum," where judges, public officials, and political candidates seek to persuade free and equal citizens to act on political values that all reasonable people may be expected to endorse.[18]

In his criticism of Rawls, Sandel suggests that the theory of public reason would have barred public arguments against slavery that were based on metaphysical or theological doctrines. This is problematic for the antislavery tradition, because public arguments against slavery in antebellum America were largely based on appeals away from the political culture to some conception of natural or divine order, which was thought to bolster or inform constitutional government. Taking issue with attempts by both the Whig and Democratic parties to silence public debate on the legitimacy and morality of the Fugitive Slave Law of 1850, Horace Mann combined appeals to natural and divine law in a synthesis that was common to such antislavery protests before declaring that one of the collateral affects of barring public deliberation concerning the law was "the promulgation from the halls of Congress, and also from – what in such cases, is not the sacred, but the profane desk – that there is no 'higher law'

[16] Ibid., 131.
[17] Ibid., 132.
[18] Ibid., 133.

than the constitution, or any interpretation which any corrupt Congress may put upon it."[19]

While antislavery arguments were often based on appeals to natural or divine law, similar arguments were, of course, made in defense of slavery as well. In a speech before the U.S. Senate, Judah Benjamin described the right to hold property in slaves as emanating from "the principles of eternal justice which God has implanted in the heart of man," and Southern intellectuals offered metaphysical and theological defenses of their peculiar institution.[20] The point is not that reasoning from foundational concepts settles the debate over slavery; rather, it is that from the perspective of many nineteenth-century Americans "discussion on the great question of human freedom ... involve[d] the whole question of free agency and human accountability and the entire plan and order of Divine government."[21]

Arguments against slavery in the twenty-first century can perhaps be made solely with reference to concepts implicit in our political culture (including, significantly, the Thirteenth Amendment), but such appeals are not decisive in an analysis of the antebellum period. The problem Sandel identifies in Rawls's theory is that, as a *political* conception, it is not grounded in anything beyond the public political culture and thus cannot assume the critical stance that was assumed by the antislavery tradition. As David Lewis Schaefer notes, there is a "central paradox running throughout Rawls's project, in that he seeks to resolve a supposed impasse in the public political culture by articulating an account of justice derived from ideas that are already implicit in that culture."[22] In other words, Rawls is left without a permanent standard of right

---

[19] Horace Mann, "The Institution of Slavery" (August 23, 1852) in the appendix to *Congressional Globe*, 32nd Congress, 1st Session, 1075.

[20] Judah Phillip Benjamin, "On the Property Doctrine" (March 11, 1858) in *Congressional Globe*, 35th Congress, 1st Session, 1069. See also Chad Vanderford, "Proslavery Professors: Classic Natural Right and the Positive Good Argument in Antebellum Virginia," *Civil War History* 55, no. 1 (2009): 5–30.

[21] Horace Mann, "The Institution of Slavery," 1072.

[22] David Lewis Schaefer, *Illiberal Justice*, 252.

against which the contradictory aspects of the political culture may be judged.

The problem of Rawls's antifoundationalism is particularly evident in his account of the freedom and equality of democratic citizens, which finds an amusing, if strained, analogy in an anecdote from Stephen Hawking's *A Brief History of Time*:

> A well-known scientist once gave a public lecture on astronomy. He described how the earth orbits around the sun and how the sun, in turn, orbits around the center of a vast collection of stars called our galaxy. At the end of the lecture, a little old lady at the back of the room got up and said: "What you have told us is rubbish. The world is really a flat plate supported on the back of a giant tortoise." The scientist gave a superior smile before replying, "What is the tortoise standing on?" "You're very clever, young man, very clever," said the old lady. "But it's turtles all the way down!"[23]

To the question of what provides the foundation for the freedom and equality of citizens in a democratic society, Rawls offers a similarly unsatisfying answer: Our public status as free and equal citizens inheres in the fact that within our public political culture we *regard* all citizens as free and equal. For the purposes of political liberalism, Rawls disavows any reliance on a metaphysical conception of man, and he therefore cannot engage the question of whether (and in what sense) all men are, in fact, morally free and equal.[24] John Finnis observes that the "question

---

[23] Stephen Hawking, *A Brief History of Time*, 2nd edition (New York: Bantam Books, 1996), 1.

[24] Additionally, Rawls's theory applies only to *citizens*, and, for the purposes of political liberalism, citizens are defined as those human beings who are engaged in mutually beneficial social cooperation over time. Such social cooperation requires that citizens have (1) a capacity for a sense of justice and (2) a capacity for a conception of the good. In addition, these two "moral powers" define "moral persons" and "moral personality." In other words, all citizens are moral persons who are regarded as free and equal, but not all human beings are citizens. Moreover, the idea of free and equal persons is "worked up" from "the public political culture of a democratic society, in its basic political texts (constitutions and declarations of human rights), and in the historical tradition of the interpretation of those texts." There is a question, then, of where slaves in the public political culture of nineteenth-century America might fit into this scheme and why, on Rawls's account, they could be regarded as moral persons absent some metaphysical view of the moral status of human

whether the opinions that overlap in this consensus are correct or true, and whether those reasons are valid or sound, is to be set aside by public reason, i.e., in decision-making on the fundamental questions of political life and legislation."[25] The foundations of political liberalism are thus laid in the shifting sands of social consensus – a consensus that affirms a political (and not a metaphysical) conception of the citizen as a free and equal moral person who is member of a fair system of social cooperation over time.[26] The "fact" of our being regarded as free and equal moral persons is a feature of modern liberal democracies, but it is not intended to be normative in a universal or comprehensive sense. Rather, "the conception of the person is worked up from the way citizens are regarded in the public political culture of a democratic society."[27]

Anyone familiar with the political history of America will recognize the difficulty in simply "working up" a liberal conception of the person as free and equal from the public political culture of the nineteenth century.[28] Yet, in response to Sandel's criticism that political liberalism lacks the tools to say why Douglas was wrong in 1858, Rawls tersely responds:

A further misunderstanding alleges that an argument in public reason could not side with Lincoln against Douglas in their debates of 1858.

---

beings as such. Rawls, of course, could appeal to his own Kantian liberalism, but this would undercut his claim that the idea of citizens as free and equal persons belongs to a "political conception" rather than to a "conception of the person [...] taken from metaphysics or the philosophy of mind, or from psychology." As Rawls admits, "it may have little relation to conceptions of the self discussed in those disciplines." See Rawls, *Justice as Fairness*, 18–24. Rawls recognizes that justice as fairness, as a political conception, does not attempt to answer "the question of what is owed to those who fail to meet this condition [i.e., possession of the two moral powers] either temporarily (from illness or accident) or permanently, all of which covers a variety of cases." See Rawls, *Political Liberalism*, 21.

[25] John Finnis, "On 'Public Reason,'" Petrazycki Lecture, Warsaw University, June 6, 2005.

[26] See Rawls, *Justice as Fairness: A Restatement*, 5.

[27] Ibid., 19.

[28] See, for example, Rogers Smith, *Civic Ideals: Conflicting Visions of Citizenship in U.S. History* (New Haven, CT: Yale University Press, 1997).

But why not? Certainly they were debating fundamental political principles about the rights and wrongs of slavery. Since the rejection of slavery is a clear case of securing the constitutional essential of the equal basic liberties, surely Lincoln's view was reasonable (even if not the most reasonable), while Douglas' view was not. Therefore, Lincoln's view is supported by any reasonable comprehensive doctrine.... What could be a better example to illustrate the force of public reason in political life?[29]

Rawls seems to have missed the brunt of Sandel's criticism, namely that the very argument he makes to justify the reasonableness of the Lincolnian position is anachronistic when judged by his own theory, which begins with a "fact" of modern, democratic political culture that, by definition, is not normative for antebellum America.

There is, however, an additional caveat to a possible Rawlsian defense of Lincoln insofar as Rawls distinguishes the idea of public reason from what he calls the *ideal* of public reason. The ideal of public reason is the realization of the initial idea. It is a state of affairs when "judges, legislators, chief executives, and other government officials, as well as candidates for public office, act from and follow the idea of public reason and explain to other citizens their reasons for supporting fundamental political positions in terms of the political conception of justice they regard as the most reasonable."[30] Additionally, when speaking of the religiously inspired abolitionists (and we might apply the same reasoning to Lincoln and other antislavery public officials), Rawls makes a distinction between an "inclusive view" of public reason (found in *Political Liberalism*) and a "wide view" of public reason (found in *Justice as Fairness: A Restatement* and *The Law of Peoples*). "The difference," Rawls writes, "is that the inclusive view allowed comprehensive doctrines to be introduced only in nonideal circumstances, as illustrated by slavery in the antebellum South and the civil rights movement in the 1960s and later."[31] The "wide view," which is found in Rawls's later works,

---

[29] John Rawls, "The Idea of Public Reason Revisited," in *The Law of Peoples*, 174.

[30] Ibid., 135.

[31] Rawls, *Justice as Fairness*, 90, n. 12.

would allow citizens to articulate reasons based on comprehensive doctrines to disclose "where they come from, so to speak, and on what basis they support the public political conception of justice."[32] At the end of the day, however, "the duty of civility requires us in due course to make our case for the legislation and public policies we support in terms of public reasons, or the political values covered by the political conception of justice."[33] In other words, reasons based on comprehensive doctrines are justified in the public forum if they are seen as anticipating a time when such reasons will be unnecessary (i.e., when the *ideal* of public reason is a reality) or if they help explain one's support for the public political conception.

Viewed in this light, Rawls asserts, the arguments put forward by the abolitionists may be viewed conceptually as anticipating a "well-ordered and just society in which the ideal of public reason could eventually be honored.... The abolitionists ... would not have been unreasonable in these conjectured beliefs if the political forces they led were among the necessary historical conditions to establish justice, as does indeed seem plausible in their situation."[34] From the view of public reason, then, one need not condemn the religious or moral public arguments against slavery, because these arguments are part of the necessary historical circumstances leading to the establishment of the ideal of public reason. As Rawls emphasizes that his analysis is conceptual, rather than historical, however, it is an open question whether the historical men putting forward these arguments would agree with Rawls's conceptual characterization. Additionally, given the public political culture of nineteenth-century America, it is not altogether clear how the ideal of public reason, in its Rawlsian form, applies at all.[35]

---

[32] Ibid., 90.

[33] Ibid., 90.

[34] Rawls, *Political Liberalism*, 250–251.

[35] By setting up the ideal of public reason (which is understood as emerging from the peculiar facts of modern, democratic societies) as a standard by which to judge a previous historical age with a different public culture, Rawls seems to be making a claim that is unwarranted by his own theory.

A further distinction, alluded to earlier, may also be made between the religious abolitionists that Rawls is primarily responding to and the antislavery public officials who articulated arguments primarily based on the authority of nature instead of the authority of a particular religious doctrine.[36] Many of the antislavery public officials were religious people, of course, but natural-law arguments for them operated as a "public reason" of sorts – that is, it was assumed that arguments based on natural law could be affirmed in light of the common authority of reason and not the authority of a particular religion. After being censured in the House of Representatives for bringing forth an antislavery petition, John Quincy Adams described his actions as a defense of "the rights of human nature," which he identified with the "inalienable rights of all mankind, as set forth in the Declaration of Independence."[37] God often was invoked as the author of the rights of human nature, but even this knowledge was thought to be accessible by "natural theology, apart from revelation" – to use Lincoln's phrase.[38]

As Robert George notes, in a different context, the natural-law tradition "proposes what amounts to its own principle of public reason when it asserts that questions of fundamental law and basic matters of justice ought to be decided in accordance with natural law, natural right, natural rights, and/or natural justice."[39] Yet inasmuch as political liberalism disallows, for the purposes of

---

[36] I distinguish here between the terms "abolitionist" and "antislavery." Many of the jurists were antislavery in the sense that they favored construing legal rules, if they believed such legal rules to be ambiguous, *in favorem libertatis*. They did not, however, intend to effect total and immediate abolition in the way favored by religious abolitionists such as William Lloyd Garrison, John Brown, and others.

[37] Quoted in Josiah Quincy, *Memoir of the Life of John Quincy Adams* (Boston: Phillips, Sampson and Company, 1859), 260.

[38] Basler, ed., *Collected Works of Abraham Lincoln*, 4: 9.

[39] Robert P. George, "Public Reason and Political Conflict: Abortion and Homosexuality," *The Yale Law Journal*, 106, no. 8 (1997): 2475. Rawls recognizes the possibility of setting up a well-ordered society that is effectively regulated by a "natural rights doctrine" that all citizens may reasonably accept. This, however, remains distinct from "justice as fairness" and certainly seems to be distinct from a natural law/right/rights/justice doctrine that assumes the

deliberation on fundamental questions of constitutional essentials and basic rights, arguments falling outside of a "freestanding" political conception of justice, natural-law arguments, along with other comprehensive philosophical, moral, or religious arguments, are disbarred from public reason.[40] This additionally calls into question Rawls's insistence that Lincoln, within the context of political liberalism, was "more reasonable" than Douglas in 1858, for arguably it was Douglas who was simply "working up" a conception of the person from the public political culture of his day.

When considering public reason in the American polity, Rawls also suggests that the paradigmatic example of public reason comes by way of Supreme Court opinions, for public reason applies "in a special way to the judiciary and above all to a supreme court in a constitutional democracy with judicial review." As Rawls explains, "This is because the justices have to explain and justify their decisions as based on their understanding of the constitution and relevant statutes and precedents. Since acts of the legislative and executive need not be justified in this way, the court's special role makes it the exemplar of public reason."[41] Rawls additionally articulates this test for whether a particular reason would be permissible in the public forum: "[W]e might ask: how would our argument strike us as presented in the form of a supreme court opinion? Reasonable? Outrageous?"[42] Therefore, it is quite appropriate to judge Rawls's theory of public reason, as he invites us to, by asking, within the context of slavery, what types of arguments public actors in the nineteenth century might have offered when reasoning about such fundamental constitutional questions. Given Rawls's defense of Lincoln

---

primacy of the good over the right. In substance, then, such a natural-rights doctrine, as a political conception, remains a close cousin of justice as fairness. See John Rawls, *Justice as Fairness*, 9.

[40] Rawls, *Political Liberalism*, 10. Rawls writes that "Political liberalism ... aims for a political conception of justice as a freestanding view. It offers no specific metaphysical or epistemological doctrine beyond what is implied by the political conception itself."

[41] Rawls, *Political Liberalism*, 216.

[42] Ibid., 254.

in 1858 – and Rawls's insistence that the Supreme Court is the exemplar of public reason – it also is relevant to consider public reason in the context of the *Dred Scott* case, which provided the immediate backdrop for Lincoln's debates with Stephen Douglas. John McLean's dissenting opinion in *Dred Scott* bears the closest affinity to Lincoln's own politics, and, between the two options of "reasonable" or "outrageous," Rawls would have to concede that McLean's reasons for opposing the majority opinion in this case were, according to the standards of public reason, particularly outrageous.

The Moral and Constitutional Wrong of Dred Scott

Nearly all contemporary legal scholars agree with Alexander Bickel that the *Dred Scott* decision "was a ghastly error."[43] Paul Finkelman indicates that the case now "is at the center of controversies that are almost entirely one-sided. Scholars debate *why* the decision was wrong, not if it was wrong."[44] Nothing like the contemporary academic consensus existed when the decision was rendered, however. The debate contemporaneous with *Dred Scott* was concerned first with *whether* the decision was wrong and then only secondarily *why*. As Edward Corwin noted, the position assumed by the Free Soil and Republican critics of the decision, "which was represented for the nonce in Justice McLean's dissenting opinion, was that there was a difference between slave property and other kinds of property which arises from the alleged fact that slavery was contrary to natural law, and that consequently, while the Constitution recognized property in slaves within the States where slavery was permitted, it did not recognize it within the territories."[45] Although

---

[43] Alexander Bickel, *The Supreme Court and the Idea of Progress* (New Haven, CT: Yale University Press, 1978), 41.

[44] Paul Finkelman, "*Scott v. Sandford*: The Court's Most Dredful Case and How it Changed History," *Chicago-Kent Law Review* 82 (2007): 3. One major exception to the scholarly consensus is Mark Graber's *Dred Scott and the Problem of Constitutional Evil*.

[45] Edward S. Corwin, "Dred Scott," in *The Doctrine of Judicial Review* (Princeton, NJ: Princeton University Press, 1914), 145.

Corwin seemed to think McLean's arguments were "erroneous and beside the point," he did correctly note that McLean's dissent was not based primarily on an alternative reading of Taney's history, but instead rested on a consideration of the nature of the thing being claimed as property. McLean did not dispute Taney's assertion that the Fifth Amendment affords substantive protection for property in the territories,[46] and he acknowledged that the "Government was not made especially for the colored race"[47]; however he did dispute whether a human being constituted a legitimate species of property and whether such a being could be claimed as property outside of some expressed provision of the positive law.[48]

Fellow dissenter Benjamin Curtis had argued that Congress's authority in the territories extended to any property whatsoever, including slave property. McLean, however, did not agree that all territorial property was constitutionally insecure. Rather, McLean insisted that property *in men* was left insecure based, in part, on the nature of the property in question, and he therefore thought, like Lincoln, that it mattered "whether a negro is *not* or *is* a man." McLean's conclusion rested on a consideration of the nature of man as such and not, consistent with political liberalism, on an interpretation of how the public political culture regarded man *qua* citizen of a democratic society. As evidence of the humanity of the slave, McLean asserted that "He bears the impress of his Maker, and is amenable to

---

[46] This supplies the ground for McLean's fellow dissenter Benjamin Curtis, who disputed Taney's conclusion by treating slave property the same as any other property, which may be regulated or prohibited from the territories by the federal government.

[47] *Dred Scott*, 537 (McLean, J. dissenting).

[48] Following a familiar formula of nineteenth-century natural-law reasoning, McLean held that a judge *qua* judge did not have authority to overturn a legislative decree based on natural law. Nevertheless, where the law was ambiguous or unpronounced, natural law could guide the reasoning of the judge. Therefore, where the positive law does not sanction a right to hold property in man, the law is construed in *favorem libertatis*. This rule of construction does not apply to horse or hog property, but only to property in man (based on the nature of the thing in question). See *Dred Scott* at 549 (McLean, J. dissenting).

the laws of God and man; and he is destined to an endless existence."[49] Man's rational nature and his amenability to law were, in other words, attributes incompatible with the characteristics of chattel.

This type of legal reasoning in American jurisprudence – reasoning that engages rather than shuns moral and philosophical questions concerning the nature of man – was not peculiar to McLean. There is a long pedigree of antislavery arguments affirming precisely what McLean affirmed, and many of these arguments are discussed in greater detail in previous chapters. By the time Lincoln took up the struggle against slavery's extension in the federal territories, however, the movement had splintered over disagreements concerning the relationship of slavery to the Constitution, with the more radical abolitionists denouncing America's fundamental law and eschewing political participation as an avenue to affect the goal of immediate emancipation. On the other side of the antislavery spectrum, activists such as Lysander Spooner and William Goodell began to venture a natural-law constitutional theory more thoroughly antislavery than anything ever offered by moderate antislavery constitutionalists such as John Quincy Adams, John McLean, and Abraham Lincoln. Because written laws admit of multiple interpretations, Spooner wrote, a proper interpretation "can be only by the aid of that perception of natural law, or natural justice, which men naturally possess."[50] In construing the laws, the private intentions of framers were accordingly irrelevant. Only the public meaning of the words interpreted in light of the principles of natural law – a "thing certain in itself [and] capable of being learned" – could legitimately be considered in the process of constitutional interpretation. "Apply this rule to the interpretation of the Federal Constitution," William Goodell concluded, "and not a single syllable can be construed in favor of slavery."[51]

[49] Ibid., 549 (McLean, J. dissenting).
[50] Lysander Spooner, *The Unconstitutionality of Slavery* (Boston: 1860), 138.
[51] William Goodell, *Our National Charter, For the Millions* (New York, 1858), 8.

Frederick Douglass's Case for the Antislavery Constitution

The more aggressive antislavery constitutional theories that arose in the mid-nineteenth century led to what William Wiecek described the "untenable thesis that slavery had usurped its preferred constitutional status."[52] Rather than conceding that slavery was limited to the municipal laws of the various states, the more radical antislavery constitutionalists began arguing that slavery was constitutionally illegitimate everywhere in the Union (and in fact had been since the document's ratification). As a unique heir to the antislavery constitutional tradition, Frederick Douglass made use of both the moderate and radical formulations in his own public arguments against slavery. Echoing similar arguments made by James Wilson, among others, Douglass asserted that the primary wrong of slavery was identical with the primary wrong of arbitrary power, whether "vested in the civil ruler" or in "a slaveholder on a plantation."[53] The wrong of slavery, according to Douglass, then, did not consist primarily in its violence, for "you may surround the slave with luxuries, place him in a genial climate, and under a smiling and cloudless sky, and these shall only enhance his torment and deepen his anguish." Rather, it was the exercise – even if benign – by one man of "absolute power over the body and soul of his brother man" that constituted the particular cruelty of slavery, because such an exercise of arbitrary power degraded the "moral nature" of both master and slave.[54]

And yet even more so than Wilson, Douglass interpreted the Constitution in antislavery terms. The Constitution, according to Douglass, was morally justified as supreme law because it was, in its essence, opposed to the exercise of arbitrary power. Against Taney's contention that the right to own and traffic in slaves was "clearly and expressly affirmed" in the Constitution,

---

[52] William Wiecek, "Abolitionist Constitutional Theory," in Leonard W. Levy and Kenneth L. Karst, eds., *Encyclopedia of the American Constitution*, 2nd ed., 6 vols. (New York: Macmillan Reference, 2000), 1:3.

[53] Blassingame, ed., *The Frederick Douglass Papers*, 3:8.

[54] Ibid., 3:11.

Douglass argued that "if in its origin slavery had any relation to the government, it was only as the scaffolding to the magnificent structure, to be removed as soon as the building was completed,"[55] and that slavery, if it were allowed a perpetual existence, would poison, corrupt, and pervert "the institutions of the country," marking out "the white man's liberty ... for the same grave with the black man's."[56] The moral and constitutional wrongs of slavery thus were identified together as one and the same.

The *Dred Scott* decision rested on the disparate conclusion that the Constitution explicitly affirmed the right to own slaves, and Douglass had to contend with the position held both by Chief Justice Taney and by his former mentor William Garrison that the Constitution itself was a proslavery document. In his 1855 autobiography, Douglass described his rejection of this doctrine: "About four years ago," Douglass wrote, "upon a reconsideration of the whole subject, I became convinced that ... the constitution of the United States not only contained no guarantees in favor of slavery, but, on the contrary, it is, in its letter and spirit, an anti-slavery instrument, demanding the abolition of slavery as a condition of its own existence, as the supreme law of the land."[57] Douglass went on to write that his new antislavery constitutional arguments were based on a considered judgment concerning "not only the just and proper rules of legal interpretation, but the origin, design, nature, rights, powers, and duties of civil government, and also the relations which human beings sustain to it."[58]

Douglass's arguments on "the whole subject" cannot be understood apart from his consideration of the nature of the

---

[55] Frederick Douglass, "Should the Negro Enlist in the Union Army?" In Foner, Philip S., ed., *Frederick Douglass on Slavery and the Civil War: Selections from his Speeches and Writings* (Mineola, NY: Dover Publications, 2003), 50.
[56] Blassingame, ed., *The Frederick Douglass Papers*, 3:169.
[57] Frederick Douglass, *My Bondage and My Freedom* (Mineola, NY: Dover Publications, 1969), 396. For an article representative of Douglass's early views, see Frederick Douglass, "The Constitution and Slavery," *The North Star* (March 16, 1849).
[58] Ibid., 398.

wrong in question. The slave, Douglass repeatedly claimed, was "a moral and intellectual being,"[59] bearing "the image of God ... [and] possessing a soul, eternal and indestructible,"[60] and slavery, as a violation of the natural moral order, constituted a peculiar "crime against God and man."[61] Douglass's arguments also presupposed a connection between the moral order and divine providence, and, like Lincoln, Douglass interpreted historical events in terms of a providential political theology. The *Dred Scott* decision, in this context, was described by Douglass as "an open rebellion against God's government" and "an attempt to undo what God [has] done, to blot out the broad distinction instituted by the *Allwise* between men and things, to change the image and superscription of the everliving God into a speechless piece of merchandise."[62]

Taney's opinion, Douglass declared, was both empirically false to the historical record and normatively false to what the law, when properly interpreted, required – "a most scandalous and devilish perversion of the Constitution, and a brazen misstatement of the facts of history."[63] Even still, the wrong of constitutionally extending slavery into the federal territories was not merely that it relied on bad history or bad constitutional law. Rather, the true wrong of expanding the reach of slavery throughout the territories consisted in its degradation of moral nature through the violation of natural moral rights and natural moral duties. The constitutional and moral wrongs were the same: Slavery, Douglass made clear, was synonymous with despotism,

---

[59] Ibid., 431.

[60] Ibid., 431.

[61] Ibid., 445.

[62] Douglass, "The *Dred Scott* Decision," 168. See Peter C. Meyers, *Frederick Douglass: Race and the Rebirth of American Liberalism* (Lawrence: University Press of Kansas, 2008). Meyers notes that Douglass's "core conviction about the universe's moral design does seem to have originated in a faith in divine Providence, and as [historian David] Blight has carefully documented, his arguments throughout the 1850s were suffused with biblical language, contributing significantly to various traditions in American political theology" (49). See David Blight, *Frederick Douglass's Civil War: Keeping Faith in Jubilee* (Baton Rouge: Louisiana State University Press, 1989).

[63] Douglass, "The *Dred Scott* Decision," 179.

and, concomitantly, a respect for natural rights was essential to free government. Summarizing this connection between private and public despotism, Peter Myers writes that the regime of slavery, in Douglass's thought, "was an antigovernment, a system of brutality impelled by its nature to do violence to the dignifying human qualities of all those within its domain and to the cause of civil government everywhere in its vicinity."[64]

After surveying the perilous state of the Union in 1857, Douglass argued that because of the encroachments of the slave power – most recently in the edict of Taney – "The ballot box is desecrated, God's law is set at naught, armed legislators stalk the halls of Congress, freedom of speech is beaten down in the Senate."[65] This was not a series of desultory thoughts but a description of the interconnectedness of morality and free government. Self-rule, symbolically represented by the ballot box, required a certain assent to the law of God revealed through nature, and recognition of the authority of the natural law, in turn, was necessary for the establishment of the rule of law (identified conceptually as the rule of reason instead of force).[66] Yet reason did not reign – legislators armed themselves, and free speech was stifled – and the genealogy of reason's demise was traced back to the advancements of slavery upon the country.

Within this context, it is difficult to imagine removing the entire framework within which Douglass made his public case against *Dred Scott*, turning instead to the political culture of the 1850s and the reasons that were to be found in its overlapping consensus. Such a move would render impotent nearly all of

[64] Myers, *Frederick Douglass*, 45.
[65] Douglass, "The *Dred Scott* Decision," 169.
[66] Douglass argued that the right to liberty was proclaimed by the "voices of nature, of conscience, of reason, and of revelation." See Douglass, "The *Dred Scott* Decision," 168. Nevertheless, he maintained that nature was epistemologically prior to biblical revelation, proclaiming that "*Should* the doctors of divinity ever convince me that the Bible sanctions American slavery ... then will I give the Bible to the flames, and no more worship God in the name of Christ." See Frederick Douglass, "Lecture on Slavery No. 7," in Philip S. Foner, ed., *The Life and Writings of Frederick Douglass* (New York: International Publishers, 1975), 5: 174.

the arguments that Douglass marshaled against the moral and constitutional wrongs of that infamous decision. In this, I suppose that Rawls would characterize the entire nineteenth century as nonideal and so would reluctantly admit arguments like Douglass's under such nonideal circumstances. But Rawls seems to neglect the other side of that coin inasmuch as what made the nineteenth century nonideal, in part, were the numerous illiberal notions of citizenship and moral personality at work in the public political culture. These illiberal notions are unnecessary to catalogue here: The majority opinion in *Dred Scott* serves as a case in point. The question to be asked, then, is how will Rawls, in 1858, decide between competing notions of citizenship and competing ideas concerning the nature of man without engaging the question of which, if either, notion is *true*? How will he contend with Lincoln's insistence that the "real issue" with the democratic policy "in the shape it takes in the *Dred Scott* decision ... [is that it] carefully excludes the idea that there is anything wrong in [slavery]"?[67]

Revisiting Rawls's Theory

By eschewing a metaphysical conception of the person, Rawls removes the only basis from which to scrutinize a given polity's *political* conception (whatever it happens to be). Nevertheless, the problem Rawls is responding to in *Political Liberalism* (i.e., the potential for violence that accompanies the existence of incommensurable comprehensive doctrines in a pluralistic society) is a real problem. The theory of public reason constitutes Rawls's attempt to respond to this problem by creating a public space that relies only on the "shared content" through which several comprehensive views coincide.[68] This, too, is a sensible response. But Rawls disavows that his theory of public reason is a *modus vivendi* or a mere way of living peaceably. Instead, he maintains that the political values that are part of the overlapping consensus

---

[67] Basler, ed., *Collected Works of Abraham Lincoln*, 3: 315.
[68] See Rawls, *Justice as Fairness*, 194.

are affirmed by individuals for *moral* and not merely for *political* reasons.[69] It is a moral agreement peculiar to modern democratic societies to bracket certain moral doctrines from public life.[70] As Sandel points out, however, "Where grave moral questions are concerned, whether it is reasonable to bracket moral and religious controversies for the sake of political agreement partly depends on which of the contending moral and religious doctrines is true."[71]

Rawls's "overlapping consensus" – and the public reason it engenders – is not helpful for analyzing the arguments put forward by men such as Lincoln, who were dealing with serious issues about the nature of man and what is owed to him by virtue of his human status as well as prudential questions about how to live together with men whom one has serious moral disagreements with and when, if ever, a resort to force in defense of the good or the right is justified. One prominent antislavery congressman, responding to the possibility of a tax imposed on Northerners for the execution of the Fugitive Slave Law of 1850, proclaimed in the House of Representatives that "when it comes to that, I, for one, shall be prepared for the *dernier ressort*, – an appeal to the God of battles. I am a man of peace, but am no non-resistant; and I would sooner have the ashes of my hearth slaked in my own blood and the blood of my children than submit to such degradation."[72]

It is scarcely possible to imagine a similar sentiment being proclaimed in the national legislature today. But how is one to

---

[69] Rawls, *Political Liberalism*, 173–212.

[70] As Robert George notes, public reason thus bears the burden of showing why "people are obligated morally, in circumstances in which they are not obliged as a matter of political prudence [i.e., in circumstances requiring a *modus vivendi*], to refrain from acting on principles that they reasonably believe to be true and that are not ruled out as reasons for political action by their reasonable comprehensive doctrines of justice and political morality." See George, "Public Reason and Political Conflict," 2475.

[71] Sandel, "Political Liberalism," 1776.

[72] Joshua Giddings, "Denunciation of Slavery" (June 23, 1852) in *Congressional Globe*, House of Representatives, 32nd Congress, 1st Session, 738–741 (1852).

retrospectively evaluate such an assertion without asking if it is reasonable to value honor or justice more than peace or whether, and for what reasons, one should be prepared to offer "resistance in defense of natural right"?[73] How is one even to begin such an evaluation without appealing to some conception of the honorable, the just, and the right that transcends any mere *political* conception? The liberalism of John Rawls does not ask such questions. When it is not the subject of consensus, it quietly resigns itself to the sidelines, refusing to fight for the principles it affirms. It certainly would not have been able to fight alongside those who denounced America's "crimes against God and man" even as they sought to extend the protection of the law to those men previously left outside of its purview.[74]

[73] Ibid.
[74] Frederick Douglass, "What to the Slave is the Fourth of July?" (July 5, 1852) in Frederick Douglass, *My Bondage and My Freedom*, 445.

7

Conclusion

The Heritage of the Antislavery Constitutional Tradition

In our own day, the constitutional and political landscape is materially altered from that of the nineteenth century. We have gone to great lengths to right the wrongs of our slaveholding past, while still wrestling with the remnants and incidents of that peculiar institution. But how did we get from there to here? Was there anything inevitable about the course of American history or the cause of emancipation? The development of American antislavery constitutionalism suggests that the eventual triumph of freedom over slavery was, at least in part, contingent on the human participants who contested constitutional meaning and engaged in constitutional politics. The antislavery constitutional theories espoused were, moreover, bound up with the idea of a higher law that undergirded the law of the state and against which the law of the state might be judged. Indeed, the anti-slavery movement in America (as in the West generally) origi-nated with, and was sustained by, the natural-law tradition. In the rhetoric and imagination of antislavery constitutionalists, the Declaration of Independence thus attained a revered status for its assertion that legitimate government was founded on the equal rights of all under the laws of nature and nature's God.

The legacy and heritage of the antislavery constitutional tradition is perhaps most evident in the civil rights legislation passed immediately after the Civil War and in the Constitution's

Fourteenth Amendment, which sought to enshrine the basic tenets of antislavery constitutionalism in the nation's fundamental law.[1] The emphasis on natural rights during congressional debates on Reconstruction was not simply vacuous rhetoric – a mere parroting of concepts fashionable in the nineteenth century – but rather reflected a free-labor and antislavery understanding of the basic social and political conditions necessary for the flourishing of human beings under a well-constituted government. The promise of freedom held out by the Fourteenth Amendment was defined by its proponents in juxtaposition to what the system of slavery had deprived – the right to raise and educate a family and to support it by entering a trade, contracting for labor, acquiring and holding property, and participating in the creation of laws that would offer equal security and protection. Such were the rights "essential to freemen," Lyman Trumbull declared, and it would take national legislation to secure these rights to the "millions of the African race in this country who were ground down and degraded and subjected to a slavery more intolerable and cruel than the world ever before knew."[2]

---

[1] When the Supreme Court began showing renewed interest in the meaning of the Fourteenth Amendment during the mid-twentieth century, Howard Jay Graham and Jacobus tenBroek prominently put forward this thesis. According to Graham, the Fourteenth Amendment was "the outcome of the organized antislavery movement in the United States" and, as tenBroek notes, the Equal Protection, Due Process, and Privileges and Immunities clauses of the Fourteenth Amendment "were intended to guarantee national constitutional and legislative protection to all men (citizens and persons) in their natural, inalienable rights." See Howard Jay Graham, "The Early Antislavery Background of the Fourteenth Amendment," *Wisconsin Law Review* (1950), 483, and Jacobus tenBroek, *The Antislavery Origins of the Fourteenth Amendment* (Berkeley: University of California Press, 1951). Perhaps the harshest critic of the Graham-tenBroek thesis is Raoul Berger. See Berger's "Supplementary Note on Abolitionist Influence" in Raoul Berger, *Government by Judiciary: The Transformation of the Fourteenth Amendment*, 2nd ed. (Indianapolis, IN: Liberty Fund, 1997), 266–270. My own criticism of Graham and tenBroek is that they overemphasized the influence of the abolitionist movement to the exclusion of the more moderate antislavery constitutionalists that have been the subject of this book.

[2] Lyman Trumbull, *Congressional Globe*, 39th Congress, 1st Session, 474 (1866). See, for example, the description of Jacob Howard concerning the condition of the slave in American law, and his conclusion that the Thirteenth Amendment,

As Congress debated whether or not justice and duty – in conjunction with sound policy – required national protection for the civil rights of freedmen, there was, additionally, a continuation of those debates concerning race and America politics that had begun prior to the Civil War. Granting full civil rights to newly freed slaves, some feared, would mark the death knell of the white republic and would hold out the prospect, as Senator Peter Van Winkle alleged, that "not only the negro race, but other inferior races" would have occasion to immigrate into the country and become citizens. In a riposte to Republicans who invoked the principles of the American Revolution in defense of the new egalitarian ethos, Van Winkle asserted that "the authors of the Declaration of Independence could have meant nothing more than that the rights of citizens of any community are equal to the rights of all other citizens of that community."[3] Van Winkle's position was, essentially, the same position espoused by Stephen Douglas in his debates with Lincoln that the Founders meant to declare all (white) American colonists to be equal to all (white) Englishmen. It was, in other words, a conventional and historical conception of equality, racially coded and understood in terms of membership in a particular political community. Garrett Davis echoed this thought: "My position is that this is a white man's Government ... it was not to establish a government in which [the Negro] was to be a party or a power that the Declaration of Independence was enunciated to the world."[4]

Against this backdrop, the issues surrounding the Supreme Court's *Dred Scott* decision again took center stage. What was the meaning and relevance of Chief Justice Taney's opinion in that case? Would it require a constitutional amendment to dislodge the principle that slaves and their descendents could

---

without further protections for civil rights, leaves the former slave "without family, without property, without the implements of husbandry, and even without the right acquire or use any instrumentalities of carrying on the industry of which he may be capable; it leaves him without friend or support, and even without the clothes to cover his nakedness." *Congressional Globe*, 39th Congress, 1st Session, 504 (1866).

[3] Peter Van Winkle, *Congressional Globe*, 39th Congress, 1st Session, 497 (1866).

[4] Garrett Davis, *Congressional Globe*, 39th Congress, 1st Session, 528 (1866).

never become citizens of the United States? Would dislodging that principle, in turn, be *revolutionary* rather than amendatory, and could such a revolution be effected by the legislature under such unique political circumstances? The Republican answer to these questions involved a re-articulation of arguments that had been developed long before the war. "No matter where slavery exists ... it is a violence and a wrong," Daniel Clark asserted to applause in the galleries.[5] And abolishing that wrong and granting citizenship to former slaves was, according to Lot Morrill, "a change precisely in harmony with the general principles of the Government." As slavery was anomalous to the theoretical underpinnings of American government, the "change which has been made [by the abolition of slavery] has destroyed that which was exceptional in our institutions."[6] In other words, civil rights provisions intended to make the abolition of slavery meaningful for freedmen represented something that was already latent in the principles of the American Founding.

"Let it be remembered," John Bingham declared, quoting an address by the Continental Congress in 1783, "that the rights for which America has contended were the rights of human nature."[7] The Fourteenth Amendment, with its emphasis on birth citizenship and equal protection, due process and privileges and immunities, was indeed understood by many of its supporters to be merely "declaratory of what *always* had been the 'true' meaning of the Constitution, declaratory of the view that slavery and race discrimination had no place in the Constitution and were outlawed by it."[8] As Iowa Congressman James Wilson contended, the 39th Congress was "establishing no new right, declaring no new principle."[9]

---

[5] Daniel Clark, *Congressional Globe*, 39th Congress, 1st Session, 529 (1866).

[6] Lot Morrill, *Congressional Globe*, 39th Congress, 1st Session, 570 (1866).

[7] John Bingham, *Congressional Globe*, 39th Congress, 1st Session, 1090 (1866). See Continental Congress, "Address to the States" (April 18, 1783) in 1 *Elliot's Debates* 100.

[8] Howard Jay Graham, "Our 'Declaratory' Fourteenth Amendment," *Stanford Law Review* 7 (1954–1955): 38.

[9] James Wilson, *Congressional Globe*, 39th Congress, 1st Session, 1117 (1866).

To revisit Lincoln's metaphor, the Fourteenth Amendment was instead the working out of a constitutional aspiration implicit in the fundamental teaching of the Declaration that "all men are created equal and endowed by their Creator with certain inalienable rights"; it represented, in other words, the reclamation for American politics of that Apple of Gold around which the Constitution was originally framed, "not to conceal, or destroy the apple; but to adorn, and preserve it."[10] America's Second Founding, involving this "new birth of freedom," was very much indebted to the idea of a law higher than the Constitution that was relevant to the purposes and animating principles of the Constitution. Although such "higher law" rhetoric was certainly ubiquitous in early abolitionist movements, it was also central to the decidedly less radical antislavery constitutionalists at the center of the establishment and to many of the Founders, who pledged their lives in defense of a revolution that took as its central aim the establishment of a regime founded on the equality of all men under the laws of nature and nature's God.

---

[10] Basler, ed., *The Collected Works of Abraham Lincoln*, 4: 168–169.

Index

CPSIA information can be obtained at www.ICGtesting.com
Printed in the USA
BVOW07s1600010315

389640BV00001B/4/P